THE DAILY GOD BOOK™
THROUGH THE BIBLE

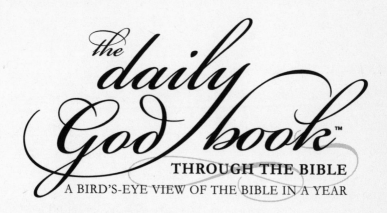

the daily God book™

THROUGH THE BIBLE

A BIRD'S-EYE VIEW OF THE BIBLE IN A YEAR

SKIP HEITZIG

TYNDALE HOUSE PUBLISHERS, INC.

CAROL STREAM, ILLINOIS

Visit Tyndale's exciting Web site at www.tyndale.com.

Visit Skip's Web site at www.skipheitzig.com.

TYNDALE and Tyndale's quill logo are registered trademarks of Tyndale House Publishers, Inc.

The Daily God Book is a trademark of Tyndale House Publishers, Inc.

The Daily God Book Through the Bible: A Bird's-eye View of the Bible in a Year

Copyright © 2010 by Skip Heitzig. All rights reserved.

Cover texture copyright © by Von Glitschka. All rights reserved.

Designed by Mark Anthony Lane II

Edited by Susan Taylor

ISBN 978-1-4143-1300-9

Printed in the United States of America

16 15 14 13 12 11 10
7   6   5   4   3   2   1

God Speaks!

In the beginning God created the heavens and the earth. . . . Then God said, "Let there be light," and there was light. GENESIS 1:1, 3

Did you know that the Bible, made up of sixty-six books and approximately thirty-one thousand verses, is the best-selling and most widely distributed book of all time? More than 2.5 billion copies have been sold since 1915, and at least part of the Bible has been translated into 2,233 dialects.

Even more important than its popularity, however, is its message: God speaks! He likes to communicate. Genesis 1 says repeatedly, "God said." God wants people to know who he is and what he is up to, and he reveals himself to us through what he has said in Scripture. No matter what issue you face, difficulty you encounter, or question you have, somewhere in the Bible "God said" something about it.

Genesis is a book of beginnings: of humankind, of sin, of marriage, of government, of nations, and most important, of God's plan to rescue the world. The Bible's landscape makes a grand sweep from eternity past to eternity future. In between are events, people, and places, all centered around one Person and two events. That one Person is Christ, and the two events are his two comings to Earth. In the first, he comes to cleanse people from sin; in the second, he will rule with those he has cleansed.

God has a lot to say in this first book—about creation, sin, redemption, and culture. And he has even more to say about people, namely Abraham, Isaac, Jacob, and Joseph. The book of Genesis is a treasure chest of God's speaking and interacting with his creatures and pointing us toward the day he would enter humanity through his Son, Jesus, when the "Word became human" (John 1:14).

Martin Luther once said, "The Bible is alive; it speaks to me. It has feet; it runs after me. It has hands; it lays hold of me!" As you read each day, listen with your heart to what "God said," and get ready for the adventure of your life!

My Father Made That!

This is the account of the creation of the heavens and the earth. . . . The LORD God made the earth and the heavens.   GENESIS 2:4

I love telescopes. They take me away from my everyday life and catapult me into the vastness of the cosmos. I don't know much about galaxies or telescopes, but I've discovered that our universe reflects God's creative order. Far from being the result of a chaotic accident, God's creation was a well-organized event! The six days of creation reveal how God created everything, from light on the first day to land animals and humankind on the sixth day. He created it all ex nihilo—out of nothing—and it's still working after all this time.

Some people say it all just happened! Really? Does the sun "just happen" to be ninety-three million miles away, with a surface temperature of twelve thousand degrees Fahrenheit? No. The sun is the perfect temperature and at the perfect distance from Earth to sustain life. Does the earth "just happen" to rotate 365.25 times in a year? No. If the rotations occurred more or fewer times per year, the temperatures on Earth would be extreme. Does the earth "just happen" to tilt just over twenty-three degrees on its axis, which gives us the balance of four seasons? Does our atmosphere "just happen" to be a perfect balance of seventy-nine parts oxygen, twenty parts nitrogen, and one part variant gases? No. None of it "just happened." Our Father made it that way!

Now, if the art hanging in the skies is so magnificent, what must the Artist be like? The creation reveals that our good Father loves to give good things. Seven times in the creative process, God noted that what he had made was "good." What's more, human beings were given the regal status of being created in God's "own image" (Genesis 1:27).

The next time you see a multicolored sunset or a snowcapped mountain or a pristine stream, pause and remember, *My Father made that!*

From Creation to Corruption

[Eve] saw that the tree was beautiful and its fruit looked delicious, and she wanted the wisdom it would give her. So she took some of the fruit and ate it. Then she gave some to her husband, who was with her, and he ate it, too. At that moment their eyes were opened, and they suddenly felt shame at their nakedness. GENESIS 3:6-7

People can be funny. If you randomly tell them there are 735,688,412,564 stars in the universe, they'll tend to believe you. But when they see a Wet Paint sign, they have to make a personal investigation to see if the paint really is wet! That's been our dilemma from the beginning of creation. God gave Adam and Eve so many wonderful gifts to enjoy. God essentially told Adam and Eve, "Enjoy the fruit I've given you. Have fun in the rivers. Take pleasure in each other and enjoy naming the animals!" God gave only one negative command, and it ended up functioning sort of like a Wet Paint sign, only this one read, "Danger—Lethal Tree!" But in spite of the strong warning, our first parents chose to make a personal investigation.

When I was a boy, I stood with my dad and three brothers on the shore of Jackson Lake one pristine summer morning. The image of the mountains was perfectly reflected on the mirrored surface of the lake, until one of us decided to skip a tiny stone across the water. Instantly the image was distorted, and the ripples continued to mar the reflection. That's what Adam and Eve did to all humanity! Their disobedience marred the reflection of God's image in every person who came after them.

Have your eyes been opened to some sin in your life? Maybe you feel ashamed because your sin has further distorted God's image in you. Adam and Eve's disobedience meant "paradise lost!" But Jesus' death on the cross brought the hope of paradise regained. When you confess your sin, Jesus' loving act on the cross becomes the covering for your sinful acts.

The Weather Channel

*The LORD said, "I will wipe this human race I have created from
the face of the earth. Yes, and I will destroy every living thing—all the
people, the large animals, the small animals that scurry along the
ground, and even the birds of the sky. . . ." But Noah found favor with
the LORD.*   GENESIS 6:7-8

I love watching The Weather Channel. I'm intrigued by the technology and
expertise used to predict climate patterns that could affect my immediate
future. Noah must have become interested in weather when God told him
that a catastrophic flood was coming and provided an evacuation plan for
Noah and his family. Noah was to build a 450-foot boat, complete with three
decks, an upper window system for ventilation, and a portal for access. Estimates are that this vessel could accommodate eighteen thousand species.

Why would God destroy the earth? Sometimes things get so bad that
before there can be something new, something old has to go. In Noah's case,
the world had become so wicked and corrupt that in order for God to fulfill
his future plan, he had to get rid of the old world and start over.

When the rain had finally stopped and the ark rested, Noah emerged
with his family alone and as the leader of this new generation. The task he
and his family faced was to repopulate the earth. In this, Noah was a symbol
of Jesus, who also is the head of the new order, a new spiritual family.

Genesis 6:8 says, "Noah found favor with the LORD." His obedience and
willingness to respond to God made him different from those who would be
destroyed in the Flood. Our lives, too, should be summed up in one word:
different! Our values, our outlooks, and our actions all should be different
from those in the world around us. When they are, others around us will
detect it, but even more, God will take notice, and his favor toward us will
be our delight!

A Tale of Two Cities

They said, "Come, let's build a great city for ourselves with a tower that reaches into the sky. This will make us famous and keep us from being scattered all over the world." GENESIS 11:4

Much of the Bible could be seen as "a tale of two cities," a contrast between the city of man and the city of God. The most frequently mentioned city in Scripture is Jerusalem, the city God chose to be the place of his name (see 1 Kings 11:36). The second most mentioned city is Babylon. In its beginning stages it was simply Babel (see Genesis 11), but its prophesied name will be "Babylon the Great" (Revelation 17:5). These two cities represent the contrast between God's redemptive agenda and humanity's rebellious agenda.

The ancient tower of Babel was a huge structure known as a ziggurat, a seven-level astrological temple probably used to worship the zodiac. It became a rallying point to keep people from scattering abroad. They were refusing to "fill the earth and govern it" as God had commanded in Genesis 1:28. Thus this tower symbolized the second great rebellion of humanity; it pictured the human race worshiping its own prowess and determination to control its own destiny.

The term *Babel* comes from the Hebrew word *balal*, which means "to confuse or mix up." That's what happens whenever people rebel against God's plan for their lives. Whenever you say no to God, you're essentially planting a rebel flag in the ground of your heart. Your heavenly Father knows best, and he knows the only way for you to live a clear, unconfused life is to obey him.

Where is *your* city? Are you sure you're wanting God's Kingdom to come and *his* will to be done? Are you building God's Kingdom by filling the earth with his message of love? Or are you building your own kingdom? The next time your life seems confused or mixed up, stop and consider, *Which city am I really at home in?*

January 6 READ GENESIS 12:1-9

Four Great People: Abraham

[God told Abraham,] "I will make you into a great nation. I will bless you and make you famous, and you will be a blessing to others. I will bless those who bless you and curse those who treat you with contempt. All the families on earth will be blessed through you." GENESIS 12:2-3

Genesis 12–50 focuses on four great people. The first of these is Abraham. He's quite an amazing guy. In fact, Genesis devotes fourteen chapters to him—pretty remarkable when you consider that it devotes only two chapters to the creation account!

In James 2:23, the Bible refers to Abraham uniquely as "the friend of God." To this day, Arabs still refer to Abraham as *Al Khalil*, which means "the friend of God."

What made Abraham so great? We could point to his great faith in God, which was noteworthy because Abraham came out of a pagan culture. But at times his faith lapsed (see Genesis 12:10-20; 16; and 20). We could point to his courage in making a long migration westward toward the new land of Canaan.

But the real reason Abraham was great is that God made him great! Notice all the "I wills" in the verses above. What a contrast to the previous chapter in Genesis! The folks in Babel wanted to make a name for *themselves*. But Abraham believed God's promise and followed where God led, and God made Abraham great. Abraham and his wife, Sarah, were old, and Sarah had a long history of infertility. But Abraham believed what God told him *in spite of the odds*. Abraham's real greatness was in the fact that "all the families on earth [were] blessed through [him]" (Genesis 12:3), because that blessing was the eventual coming of Jesus.

God knows your shortcomings, hang-ups, and handicaps. He knows your deep longing for significance. And your life becomes significant when you become a channel for God's blessings to flow to others. As Christ's character is formed in you and flows through you, God will regard your life as great.

Four Great People: Isaac

*[God told Abraham,] "Take your son, your only son—yes, Isaac, whom
you love so much—and go to the land of Moriah. Go and sacrifice
him as a burnt offering on one of the mountains, which I will
show you."* GENESIS 22:2

After my only son, Nathan, was born on a windy May morning, I couldn't
imagine life without him. But think of how Abraham and Sarah must have
felt about Isaac! They were both of geriatric age when Isaac was born. Just
the unusual and supernatural aspects of Isaac's birth indicated that his life
was destined for greatness.

Isaac wasn't Abraham's only son; Ishmael had been born to him by Hagar.
But God recognized only Isaac as the child of promise: "Take your son, your
only son." Remember that Jesus was known as God's "only Son." The parallel
is fascinating.

The word *love* first occurs in the Bible in Genesis 22:2. Notice that the
context is the *father of a miraculously born son offering that son in sacrifice*!
And the place where it occurred is significant as well. Moriah is the same
mountain where the Temple was later built, and the peak of Mount Moriah,
just to the north, is also known as Golgotha—the place of Jesus' crucifixion.
Jesus, God's only Son, was sacrificed on the same mountain where God had
directed Abraham to sacrifice Isaac! The trip to this mountain for Abraham
and Isaac took three days. So in Abraham's mind, Isaac was as good as dead
for three days before the angel told Abraham not to kill him. Hebrews 11:19
says, "Abraham reasoned that if Isaac died, God was able to bring him back
to life again"—just as God raised Jesus on the third day.

God's plan to redeem you started before you were born and before Jesus
came. Before God ever made the world, he had you in mind and your salvation ready to be set in motion (see Ephesians 1:4). So rest today, dear one,
and know how firmly God holds you in his hand.

Four Great People: Jacob

The two children struggled with each other in [Rebekah's] womb. So she went to ask the LORD about it. "Why is this happening to me?" she asked.   And the LORD told her, "The sons in your womb will become two nations. From the very beginning, the two nations will be rivals. One nation will be stronger than the other; and your older son will serve your younger son."   GENESIS 25:22-23

Some sociologists suggest that the order in which we and any siblings are born affects our personalities—for life! They tell us that firstborns are usually natural leaders and high achievers. As a rule, they tend to be precise, organized, detail oriented, and somewhat picky. But there are exceptions.

Jacob and Esau were twins. Esau arrived first, but Jacob was the one who would be in charge and the one through whom God would pass down the family blessing. When Jacob was born, he was holding onto his brother's heel, as if he were destined to make Esau stumble and fall. In fact, right about now, you may be thinking, *What's so great about that?* The marvel of Jacob's life was that God used him *in spite of* who he was, not *because* of who he was. Jacob tricked his brother into giving up his birthright and lied to his father, yet Jacob, the second-born son, was God's choice, contrary to the custom of those times.

God knows who you are and what sociological factors make you the way you are. But he also deals with you graciously, apart from your goodness or lack of it. "God saved you by his grace when you believed. And you can't take credit for this; it is a gift from God" (Ephesians 2:8). Maybe your birth order contributes to your being confident or insecure, optimistic or pessimistic, driven or passive. But just as God did with Jacob, he can make you into a person you never would have been naturally. Treat God's promises as gold, because nothing is more important.

Four Great People: Joseph

Joseph had another dream, and again he told his brothers about it. "Listen, I have had another dream," he said. "The sun, moon, and eleven stars bowed low before me!" GENESIS 37:9

Most people over the age of ten dream a lot. And although we may not remember doing so, we dream at least four to six times per night during a stage of sleep called REM, which stands for rapid eye movement. During these episodes, which last from five to ten minutes, our brains are as active as they are when we're awake. Why we dream is still not exactly known, but dreams may allow our subconscious to deal with things we don't address when we're awake.

Dreams can also be supernatural messengers. God used dreams several times in Joseph's life. Some of those dreams got Joseph into trouble with his own family, but others got him out of trouble with the king of Egypt and eventually led Joseph to occupy the envied position of second-in-command over that country (see Genesis 41:41-43).

God can use what may seem trivial to accomplish something monumental. Little did Joseph know that his dreams were a picture of God's sovereign plan for the nation of Israel to be nurtured and grow in the land of Goshen until it was time for them to occupy their own land!

Like Joseph's, your life is a tapestry. God is weaving all the events together to fulfill his perfect will. You may look at God's weaving and not like what you see: *Why this pain? Why these circumstances? Why have the dreams of the past become the drama of the present?* But wait awhile, because the Master Weaver isn't finished yet. You're seeing only part of the tapestry that is your life. "We know that God causes everything to work together for the good of those who love God and are called according to his purpose for them" (Romans 8:28). God can take the threads of life's worst experiences and weave them together into something truly beautiful.

Shiloh

The scepter will not depart from Judah, nor the ruler's staff from his descendants, until the coming of the one to whom it belongs, the one whom all nations will honor. GENESIS 49:10

Someone once said that promises may get you friends but performance keeps them. Genesis 49 appears to be Jacob's last will and testament for his children. But a closer look shows Jacob actually prophesying over his twelve sons. When Jacob comes to his son Judah, he makes an interesting promise.

The word *scepter* represents the sovereign right to rule and to enforce law. But the promise refers to "the one to whom it belongs" as a ruler who will come from the tribe of Judah. The Hebrew renders it *Shiloh*, which ancient rabbis considered to be a reference to the Messiah. They took Jacob's statement to mean that the national identity and the right to enforce Mosaic law would remain with the tribe of Judah until the Messiah came.

Around AD 7, Caponius, a Roman governor, took away the Jews' ruling authority in Judea, including the right to impose capital punishment. (That's why they had to ask Pilate's permission to execute Jesus.) The Babylonian Talmud records that when this happened, Jewish leaders donned sackcloth, sprinkled ashes on their heads, and walked the walls of Jerusalem, shouting, "Woe unto us, for the scepter has departed from Judah, and the Messiah has not come!" They actually thought that God hadn't kept his promise from Genesis 49 to send the Messiah! Little did they know that a young boy from the tribe of Judah, growing up in Nazareth, would soon put down his adoptive father's carpentry tools and take up his true Father's business of redemption. Shiloh *had* come and would soon present himself to the nation as deliverer.

You need never doubt God's promises because he keeps every one. Like stars, the darker the world gets, the brighter those promises shine. As you read God's promises in the Scriptures, you'll discover why God has made so many friends over the years—and kept them.

Exodus: From Groaning to Glory

These are the names of the sons of Israel (that is, Jacob) who moved to Egypt with their father, each with his family.   EXODUS 1:1

All Christians have testimonies—personal stories of how Christ delivered them from an empty past or difficult circumstances and brought hope and salvation. Some were saved out of drug addiction, others from lives of crime or illicit relationships. Still others speak of having a religious past, of trying to work their way to heaven by sincere and rigorous discipline. Some testimonies sound more dramatic than others, but whatever the details of the stories, the theme is always the same: *We've been rescued!*

The book of Exodus is the Israelites' personal testimony. Seventy descendants of Jacob made their way to Egypt during a famine and grew to a multitude of about two million. As the political landscape changed over time, the Israelites went from being honored guests in Egypt to the desperate position of providing slave labor for the Egyptians. The worse things grew for God's people, the louder they cried for help and rescue. God heard and delivered them, and this personal testimony became their spiritual rallying cry throughout every succeeding generation, even to the present day.

Exodus tells of the Israelites' going out from Egypt. The writer tells the story of domination *in* Egypt, liberation *from* Egypt, and revelation *after* Egypt. The story could also be told emotionally: from groaning to grumbling to glory! God's people groaned in Egypt and grumbled in the wilderness, but they experienced God's glory at Sinai.

Perhaps you have your own testimony, your own personal story. Stay in touch with it, and pull it out every now and again and tell someone of your own journey from groaning to glory. Tell them about how God delivered you from the past and filled you with his hope. Today might be a perfect day to do that!

Your Tax Dollars at Work

"Take this baby and nurse him for me," the princess told the baby's mother. "I will pay you for your help." So the woman took her baby home and nursed him.   EXODUS 2:9

Michael Shapiro, in his book *The Jewish 100,* considers Moses the most influential Jew in all of history. Jesus Christ and Albert Einstein rank second and third, respectively, on Shapiro's list. Jews everywhere esteem Moses greatly as prophet, leader, and lawgiver. One of the most fascinating things about his life is his upbringing in Egypt. The same day his mother released him into the Nile River to keep him from a death sentence, Pharaoh's daughter discovered him and instructed her maid to hire a Jewish woman to nurse the boy. God made sure that his plan got government subsidy when the maid "just happened" to hire the baby's own mother.

God has a way of supernaturally arranging things in surprising ways. He can make sure that Paul gets to Rome with all expenses paid by the Roman government. He can arrange a worldwide census to be taken so that Jesus gets born in Bethlehem as the prophet predicted. And he can ensure that a tiny Hebrew boy gets the finest education in Egypt while being cared for and learning the values of his godly mother. When Moses' mother and father married, they had no idea that God would use their tiny Moses to shift the Israelites' status from domination in Egypt to liberation from Egypt.

That's what makes life such an adventure! When you start to discover the supernatural design within natural events, you begin to live life with a bit more excitement. There's a sparkle in the eye of trust and a kick in the step of faith that will put you on the lookout to see what else God could be up to. Look around today to see if you can spot any of God's precious providences in the affairs of your life.

Excuses, Excuses

Moses protested to God, "Who am I to appear before Pharaoh? Who am I to lead the people of Israel out of Egypt?" EXODUS 3:11

Someone once said, "Whoever wants to be a judge of human nature should study people's excuses." Excuses reveal how people think and what's important to them. Evangelist Billy Sunday used to say, "An excuse is the skin of a reason stuffed with a lie!"

When God called Moses to be his representative to the Israelites, Moses had his list of excuses ready. His first one was, "Who am I to appear before Pharaoh? Who am I to lead the people of Israel out of Egypt?" (Exodus 3:11). Sounds humble, right? Think again. God's reply gives us insight: "I will be with you" (Exodus 3:12). Moses was making it all about him and his own lack of experience, confidence, and status. But God was saying, in effect, "It's not about you and your inabilities; it's about me and my abilities working through you!"

Moses had more objections: "What if they won't believe me or listen to me?" (Exodus 4:1) and "I'm not very good with words" (Exodus 4:10). All these excuses appear to be legitimate. But Moses' real heart was revealed when he finally uttered, "Lord, please! Send anyone else" (Exodus 4:13). Now we see that the real problem wasn't his ability but rather his *avail*ability; it was an issue of his will, not his aptitude.

What excuses have you been nurturing for God not to use you? Have you hidden behind your age, your busy schedule, or your lack of talent or ability? The truth is, when God wants to use you, it's more about his working through you than about you working for him. He promises to equip you with whatever you need to do the task. Remember, you're just the tool; the real genius is what the all-powerful God can accomplish through a yielded instrument. So throw away every excuse, and ask him to use you today. You might be surprised where that will lead.

The Great Confrontation

*[Pharaoh retorted,] "Who is the L*ORD*? Why should I listen to him and let Israel go? I don't know the L*ORD*, and I will not let Israel go."*   EXODUS 5:2

Never pick a fight with God—the odds are against you! But that's exactly what Pharaoh did. He openly defied God and would feel the full power of God's almighty hand.

In those days a nation gave credit to its gods for its power and success. Egypt prided itself on its success as a world power and its religious worship of the pantheon of Egyptian deities. But since Pharaoh defiantly questioned who the Hebrew God was, God revealed himself in ways that Pharaoh and Egypt would never forget.

Through ten plagues, God demonstrated the phoniness and impotence of Egypt's false gods. The first plague (see Exodus 7:19-25), which turned the Nile River to blood, was an attack on Egypt's principal natural resource and on the god Osiris, who supposedly ruled over it. God used the second plague to show the Egyptians how false was their belief in Heket, the frog goddess. God tailored every plague against the Egyptians to correspond to Egypt's false worship system.

It would seem to have been enough to make anyone cry uncle, but not Pharaoh. He hardened his heart with each successive plague until the final confrontation resulted in the death of his firstborn son. Moses and Aaron may have wondered why deliverance was taking so long. But God had more in mind than just getting Israel *out* of Egypt; he wanted to make a spiritual impact *on* Egypt.

When success comes too quickly, you may forget about God. So he may take longer than you'd like to accomplish something so that you'll lean harder on him and learn to trust him more. Then, when deliverance comes, you'll recognize his mighty hand in it. Let God do his work; he might just be using your situation to deal with someone who, like Pharaoh, is still fighting God.

Passover!

The blood on your doorposts will serve as a sign, marking the houses where you are staying. When I see the blood, I will pass over you. This plague of death will not touch you when I strike the land of Egypt.

EXODUS 12:13

Many people can't stand the sight of blood. But one particular night in Egypt, God was actually *looking* for blood.

The tenth plague—the death of the firstborn sons in Egypt—is the climactic one. This would strike the hardest blow at the dynasty of Pharaoh, because his own firstborn son, his successor, would die.

On the Israelites' last night in Egypt, they were to kill a lamb and smear its blood on the sides and tops of their door frames. When the death angel saw the blood, he would "pass over" their houses and not kill their firstborn. Only the blood would save them, not the fact that they were Israelites. In fact, if an Egyptian was visiting a Jewish home on that night, he, too, would be safe. This event would rearrange the Hebrews' entire calendar so their year would begin with the Passover month. Jewish families still annually celebrate God's great deliverance of their forefathers.

God wants us to celebrate the day or night of our deliverance too. The moment we first received Jesus Christ, all of life changed. It becomes our spiritual birthday! If you remember when it happened for you, mark it on your calendar, and each year recall the event. God saved you not because you're superior, smarter, or more likable than other people. He saved you because the blood of his Son was smeared on a cross, and through his death, you can have life.

In 1835 Charlotte Elliott penned these famous words, still sung by those who love God's salvation:

> Just as I am, without one plea,
> But that Thy blood was shed for me,
> And that Thou bidd'st me come to Thee,
> O Lamb of God I come! I come!

The Line in the Sand

*The people of Israel walked through the middle of the sea on dry ground,
with walls of water on each side!*   EXODUS 14:22

The Red Sea divides the vast desert of Upper Egypt and the Sinai Peninsula.
In aerial photographs it appears to be a bright blue line in the sand. God
led his people to this watery "line in the sand" to demonstrate to both them
and their enemies that nothing is too hard for him. This would be the ultimate deliverance and become an event that the Israelites would remember
throughout their history.

Some people have trouble believing this story. They prefer to naturalize
it rather than take it at face value as a miracle. It could be that since they've
never seen God's power, they naively assume it doesn't exist. How big is *your*
God? Can he do anything? Most of the Israelites on a good day would have
said he could. But on that day, when they saw the dust of Egypt's army on
the horizon, they panicked. They forgot that God had punished Egypt with
plagues. They forgot that God had brought them this far out of Egypt. This
crisis made them second-guess their own history!

Irish preacher and author C. H. Mackintosh (1820–1896) once noted that
"10,000 mercies are forgotten in the presence of a single, trifling moment."
But every moment of crisis can crystallize your faith; it can become a line in
the sand. God may be showing you a similar line and nudging you to cross
it. Maybe it's a line in a relationship moving toward reconciliation. Maybe
it's a line of commitment that would require more of your time and incur
the disdain of onlookers. Perhaps the line is a move to another location,
perhaps even to the mission field. Will God meet you there? Will he sustain
you and deal with the obstacles? You'll never know until you cross the line!

In-Law or Outlaw?

When Moses' father-in-law saw all that Moses was doing for the people, he asked, "What are you really accomplishing here? Why are you trying to do all this alone while everyone stands around you from morning till evening?" EXODUS 18:14

I love my father-in-law. He has always been supportive and encouraging. But I didn't always think so. In the early years of my marriage, I wondered about ulterior motives and competitive intentions. But that was all a reflection of my own insecurities.

Moses may have felt the same way. He no doubt wanted to impress Jethro, his father-in-law, so he "took him to work." Jethro watched all day as his son-in-law filled the role of "problem shuffler" for Israel. He must have heard it all, from "So-and-so stole my sheep" to "He snores and wakes up our neighbors in the next tent!" Moses was trying to meet too many needs of too many people—alone!

Jethro was a good father-in-law. He gave Moses a golden principle: *No one person, no matter how gifted, can do ministry alone!* He watched as his son-in-law tried to wear the hats of the judicial, the legislative, and the executive branches of government. By the end of the day, he was worn out. Jethro's advice was to delegate: find other capable people to help. So Moses did, and he discovered that he got more done and made everyone else happier.

Take a fresh look at your family. It could be that God has placed an uncle, sister, stepbrother, or father-in-law in your life to help you grow. Maybe a new perspective from one of them could initiate a breakthrough in your career or an area of ministry. Jethro's advice helped Moses to have longevity in his service to God. Jethro wasn't a meddling outlaw but rather a masterful in-law, sent by God to make Moses a better leader. Why not build a bridge with someone in your family? Ask that person for prayer at least and perhaps even for a little piece of instructive advice.

God's "Top Ten" List

God gave the people all these instructions: "I am the LORD your God, who rescued you from the land of Egypt, the place of your slavery. You must not have any other god but me."   EXODUS 20:1-3

Since 1993, David Letterman has sported a "Top Ten" list on his nightly TV show. Normally wacky, and sometimes crude, the list can range from the Top Ten Signs You're Not Getting a Year-End Bonus to the Top Ten Promotional Slogans. What if you were to compose a list of the top-ten important things about life? What would they be? God gave his own top-ten list when he gave his commandments.

The Ten Commandments have both a vertical focus (God-ward) and a horizontal focus (people-ward). The first four commandments show us how to relate to God; the last six tell us how to treat our fellow humans. Much of our modern system of jurisprudence has been based on these foundational principles.

Memorize these top ten—only 40 percent of Americans can name even four of them!—and then use them. Let them be a *compass* to help you plot your direction in life. Use them as a *thermometer* to gauge the warmth of your love for God. Use them as a *mirror* that helps you to see your own flaws and your failure to keep God's commands. But don't try to use the mirror that shows the flaws as soap to clean those flaws. Paul said, "No one can ever be made right with God by doing what the law commands. The law simply shows us how sinful we are" (Romans 3:20).

Finally, let God's law be a *road sign* to point you to Jesus for cleansing and change. Whatever dirt these commandments point out in you, run to the shower of the cleansing blood of Christ. He will do for you what the law could never do.

Camping Out with God

[God said,] "Have the people of Israel build me a holy sanctuary so I can live among them. You must build this Tabernacle and its furnishings exactly according to the pattern I will show you." EXODUS 25:8-9

I used to go camping every year in either the majestic Sierra Nevadas in California or the vast, empty desert around Death Valley. Those trips were a chance to get away from the distractions of the city and get alone to hear God. Thirty-five hundred years ago, God went camping in the Sinai desert with the children of Israel. While they were living in tents, God was present with them in a tentlike structure called the Tabernacle. The outer courtyard housed a closed tent, which became God's residence and provided a picture of how the gospel was portrayed in the Old Testament.

There was only one door into the Tabernacle, just as there is only one way into heaven, through Jesus Christ (see John 14:6). The entrance was on the east side, which meant one had to pass through the encampment of Judah to get in. (Jesus' genealogy was from this tribe.) From the outside, the Tabernacle wasn't particularly attractive, but the inside was adorned with ornate hangings and gold. Isaiah prophesied of Christ that "there was nothing beautiful or majestic about his appearance, nothing to attract us to him" (Isaiah 53:2). But Jesus' life and nature are pure and divine and life-giving. The only light source in the Tabernacle, the golden lampstand, also pointed to Christ, who said, "I am the light of the world" (John 8:12). Across from the lampstand was a golden table holding the Bread of the Presence, which pointed to Jesus, who is the Bread of Life (see John 6:35).

God lived with his people! Wherever they went, he went. Wherever they stopped, he did too. God still "camps" among his people, inside everyone who believes in him. When was the last time you celebrated the fact that God has taken up residence in you?

More! More! More!

Moses responded, "Then show me your glorious presence." EXODUS 33:18

Moses wanted more of God. He wanted to see more glory, and he wanted more of the joy that comes from being in God's presence. On one hand, we can understand that. On the other, we may wonder about Moses. What more could he need? He had already heard God's audible voice. He had seen God's mighty hand in sending plagues on Egypt, opening the Red Sea, and providing water from rocks! He had experienced more than any of us ever will in a lifetime. So why was Moses asking for more? It's not because Moses wasn't satisfied with what he already had; it's because he had tasted something so good that he wanted to be a repeat customer.

When you go to a good restaurant and have an exceptional meal, you don't leave saying, "I'll never be back to this place. The food was so great that I'll never want to eat here again!" No, you'll be a return customer because you want more of what you've already tasted. Maybe the next meal will even top the previous one!

Moses so enjoyed what he'd already encountered with God that he wanted to visibly experience God's full and unfolded glory. But God told him that was impossible. His unshielded glory was too grand and glorious for Moses to handle. Moses longed for an experience that only heaven will afford.

No matter how spiritually well informed or biblically mature we are, at our core, we long for God himself. Every sweet time of intimate devotion with God, every powerful episode of corporate worship, every palpable experience of divine fellowship only intensifies our longing for God on a deeper level. God designed it that way. He wants us to long for heaven, where we will stand in his glorious presence. Until then, we cry out for as much as we can get right now!

How Do I Approach God?

Lay your hand on the animal's head, and the LORD will accept its death in your place to purify you, making you right with him.   LEVITICUS 1:4

How many times have you heard someone say, "All roads lead to God"? In our age of relativism, truth is measured on the sliding scale of individual experience. People begin with themselves and make personal discovery about their universe the basis for belief. Consequently, absolute truth has no place, and neither do the exclusive claims of Christ.

But in the book of Leviticus, God establishes an important principle: *The approach that God accepts is the approach that God prescribes!* You can't make up just any old way to come to God. God begins with himself and builds downward to people by revealing who he is and how he is to be worshiped, and he makes it clear that the only way to approach him is through sacrifice. In the Old Testament, the blood of animals was shed as a sacrifice for sin in a visual communication of the truth that "without the shedding of blood, there is no forgiveness" (Hebrews 9:22).

In the book of Leviticus, the Israelites don't move anywhere. The book opens and closes with the people in the same spot, learning how to draw near to God and how to be God's people through personal and national holiness. And here's the truth all of us must face: Sin, the great obstacle to our approaching God, must be dealt with first, and we must confess it frequently.

Though Jesus shed his blood for our sins once and for all, it's a good idea to begin each day with a clean slate: "If we confess our sins to him, he is faithful and just to forgive us our sins and to cleanse us from all wickedness" (1 John 1:9). That may not be man's way, but it *is* God's way.

Oops! I Didn't Mean to Do That!

Give the following instructions to the people of Israel. This is how you are to deal with those who sin unintentionally by doing anything that violates one of the LORD's commands.   LEVITICUS 4:2

Dwight Moody was to speak at a church where people were notorious for leaving before the end of the sermon. He was informed about this ahead of time, so he began his sermon this way: "I'm going to speak to two classes of people this morning: first to the sinners and then to the saints."

A few minutes into the sermon, Moody announced, "I'm done speaking to the sinners, so if they would like to leave, that's fine; I will now address the saints!" For once, no one in the congregation dared to leave early.

We are sinners, both by nature and by choice. Sometimes we sin intentionally, and other times we do it in ignorance, but we all do it.

Sin is not a popular subject. It never has been. Hinduism regards good and evil as relative terms and declares that people can't help but stumble as they strive to know themselves and move toward nirvana. If they fail in this life, they can always try again in their next reincarnation. Unitarians believe that people are essentially good and can save themselves by personal improvement. In Christian Science, sin, death, and evil do not even exist. These kinds of denials and truth tweaking only drive people further from the solution, which is an honest admission of failure.

The Bible declares, "People who conceal their sins will not prosper, but if they confess and turn from them, they will receive mercy" (Proverbs 28:13). This passage presses us to reevaluate our concepts of sin and responsibility. If we committed it, then we are responsible for it, whether it was intentional or not. Sit quietly for a moment and allow the Holy Spirit to sift through yesterday's thoughts and actions and bring your sins to the light. Then confess them. Honestly admitting sin and weakness is a sign of maturity.

The First Ordination

Moses took some of [the ram's] blood and applied it to the lobe of Aaron's right ear, the thumb of his right hand, and the big toe of his right foot.

LEVITICUS 8:23

I will never forget one Christmas service when, after I invited people to come to Christ, a man came to me and stated, "I've been a pastor for years, but until now it's never been personal. I've preached about it, but I've never lived it!" His statement struck me profoundly. I wondered how one could preach about the need to be cleansed without having experienced that cleansing. But I was grateful for this man's humility and honesty.

God wanted to make sure that his priests, who would officiate at the sacrifices, had applied the cleansing of the sacrificial blood in their own lives. When a priest was ordained, blood was smeared on his right ear to symbolize that he should be sensitive to the voice of God above all others'. Blood was rubbed on the priest's right thumb, committing the person to skillfully perform God's work. Finally, blood was placed on his big toe to show that he would walk in God's ways. The priest was consecrating his body to God.

A helpful exercise is to take the various parts of your body and consecrate them to God for his purpose. The New Testament encourages us to do this: "Dear brothers and sisters, I plead with you to give your bodies to God because of all he has done for you. Let them be a living and holy sacrifice—the kind he will find acceptable. This is truly the way to worship him" (Romans 12:1). Just as God used Moses' mouth to speak his laws, David's hands to defeat Goliath, and Paul's feet to spread the Good News, he wants to use your body as his instrument. A simple prayer might be, "Here I am, Lord. Use my body to do your work today. Help me to faithfully allow you to direct my steps, speak your message, and do your will."

January 24

I Wouldn't Eat That

Give the following instructions to the people of Israel. Of all the land animals, these are the ones you may use for food. LEVITICUS 11:2

When my three brothers and I were growing up, our parents loved to surprise us at mealtimes. Once, Mom served an oddly textured entrée with a brownish sheen. "What's that?" I queried, to which Mom replied, "Just eat it; it's fine!"

One of my brothers, wanting me to be fully aware, shouted, "It's cow brains!" I almost gagged. There are some things people should stay away from!

Chapters 11–15 of Leviticus illustrate the principle of *worship as separation*. The Israelites were to follow certain dietary laws.

What's the big deal about Israel's diet? Why would God make what they ate a part of their worship system? There were two reasons: First, they simply were to be *set apart* from other nations: "I, the LORD, am the one who brought you up from the land of Egypt, that I might be your God. Therefore, you must be holy because I am holy" (Leviticus 11:45). Second, for sanitary reasons: "By these instructions you will know what is unclean and clean, and which animals may be eaten and which may not be eaten" (v. 47). There was no FDA in ancient times. Modern science has confirmed that the Jewish diet, during these wilderness years and even in later years during the plagues of Europe, helped the Jewish people to escape infections brought on by animal parasites. Moses, Aaron, and the rest of Israel may not have known that at the time, but God did, and he was watching out for his people.

Leviticus 11–15 illustrates an overarching principle: *All of life is to be lived under the watching eye of God.* Public and private life, whether in the kitchen, the boardroom, or the bedroom, must be lived consistently. God doesn't want to be compartmentalized into an hour or two on Sunday. He wants to share *every* part of your life. That's what it means to be holy.

Wholly Holy!

[God said,] "Give the following instructions to the entire community of Israel. You must be holy because I, the LORD your God, am holy."

LEVITICUS 19:2

Holiness is sometimes thought of as God's least "attractive" attribute. Folks tend to gravitate toward his other qualities, such as his love, his goodness, his sovereignty, or his creativity. But the Bible discusses holiness more frequently than any other attribute of God. God is called *holy* more than he is called anything else. And lest you think that holiness is just some Old Testament quality that God abandoned in the New Testament, remember that Jesus taught his followers to pray, "Father, may your name be kept holy" (Luke 11:2). The third person of the Trinity is also closely connected with this attribute: He is known not as the Loving Spirit or the Creative Spirit but rather as the *Holy* Spirit.

Just as Leviticus 1–17 showed the way to God through sacrifice, chapters 18–27 describe a walk with God through sanctification (growth in holiness). We are to reflect this characteristic of God in our own lives. In fact, this reminder to be holy like our God is found a total of nine times in Leviticus and nearly sixty times in the rest of the Old Testament.

Though definitions of holiness abound, perhaps it's best to see it as *wholeness*. To be holy is to be *whole*. We are really not whole, or complete, until our lives are devoted to God, set apart for his use. To be wholly holy is to live as nonconformists in an unholy world. It is when we walk in holiness that we begin to really live! How do we do that? Simply by consistently evaluating everything we do and asking, "Does this turn me toward God or away from him?" This kind of self-evaluation is a lifelong process—and today is a perfect day to start.

Rejoice!

On the first day gather branches from magnificent trees—palm fronds,
boughs from leafy trees, and willows that grow by the streams. Then
celebrate with joy before the LORD your God for seven days.

LEVITICUS 23:40

Do you remember Bobby McFerrin's 1980s song "Don't Worry—Be Happy"?
With a whimsical reggae beat, the cheerful words rang out:

> In every life we have some trouble
> But when you worry you make it double
> Don't Worry—Be Happy.

But happiness isn't something we can just turn on. It must be objective, that
is, based on some reality.

The Israelites had the best reason—*they were God's people!* And God wanted
them to live like it. Three times a year, the Israelites were to leave their homes
and gather together to celebrate before the Lord. At the festivals of Passover,
Pentecost, and Shelters, joy was mingled with the pageantry of offerings and
thanksgiving. There were no convocations of mourning except one, and that
was on the Day of Atonement. On the other occasions, joy was to be the emotion of the day. Each festival was a reminder of God's power or provision.

So joy was to mark God's people. Does it mark you? Do you rejoice when
you gather for corporate worship? Or do you just fold your arms, sit back,
and shift into neutral? Being around some church folks is like witnessing an
autopsy. You begin to wonder, *Does that person know that God is alive and*
active?

When I was growing up, church felt like an obligation rather than an
opportunity. It was something I had to do, not something I wanted to do.
But when the relationship with God became real, I discovered I had every
reason for joy.

Charles Spurgeon once remarked, "Our happy God should be wor-
shipped by a happy people; a cheerful spirit is in keeping with His nature."
Bars have happy hours. Shouldn't the hours we spend at church in the community of worship be happy hours? After all, God's redeemed people are
really the ones who have something to sing about!

The Four-Sided Campground

When the Israelites set up camp, each tribe will be assigned its own area.
The tribal divisions will camp beneath their family banners on all four
sides of the Tabernacle, but at some distance from it. NUMBERS 2:2

The book of Numbers is a wanderer's travelogue. It's the honest narrative of what happens when people refuse to believe God's promises. From Sinai, the Israelites could have arrived in Canaan in two weeks, but they wandered in the wilderness for an entire generation.

But how they camped as they traveled is noteworthy. The twelve tribes were organized into camps on the four sides of the Tabernacle. Each tribe had a standard, a symbol that denoted which tribe it was. On the east, three tribes gathered under the standard of Judah, which was a lion. On the south, three more tribes met under Reuben's standard, which was a man. To the west congregated three tribes under Ephraim's symbol, an ox. And on the north, the remaining three tribes assembled under the tribal symbol of Dan, an eagle.

The prophet Ezekiel saw a vision of the throne of God and noticed that each of the living beings had "a human face in the front, the face of a lion on the right side, the face of an ox on the left side, and the face of an eagle at the back" (Ezekiel 1:10). John described them this way: "The first of these living beings was like a lion; the second was like an ox; the third had a human face; and the fourth was like an eagle in flight" (Revelation 4:7). Some scholars suggest that these four figures represent the four Gospels: Matthew revealed Christ's kingliness (lion), Mark his servanthood (ox), Luke his humanity (man), John his deity (eagle).

The Bible you hold and read is the revelation of the living God and especially his Son, Jesus Christ. When we are in disarray and confusion, God uses the fact that he is a God of order to remind us of his presence.

Chasing Clouds

Whenever the cloud lifted from over the sacred tent, the people of Israel would break camp and follow it. And wherever the cloud settled, the people of Israel would set up camp. NUMBERS 9:17

Today's verse sums up the daily experience of the children of Israel in the wilderness. The cloud that towered above the Tabernacle wasn't some natural formation of cumulus, stratus, cirrus, or nimbus clouds. It was a supernatural wonder that looked like a pillar of cloud by day and a giant column of fire at night! Often called God's *shekinah* (a Hebrew word that means "presence"), it made the people of Israel different from every other ancient nation. When the cloud moved, the people moved. When the cloud stopped, they stopped. God's people spent their wilderness lives looking up. In other words, they were looking to God for guidance.

I love seeing people receive Christ, especially when it's obvious that God has touched their lives. But conversion is just the beginning; there are many more steps of obedience to be taken. Now they begin a pilgrimage of faith, learning to discern the will of God and to obey his leading.

A pilot inexperienced at instrument navigation was flying his single-engine plane on a cloudy day. When the control tower was giving him directions on how to land, he started getting tense as he thought of the hills, towers, and buildings in the area. The more he thought about them, the more he panicked. Finally, in a calm but stern voice, the tower director said, "You just obey the instructions, and we'll take care of the obstructions."

God has no shortage of methods he can use to guide us, including the principles of his Word, the counsel of mature believers, and circumstances that take place on any given day. But the secret to being led by God is focusing on the Master more than on the methods. Learn to tap into God's navigational system, the Holy Spirit, who Jesus assured would guide you (see John 16:13). Looking up is more important than looking around.

Is the Majority Always Right?

*We even saw giants there, the descendants of Anak. Next to them we felt
like grasshoppers, and that's what they thought, too!* NUMBERS 13:33

Abraham Lincoln is credited with saying that you can fool some of the
people all of the time, and even all the people some of the time, but you
can't fool all the people all the time. In today's reading, all the Israelites were
fooled by only ten people. Twelve representatives, one from each tribe, went
on an exploratory mission to the Promised Land. These spies all agreed
that the land was a great place, exceedingly rich in resources. They all also
agreed that there were some sizable enemies there. What they disagreed on
was what that meant for the Israelites. Ten of the twelve got scared and were
fooled by what they saw. Only two, Joshua and Caleb, saw their enemies
through the lens of God's character and promise. When it came to decision
time, whether to enter the land, the majority of Israelites chose to listen to
the unbelieving majority.

Once unbelief begins to spread, the momentum is hard to stop. The
amazing thing was that the situation was the opposite of what the ten spies
had said: The *Canaanites* were afraid of the *Israelites*. We know this because
when Joshua entered the land years later, a woman from Jericho said, "We
are all afraid of you. Everyone in the land is living in terror. For we have
heard how the Lord made a dry path for you through the Red Sea when you
left Egypt. . . . No wonder our hearts have melted in fear! No one has the
courage to fight after hearing such things" (Joshua 2:9-11).

Life will always pose challenges, and we can easily misinterpret those
challenges and fall prey to unbelief. Dare to go against the flow of popular
belief. Dare to view life through the lens of faith. Not many people are doing
it these days. But even all the people can be fooled some of the time.

I Hate *Snakes!*

Moses made a snake out of bronze and attached it to a pole. Then anyone who was bitten by a snake could look at the bronze snake and be healed! NUMBERS 21:9

At one point in Steven Spielberg's film *Raiders of the Lost Ark*, Indiana Jones looks into a pit filled with writhing snakes and exclaims, "I *hate* snakes!"

I agree. Indiana Jones would've hated being in camp with the Israelites the day God sent poisonous snakes in response to the people's grumbling. Their walking had turned into wandering and then degenerated into murmuring. Now they would be wailing as snakes bit them. But God told Moses to make a bronze snake, hang it on a pole, and have people look at it.

Why would God do such a thing? God was using the snakes as discipline to turn his children's hearts to him. He was also providing a way for them to be cured. It must've sounded crazy to them, but all they had to do was look at the bronze serpent, and they would be cured of the effects of the venom ravaging their bodies.

Jesus referred to this incident in predicting his crucifixion: "As Moses lifted up the bronze snake on a pole in the wilderness, so the Son of Man must be lifted up, so that everyone who believes in him will have eternal life" (John 3:14-15). Just as the Israelites looked in faith at the snake on the pole, people would look in faith to the cross for salvation.

Faith must be carefully tended. As Israel's history unfolded, the people turned the bronze serpent into an object of worship. The look of faith became a look of false devotion.

A snake on a pole or a cross at the front of a church can become an object of worship rather than a signpost that directs our worship. Is there any place, person, or object to which you have ascribed too much meaning? Be careful never to let the instrument eclipse the source.

Let the Donkey Talk

The LORD gave the donkey the ability to speak. "What have I done to you that deserves your beating me three times?" it asked Balaam.

NUMBERS 22:28

If you're old enough, you might remember Mr. Ed, the animal star of the 1960s TV show of the same name. Ed was one smart horse, often wiser than his human owner, Wilbur. The Bible had a donkey that was wiser than his master, Balaam, and it, too, could talk.

Balaam was a mercenary, a hired gun. The king of Moab wanted him to curse the Israelites. But God refused to give him permission to curse his people. When Balaam finally did speak, this pagan diviner spoke like a golden-tongued orator to bless God's inheritance instead.

But most people forget that God didn't speak just through Balaam; God spoke *to* Balaam through Balaam's donkey!

The Bible says more about Balaam than it does about Mary the mother of Jesus or any of the twelve apostles, mentioning him fifty-nine times. His life is full of lessons, but what people often overlook as they focus on the idea of a talking donkey is the amazing reaction of Balaam—he talked back to the donkey! Never once did he stop to think, W*ait a minute. Donkeys can't talk!*

God has used patriarchs, prophets, seers, angels, and even a donkey to speak to people. What a privilege to be his representative. What a thrill to be his spokesperson. But Paul wrote, "If I could speak all the languages of earth and of angels, but didn't love others, I would only be a noisy gong or a clanging cymbal" (1 Corinthians 13:1). God can use anyone to speak for him, even Balaam and Balaam's donkey! It's not eloquence or brilliance that marks a true man or women of God. It's love! Ask God to help you to be one of his faithful representatives. Anyone can be, for God chooses "things the world considers foolish in order to shame those who think they are wise" (1 Corinthians 1:27).

February 1

This Land Is Your Land

These are the boundaries of your land.   NUMBERS 34:12

My father loved land. He bought it and sold it; he parceled it and improved it. As a real estate developer he always made sure that in every transaction the land was properly platted, or plotted out. Even though boundary lines were carefully marked, some people never cared about the exact proportions of their own land, and often they never used the full extent of what they owned. They simply wanted the "space."

As Israel reached the border of the Promised Land, God fixed their boundaries for them and instructed them to drive out their enemies completely and occupy their inheritance.

It's regrettable that the Israelites never fully "possessed their possessions." They crossed the Jordan; they entered their land; they even marked it off as God had instructed. But they never were able to fully enjoy all of it. The boundaries that God prescribed for his people totaled *three hundred thousand* square miles. God promised Abraham that Israelite real estate would extend all the way to the Euphrates River (see Genesis 15:18). But they never appropriated it all. You might say they never opened all their presents! At Israel's political zenith, the people enjoyed only thirty thousand square miles, one-tenth of what God had promised.

The Christian life can be like that. We can receive the gift but never fully open it. We might conclude, "I'm saved—that's all I care about!" But that would be a tragedy. God has given his people "every spiritual blessing in the heavenly realms" (Ephesians 1:3). Are you fully experiencing your inheritance in Christ?

British preacher Charles Spurgeon once remarked, "Most Christians as to the river of experience, are only up to the ankles; some others have waded till the stream is up to the knees; a few find it breast-high; and but few—oh! how few!—find it a river to swim in, the bottom of which they cannot touch." Ask God to show you your boundaries so that you can live your life to the fullest!

The Desert "Briefing"

Forty years after the Israelites left Egypt, on the first day of the eleventh month, Moses addressed the people of Israel, telling them everything the LORD had commanded him to say. DEUTERONOMY 1:3

History proves how easily people can forget truth and principle. Many great institutions once based on solid values have eroded to the point of being unrecognizable from their original intent.

The history of the Jewish nation shows us that truth and principle must be reinforced by repetition and frequent reminders. The word *Deuteronomy* means "second law." The values taught in the Bible's previous four books are repeated in this one because a new generation is rising and the people need to hear what God did and said in the previous thirty-eight years. God didn't want them to forget their history or their calling.

So, on the plains of Moab, Moses spends a whole month giving three farewell speeches to brief this upcoming generation. He *reviews* their past (chapters 1–3); he gives *regulations* for the present (chapters 4–26), and he *readies* them for their future (chapters 27–34). Without this briefing, the people would be in danger of forgetting their heritage.

What about your spiritual experience? Are you moving forward spiritually, understanding your heritage in Christ, and reaching toward the future? Or are you merely wandering? An understanding of biblical truth and of God's plan for you is essential for your spiritual vitality and growth. Without that solid foundation, you're in danger of forgetting that your purpose in life is to please God. Don't be impatient when the Bible repeats itself. (It does so quite a bit: repeated stories in both 1 and 2 Kings and 1 and 2 Chronicles, repetition in Psalms and the four Gospels.) In fact, Deuteronomy is quoted some eighty times in the New Testament. So rather than think, *I'll skip this part; I've read it before,* say, "I guess this is important enough for me to remember!" Then ask God for patience and humility to listen carefully and obey fully.

February 3

King-Size Bed!

King Og of Bashan was the last survivor of the giant Rephaites. His bed was made of iron and was more than thirteen feet long and six feet wide. It can still be seen in the Ammonite city of Rabbah. DEUTERONOMY 3:11

The children of Israel had a few king-size enemies. But they also had a King-size God! The question was, where would their focus be? As Moses reviewed the various geographical locations their forefathers had visited on their journey toward the Promised Land, he mentioned an interesting leader. Og was the king of Bashan, the rich and verdant land east of the Sea of Galilee. This area, known also as Gilead, was where the tribes of Reuben and Gad and the half-tribe of Manasseh eventually settled.

Og was an unusually big man. Moses mentions that Og's bed was more than thirteen feet long and six feet wide!

Apparently the Israelites decided to preserve it in some sort of museum-like setting in a local town. Maybe Moses wanted future generations to be able to see the size of some of the enemies God had defeated for them. Certainly many formidable foes had faced off against God's people in their history. The twelve spies who had canvassed the new land some thirty-eight years before had reported that some of its inhabitants were giants. Even David would face a giant in the future.

But what are such enemies before a King-size God? When we look with the eyes of faith at a seemingly impossible situation, we can see a big God looming over it. That makes all the difference. If you see giants fighting ordinary people, you'll think, *Those poor people.* But if you focus on God, who is actually fighting the giants, you'll say, "Those poor giants!"

As you look at your problems, obstacles, and giant issues, remember that "the Spirit who lives in you is greater than the spirit who lives in the world" (1 John 4:4). Martin Luther discovered this truth and remarked, "With God, one is a majority."

Teach Your Children Well

Repeat [God's commands] again and again to your children. Talk about them when you are at home and when you are on the road, when you are going to bed and when you are getting up.   DEUTERONOMY 6:7

As a father and son climbed a hill together, the trail was becoming steeper and more dangerous. When Dad stopped to consider which was the best way up, he heard his young son say, "Choose the good way, Daddy; I'm coming right behind you!"

Passing the spiritual baton to the next generation is part of obeying God's commands. The Israelites were not only to remember what God had done in their own history; they were also to teach it to their children.

Someone once remarked that a parent is "a partner with God in making disciples of his or her children." The book of Proverbs is primarily a record of a father's instruction to his children. By both precept and principle, parents can show their children how to choose the right way.

Are you a father or a mother? It's not an easy task, but it is an essential one. In fact, your role is indispensable. Parents must never allow the urgent demands of life to crowd out the important calling of training, mentoring, and molding their children. Even Socrates once said that he wondered how men who were so careful in training their horses could be so indifferent to the training of their own children.

In the Middle East, Bedouin mothers would put a dab of date syrup on one of their fingers and touch the lips of their newborn infants to encourage the sucking reflex. This would stimulate the desire for feeding. Parents have a significant opportunity to stimulate their children's taste for godliness by talking about God and living for God at home. When children see their parents reading the Bible and praying and talking about their faith, they will develop a desire to "taste and see that the LORD is good" (Psalm 34:8).

When Moses Introduced Jesus

The LORD your God will raise up for you a prophet like me from among your fellow Israelites. You must listen to him.   DEUTERONOMY 18:15

Jesus Christ is the undisputed champion of Scripture and the figure that dominates every story and every setting. The entire Old Testament looks forward to his coming. That's why the "scarlet thread of redemption," as it is sometimes called, can be traced throughout the Bible.

As Moses was delivering his second speech to the up-and-coming generation of Israelites, he made a prediction about *another* prophet, *another* spokesman, *another* deliverer who would be similar to him. Israel should look for and listen to a Moses-like spokesman who would be coming.

The lives of Moses and Jesus display amazing parallels. Both Moses and Jesus were in danger in their childhoods: Moses from Pharaoh's edict against Hebrew baby boys, and Jesus from Herod's command against baby boys in Bethlehem. Both Moses and Jesus were deliverers: Moses was God's instrument to deliver the Israelites from bondage in Egypt, and Jesus came to save people from the bondage of sin. Both were intercessors for sinners: Moses prayed for the calf worshipers to be forgiven (see Exodus 32:31-32), and Jesus prayed for his executioners (see Luke 23:34). Finally, both Moses and Jesus knew rejection: The Israelites initially rejected Moses' appointment by God, and Jesus was condemned and crucified by his brethren.

Moses also spoke God's message, but when God the Father sent Jesus the Son, he put a period at the end of the salvation sentence. He has nothing more to say to the world than what he has said in Jesus Christ. Now we have a choice. In a world in which entertainments, advertisements, and amusements vie for our attention, will we choose instead to "tune in" to God's frequency in Christ? Do you desire to hear your Shepherd's voice? Will you listen carefully as he speaks? Make Psalm 119:18 your prayer today: "Open my eyes to see the wonderful truths in your instructions."

The Big If

If you fully obey the LORD your God and carefully keep all his commands that I am giving you today, the LORD your God will set you high above all the nations of the world. DEUTERONOMY 28:1

I have a rather large front door at home. Recently I was fascinated by its relatively small hinges. Those small devices serve to open a portal through which friends can enter.

In today's verse, the word *if* was a literary hinge. It was also a theological and practical hinge that would allow the Israelites to experience God's blessing. This little word represented the conditional part of the covenant God was making with his people. Moses instructed that once the people got to the Land of Promise, they should travel to Samaria, its geographic center, and recite these principles. Six tribes were to stand by Mount Gerizim to recite the blessings, while six tribes stood by Mount Ebal to recite the curses. Both the blessings and the curses were dependent on the little word *if*. *If* the people obeyed God, he would bless them. *If* they disobeyed God, he would curse them. It was that simple. Only the proper response to God's commands would bring God's favor. That's why *if* was such an ominous word. The Israelites' future in the new land was dependent on their performance.

In contrast, the new covenant in Christ is joyful and life-giving because God's favor isn't dependent on our performance. The big "if" isn't the hinge any longer. Jesus came to take the "if" out of humanity's relationship to God and replace it with the word *because: Because* Jesus paid the debt for my sin, I can have eternal life. *Because* I'm in Christ, I can enjoy the fullness of his favor. *Because* there is nothing to add to the Cross, the only "if" is whether I belong to Christ.

Have you honestly received Christ, God's solution for your sin? If so, the door of God's grace is hung on hinges reading "because" rather than "if"!

Moses' Birthday Party

[Moses] said, "I am now 120 years old, and I am no longer able to lead you. The LORD has told me, 'You will not cross the Jordan River.'"

DEUTERONOMY 31:2

Maria Capovilla, who died in 2006 at the age of 116, was the oldest woman alive according to *Guinness World Records.* This Ecuadoran woman thanked God every day that she was alive. Until approximately a year before her death, Maria was in good health, had great eyesight (she was able to read the newspaper and watch TV), and walked with assistance but without a cane!

As striking as Maria's story is, Moses had Maria beat by four years: He was still vibrantly serving God at 120! In his last public speech before his death, Moses addressed the twelve tribes of Israel as the elder statesman of that nation, knowing that he himself would not be going into the Land of Promise. Yet Moses' faith in God was steadfast and exemplary.

The genius of the Christian life is that the second half of life can be the richest, fullest, and most productive, even though our culture seems to value only the youthful first half. John Wesley was still preaching eloquently at eighty-eight, and that's after years of traveling on horseback! Since 1949, Billy Graham has preached to more than one hundred million people worldwide, and he continues to do so in his later years, although on a very limited basis.

Moses was just getting started at age 80 and was only winding down at 120, the latter one-third of his life being the most productive.

Counting the years is not nearly as important as making the years count. Make sure that you're not just marking time. Don't merely *spend* your life doing things; *invest* your life for God's purposes. I suggest keeping a journal to chronicle lessons, prayers, and yearnings that are in your heart. Then write down what you've learned and ask God to give you opportunities to share those lessons with the next generation. This way every birthday will become an adventure in faith!

The Most Unlikely *to Succeed*

Joshua secretly sent out two spies from the Israelite camp at Acacia Grove. He instructed them, "Scout out the land on the other side of the Jordan River, especially around Jericho." So the two men set out and came to the house of a prostitute named Rahab and stayed there that night.

JOSHUA 2:1

Many high school yearbooks have a section that lists exemplary students in various categories: Best Dressed, Most Athletic, Most Spirited, Best All-Around, and Most Likely to Succeed. If there had been a Jericho High School yearbook, Rahab would have probably never made that list. If anything, she would've been voted Most *Unlikely* to Succeed! Yet she displays an unusual depth of faith in the God of the Israelite spies sent to Jericho. She hid them from the city officials because she knew that the God of the Hebrews would give Jericho and the rest of the land to the Hebrews.

Her faith became so renowned that the author of Hebrews included her as a model of faith in God: "It was by faith that Rahab the prostitute was not destroyed with the people in her city who refused to obey God. For she had given a friendly welcome to the spies" (Hebrews 11:31). She even appears in the family tree of Jesus himself (see Matthew 1:5). The individual most unlikely to become an example of confidence in God became just that.

God is full of surprises. Those whom others despise and reject, God repairs and uses. If a doctor performed successful cranial surgery in a pickup in the African savannah using a Swiss Army knife, he would be hailed an unsurpassed expert because he was limited to tools of poor quality. But God likes to "operate" that way. When he limits himself to broken tools (imperfect and deficient people), he gets more glory.

Don't look at the smallness of your talent or at the limitations of your ability; look to the greatness of the limitless God. In God's hands, you will become *very likely* to succeed!

Get Your Feet Wet

The priests will carry the Ark of the LORD, the Lord of all the earth. As soon as their feet touch the water, the flow of water will be cut off upstream, and the river will stand up like a wall.   JOSHUA 3:13

The Jordan River crossing has been the subject of many an old hymn. One song refers to this event as a metaphor for going to heaven:

> I looked over Jordan, and what did I see
> Coming for to carry me home?
> A band of angels coming after me
> Coming for to carry me home.

But as soon as the Israelites crossed the Jordan, they faced multiple battles. That doesn't sound heavenly!

Before the Israelites could set foot on the new land, the priests had to get their feet wet. During the season this crossing was made, the Jordan overflows and can get up to a mile wide. Carrying the Ark of the Covenant, the priests had to walk *into* the water as an act of faith. Once they showed their willingness to obey, God made the river dry up, and the people were able to walk across on dry ground. We could say that the crossing of the Red Sea signifies believers' deliverance from the bondage of sin, and the crossing of the Jordan River signifies believers' claiming their inheritance in Christ. In fact, Joshua (whose name is the Old Testament equivalent of *Jesus*) is like Christ, who leads believers into victory.

God has a purpose for his people beyond merely giving us tickets to heaven. He wants us to gain spiritual ground, to take what was once enemy territory and plant the flag of God's Kingdom there through evangelism and service.

Sometimes the first step of faith or obedience is the hardest one, but we'll never make any progress without it. What difficult assignment is God calling you to? What spiritual adventure is he directing you into? Take the first step. Trust him today for strength to make the right choices. As you do, exciting, new Kingdom opportunities will unfold before you.

Who's in Charge Here?

When Joshua was near the town of Jericho, he looked up and saw a man standing in front of him with sword in hand. Joshua went up to him and demanded, "Are you friend or foe?" JOSHUA 5:13

I have a friend who served as a marine colonel in the Gulf War. When I was going through a difficult time, my friend shared a wartime principle: "Nothing is ever as bad as first reported." I took that to heart and soon discovered that it was true. My trial began to shrink, and I was able to rest in the strength of Christ, my Commanding Officer.

In today's reading, the battle for Jericho was about to begin. Joshua was preparing for battle when he discovered that he wasn't really in charge—Someone else was. A soldier with a drawn sword stood before Joshua. "Are you friend or foe?" Joshua asked suspiciously. On learning that he was standing face-to-face with the Lord, he took off his sandals, like Moses, and fell down and worshiped this heavenly Officer. What he had thought was an upcoming battle, he now knew would be a total victory!

When life's battles come at us hard and fast, we usually jump into defense mode and begin to fight—alone. But the secret in spiritual warfare is to acknowledge whose battle it really is. As one of Israel's kings was told, "the battle is not yours, but God's" (2 Chronicles 20:15). Jesus told his disciples, "Apart from me you can do nothing" (John 15:5). If we forget this, we're already defeated. If we remember it and worship before we do battle, we'll be fine.

Public victories are the result of private visits with God! Mary, Queen of Scots admitted that she feared the prayers of John Knox more than all the armies of Europe. Satan loves it when we forget to call on Jesus and try to fight in our own strength. But as William Cowper wrote, "Satan trembles when he sees the weakest saint upon his knees."

February 11

And the Walls Came Tumbling Down

When the people heard the sound of the rams' horns, they shouted as loud as they could. Suddenly, the walls of Jericho collapsed, and the Israelites charged straight into the town and captured it. JOSHUA 6:20

Jericho's Canaanite neighbors thought it unconquerable. As the Israelites gazed across the Jordan River and saw the city's high and apparently impenetrable walls, they trembled. They were just a ragtag throng of ex-slaves facing an impossible task. Yet God instructed them to march around Jericho once a day for six days. On the seventh day, the priests were to blow their rams' horns, and the Israelites were to shout. When they did, God promised, the walls would simply fall down, and the Israelites could enter and take the city.

Why did God use this strategy? Perhaps it was to test the Israelites' faith, as they would be exposed to the ridicule of Jericho's citizens and perhaps a preemptive attack. Maybe God wanted to test their humility. Trained soldiers wouldn't enjoy running around a town and then yelling at it; they would want to taste the battle. Whatever the reason, the Israelites had their marching orders, and off they went.

All Christians have a "Jericho"—some looming, unconquerable thing. It could be internal: a character weakness or a sinful propensity. It could be external: a physical disability or an unbelieving friend they deem an impossible case. It could even be a spiritual task. Because we feel inadequate, we're intimidated by the largeness of the mission.

But as we move out in obedience to God's marching orders, we make an astonishing discovery: Things we thought were impossibilities seem to shrink; things we saw as barriers are removed, and the task gets accomplished.

Does today's agenda seem overwhelming? Do you dread what you're facing? Joshua had a wonderful "perspective check" as he worshiped before the battle (see Joshua 5:13-15), but he didn't stay there. He went from adoration to action, from meditation to marching. So just get marching, and leave the walls up to God!

God the Sharpshooter

*As the Amorites retreated down the road from Beth-horon, the LORD
destroyed them with a terrible hailstorm from heaven that continued
until they reached Azekah. The hail killed more of the enemy than the
Israelites killed with the sword.*   JOSHUA 10:11

When I was a boy, my dad signed me up for rifle classes at the local shoot-
ing range. He wanted to be sure that if I ever had to use a gun, I would be
both cautious and accurate. I had fun, but I never got good enough to be
considered a sharpshooter. Since those days, I've been to the range with
firearms instructors from SWAT teams, and I've concluded that if I'm ever
in a life-threatening situation, I want *them* around!

The ancient town of Gibeon was attacked by a coalition of five Canaanite kings. The Israelites came to Gibeon's defense even though the crafty
Gibeonites had earlier deceived them. Israel did what it could to put their
ally's enemies to flight, but God had a better view of the battle and much
better aim. Using a hailstorm and the equivalent of a smart-bomb guidance
system, God directed those hailstones selectively to hit only the enemy.

Revelation 16:21 says that one day God will unleash his wrath on the reb-
els of the earth with hailstones weighing as much as seventy-five pounds!
I take comfort in the fact that heaven's Sharpshooter will be the one to
execute the final judgment. He alone knows whom to attack and whom to
spare.

As Christians, we can't be spiritual pacifists; our enemy is always in attack
mode. In fact, Charles Spurgeon once said, "There is something comforting in the thought that the devil is an adversary. I'd sooner have him for an
adversary than for a friend." But we need to realize that we fight the real
battle with God's Word and with prayer (see Ephesians 6:17-18). So do your
best; then leave it to God to inflict the decisive damage to your enemy's
cause.

February 13 READ JOSHUA 14:1-12

Old Dog, New Trick

[Caleb said,] "I am as strong now as I was when Moses sent me on that journey, and I can still travel and fight as well as I could then. So give me the hill country that the LORD promised me." JOSHUA 14:11-12

Caleb is a fine, strong name. It can mean "bold," but in its original form it also meant "dog." I don't see that as an insult—I love my dog! Dogs can be tenacious and courageous. The Caleb in today's reading is now an old man, but he's ready for a new adventure. Forty years earlier, he and Joshua had bold faith that stood strong against the majority of murmuring, faithless ones who filled the camp of Israel. Now, at age eighty-five, the old guy is ready to take on another battle, to scale another mountain, and to tackle life with an even greater enthusiasm.

What was Caleb's secret? It was twofold: First, *he refused to live only in the past.* He didn't sit around looking back over his shoulder and saying, "Remember the good old days when we saw God do great things?" He lived in the present reality of the *living* God who could still use him to accomplish even greater things.

Second, *he viewed himself as valuable.* Many folks, as they age, are overcome by feelings of uselessness and inadequacy. Not Caleb! He declined the temptation to become a couch potato and sit around watching Monday-night camel races. He wasn't washed up. He didn't see himself as unimportant. He had the same enthusiasm he had when he first entered the Promised Land to spy it out. He was only just beginning.

There are none so old as those who have outlived their own enthusiasm. How's yours? Has your sense of adventure cooled a bit from earlier in your life? If so, ask God to renew a sense of godly adventure in you. What new exploits might he have in store for you?

What about **My** *Needs?*

The descendants of Joseph came to Joshua and asked, "Why have you given us only one portion of land as our homeland when the LORD has blessed us with so many people?" JOSHUA 17:14

An old Jewish proverb reads, "There is no room for God in the man who is full of himself." Self-betterment, self-exaltation, and self-preservation rank pretty high when it comes to what motivates most people. Once the people of God started to settle in their new land, they quickly turned inward toward themselves. Joseph's two tribal shares were assigned to the descendants of Ephraim and Manasseh. They were given areas of rich land in central Canaan suitable for their needs.

But tribal representatives complained that they weren't given enough. They felt their sheer numbers justified their request for more land. Perhaps they felt that since their forefather, Joseph, was once the prime minister of Egypt and saved the Hebrew bloodline, they deserved payback. They also complained that the Canaanite inhabitants were too strong for them to drive out.

Joshua assured them that they *could* expel these enemies: "Since you are so large and strong, you will be given more than one portion. The forests of the hill country will be yours as well. Clear as much of the land as you wish, and take possession of its farthest corners. And you will drive out the Canaanites from the valleys, too, even though they are strong and have iron chariots" (Joshua 17:17-18).

The principle is clear: *When we long for more than we have, we must first use what we have; then perhaps God will give more.* Is your spiritual engine operating on all cylinders? Are you putting everything you can into serving God right where you are? If so, relax. Jesus said, "To those who use well what they are given, even more will be given, and they will have an abundance. But from those who do nothing, even what little they have will be taken away" (Matthew 25:29). In other words, use it or lose it!

Sanctuary!

Tell the Israelites to designate the cities of refuge, as I instructed Moses.

JOSHUA 20:2

Some cities are known for entertainment, others for picturesque beauty, and still others for their architecture. Six ancient Israelite cities were set aside as judicial sanctuaries. These cities of refuge, three to the west of the Jordan River and three to the east, offered asylum to individuals who had unintentionally killed someone. The law protected the accidental criminal from relatives of the victim, who had the right to kill the guilty parties if they should ever leave their designated places of protection.

To this day in the Middle East there is said to be "blood between the tribes" if a slaying has been left unpunished. According to the Talmud (Jewish oral law), every major crossroad in ancient Israel had a sign pointing the direction to the nearest city of refuge.

These six cities were hints of the refreshment and forgiveness found in Jesus Christ. They were *available to everyone*, and Jesus is always available for anyone who calls out to him.

These cities were also *accessible to everyone.* When Jesus died on the cross, he cleared the path. There are no longer any obstructions on the road to him. The only thing that can keep you away is unbelief, pride, or disobedience.

Do you feel trapped by a situation you're in? Do you feel the weight of your sin? You need the protective refuge of the love of Christ. When you run to him, your soul will be safe there. Let the words of the classic hymn "How Firm a Foundation" reaffirm that your perfect sanctuary is in him:

> How firm a foundation, ye saints of the Lord,
> Is laid for your faith in His excellent Word!
> What more can He say than to you He hath said,
> To you who for refuge to Jesus have fled?
>
> "The soul that on Jesus still leans for repose,
> I will not, I will not desert to his foes;
> That soul, though all hell should endeavor to shake,
> I'll never, no, never, no, never forsake!"

The Sin of Assumption

The whole community of Israel gathered at Shiloh and prepared to go to war against them.   JOSHUA 22:12

During the American Civil War, rival armies camped on opposite banks of the Potomac River—and a musical contest erupted. Whenever the Union band played one of its national tunes, Confederate musicians would strike up a Southern melody. On one occasion, one of the bands started to play "Home, Sweet Home," and the contest stopped. Soon voices from both sides of the river could be heard singing the refrain, "There's no place like home." Whatever differences each side had assumed, they were diminished by a shared understanding that both sides would rather be at home with their families.

It has been said that assumption is the lowest form of communication. If that is true, then in today's reading, Israel was at an all-time low! When two and a half of the tribes were returning home east of the Jordan after fighting and helping to settle the land, they built an altar to God's faithfulness. But the other nine and a half tribes viewed it as "competition" to the central sanctuary where all of Israel was to worship. What was intended as a symbol of *unity* was mistaken for a symbol of *apostasy*. This assumption led to hearsay, and the hearsay almost led to civil war. Finally, a committee made an investigation, and the accused were cleared—in the nick of time.

How many times do we assume the worst? How often do we form a conclusion after hearing only one side of a story? We can become jury and judge on the basis of nothing but sinful assumption. Rather than personally speak to those involved firsthand, we go to others, many of whom have the same insufficient information we do. We need to remember the words of Proverbs 18:13: "Spouting off before listening to the facts is both shameful and foolish." Before fighting with fellow believers, remember that you'll be spending eternity with them, and ask God to help you get things straightened out here first.

Make Up Your Mind!

If you refuse to serve the LORD, then choose today whom you will serve. . . .
But as for me and my family, we will serve the LORD.   JOSHUA 24:15

Indecision is frustrating and debilitating, and Joshua knows it. In his final message to the people before he dies, he begins with the patriarchs and reviews their history, highlighting the things God has done for them. That should be enough for them to declare their absolute allegiance to their Lord.

Joshua not only offers the challenge; he also is the first to accept it, speaking as leader of the nation of three million people and leader of his own home. He pledges that he and his household will honor and serve only Yahweh, the covenant God of Israel. What an example he is, for a nation cannot be stronger than its individual families. As the family goes, so goes the nation.

If you are a husband and/or a father, are you the spiritual leader in your family? Do you lead by example and by teaching? If you are a mother or father, do your children see you serving God? Our personal spiritual commitment should affect every relationship in our lives.

Are competing projects or commitments vying for your attention and cutting into your family time? Researchers at the National Institute of Mental Health (NIMH) studied high-risk, inner-city neighborhoods and discovered that only 6 percent of children from stable, safe families become delinquents, but 90 percent of the kids from unstable families who lacked supervision followed a criminal lifestyle. In other words, it isn't poverty or race that causes crime but rather the misplaced priorities of family leaders. Chuck Colson added, "Take away the family, and we might as well build prison cells right now!"

Why not make a firm decision today, right this minute, that by God's strength and grace you will lovingly lead your family spiritually and morally? The legacy of serving God is the greatest gift you can pass on to the next generation.

The Sin Cycle

The Israelites did evil in the LORD's sight and served the images of Baal.

JUDGES 2:11

Bad habits are hard to break. Over time, the choices we make become routines. This occurred with God's people during the time of the judges.

This sin cycle had four phases to it: (1) *Rebellion*. Israel began to flirt with deities of other countries, often the fertility gods of the Canaanite pantheon. (2) *Retribution*. Because the Israelites worshiped other nations' gods, God allowed his people to become the slaves of those nations. (3) *Repentance*. In the midst of their suffering, Israel would cry out to God for deliverance from the oppression of these nations. (4) *Restoration*. God would send a deliverer (called a judge) to bail his people out of their affliction.

This pattern, repeated several times over a 350-year period, was often preceded by a time of prosperity during which Israel took God's blessing for granted. Why would God continue to send judges and restore these rebellious people? The answer lies in the character of God and in the nature of God's love. God's love is inexhaustible. His is a pursuing, incessant, and unrelenting love.

In 1917 Frederick Lehman penned some of the finest words that describe God's love:

> Could we with ink the ocean fill,
> And were the skies of parchment made,
> Were every stalk on earth a quill,
> And every man a scribe by trade,
> To write the love of God above,
> Would drain the ocean dry.
> Nor could the scroll contain the whole,
> Though stretched from sky to sky.

Perhaps God has been pursuing you to interrupt a pattern of sin. Let him help you break that cycle in your own life. Make right choices that will become godly habits.

February 19

Faith of Our—Mothers

There were few people left in the villages of Israel—until Deborah arose as a mother for Israel. JUDGES 5:7

An old Scottish proverb says, "An ounce of mother is worth a pound of clergy." Moms have ways of shaping children's lives that no preacher can compete with. One such mother was Deborah, the only female judge during Israel's sin cycle. Like the ancient equivalent of Golda Meir, modern Israel's fourth prime minister, Deborah was a deliverer of her people.

The Bible is filled with examples of great women. The deliverance from Egypt began with the foresight of Moses' mother (see Exodus 2:1-4). The lineage of King David resulted from Ruth's obedience to God's plan for her (see Ruth 1). The miraculous preservation of the Jews in Persia came about through the obedience of Esther (see Esther 4:16). Miriam, Moses' sister, was a prophet (see Exodus 15:20-21), and Huldah was a prophet in the days of King Josiah (see 2 Chronicles 34:22).

The theme of the book of Judges might be called "From Conquest to Compromise." Deterioration is seen in three cycles (see chapters 1–3); God's deliverance is seen in seven cycles (see chapters 3–16); and wickedness is seen in four cycles (see chapters 17–21). Into the midst of so much corruption steps Deborah, a woman who had the kind of faith the Jews of today still recall. The old hymn "Faith of Our Fathers" could just as easily be sung using the words "faith of our mothers."

If you are a mother, you hold one of the most important roles on the planet. The influence you wield is enormous; the weight of the future rests, in part, on your shoulders. President Theodore Roosevelt once remarked, "The mother is the one supreme asset of national life. She is more important by far than the successful statesman, or businessman, or artist, or scientist."

May God strengthen the hand of today's moms to be the guiding influence for this generation.

When God Stacks the Odds against You

The LORD said to Gideon, "You have too many warriors with you. If I let all of you fight the Midianites, the Israelites will boast to me that they saved themselves by their own strength." JUDGES 7:2

Three boys were bragging about their dads. "My dad writes a couple of lines," the first boy said, "calls it a poem, and gets fifty dollars for it."

The second boy said, "My dad makes dots on paper, calls it a song, and gets seventy-five dollars for it."

"That's nothing," said the third boy. "My dad writes a sermon, gets up in the pulpit and reads it, and it takes four men to bring in the money!"

Because God knew that bragging is part of human nature, he told Gideon that he had too many soldiers to fight the Midianites. The reality was that Israel was both outgunned and outnumbered by more than four to one. There were 135,000 Midianites and only 32,000 untrained Israelites. But God wanted to stack the odds against his people so that they could never brag about "their" victory. So God reduced the army to a mere three hundred courageous men, and he would get the glory.

If you were to view this battle from a human perspective, you'd look at those 300 going against 135,000 and say, "Those poor Israelites!" But if you saw it from God's vantage point, you'd have to say, "Those poor Midianites!"

You need a healthy respect for the greatness of the living God. Nothing is too hard for him. Nothing strikes him as impossible.

In church work I often hear people say, "We need more people to do this project, Pastor. No one is here to help us—just us poor, faithful few." But more or bigger isn't necessarily better. Sometimes God wants to test our faith by stacking the odds against us, because *faith that is not tested cannot be trusted.* Concentrate on passing the test today by believing that against all odds, God can do anything. His power is limitless.

Live by the Stone, Die by the Stone

A woman on the roof dropped a millstone that landed on Abimelech's head and crushed his skull. JUDGES 9:53

Twentieth-century British historian Arnold Toynbee noted that of the twenty-two civilizations that have appeared on the stage of world history, nineteen collapsed when they reached the present moral condition of the United States. The book of Judges is so relevant to us today because at one time, Israel was "one nation under God" and then slowly began to turn away from that God. Israel became a permissive society without restraints, a purely existential civilization (see Judges 17:6).

During that time, when people made up their own rules, Abimelech, the son of the venerable Gideon, appointed himself as leader. As an opportunist, he lusted for power and had his seventy brothers murdered so there would be no competition. Over time, this treacherous act brought civil unrest and ill will between the city where these murders happened and Abimelech's political staff. One day, as Abimelech prepared to destroy the inhabitants of Thebez, who had taken refuge in a tower, a woman on the roof dropped a grinding stone over the edge, and it landed on Abimelech below, thus ending Abimelech's self-proclaimed rule.

Abimelech's sin had finally caught up with him, and his death had a certain poetic justice to it. He had killed his seventy brothers on a stone, and then he was killed by a stone. Jesus said, "The standard you use in judging is the standard by which you will be judged" (Matthew 7:2). You might paraphrase it this way: If you live by the stone, you will die by the stone.

God has a way of settling scores and bringing justice to even the most wicked situations. The psalmist declared, "Calamity will surely overtake the wicked, and those who hate the righteous will be punished" (Psalm 34:21). Commit the injustices and wrongs you see around you to God, and let him administer his hand of fair play. And be faithful to pray that our country would recover the sense of righteousness that was once a part of our national fabric.

Help!

The Israelites pleaded with the LORD and said, "We have sinned. Punish us as you see fit, only rescue us today from our enemies." JUDGES 10:15

When the Beatles released their famous hit "Help!" in 1965, most people who heard it didn't realize that the song reflected John Lennon's own personal cry for help. Audiences roared with excitement when the lads from Liverpool performed, unaware that beneath the smiles were young men imprisoned by their own fame.

Israel's cries for help were much more apparent. They writhed in the pain inflicted by their oppressors and called out to God for help. They went from having a lack of authority to anarchy and then to captivity. When they cried out, God heard, and God acted. The irony was that these weren't uninformed pagans; they were the people of God crying out from a prison of their own making.

I read a true story about a sixteen-year-old girl who was kidnapped and held prisoner for four months in the attic of a church in Memphis, Tennessee. Week after week the congregation gathered to worship. And week after week, in the very same building, was a terrified human being who needed to be rescued. Until she was discovered by the maintenance staff, she was a helpless captive.

Perhaps there are more prisoners in church than we realize. Maybe you grew up going to church and have been active and involved week after week for years. But maybe you aren't freed from the bondage of sin. Maybe what started as a habit has now become an impediment to your spiritual growth. Is it anger or lust or greed? Does the veneer of church attendance fail to cover the pain deep inside? If so, tell God how you really feel. Approach him the way hymn writer Augustus Toplady (1740–1778) described: "Nothing in my hand I bring, simply to the cross I cling." Your burden will lift, and God's forgiveness will flow.

Old Testament Superhero

You will become pregnant and give birth to a son, and his hair must never be cut. For he will be dedicated to God as a Nazirite from birth. He will begin to rescue Israel from the Philistines. JUDGES 13:5

As a boy, I loved the character of Superman. He was invincible until his nemesis, Lex Luthor, devised a plan to defeat him using kryptonite, debris from Superman's home planet of Krypton. The substance was lethal to Superman, and he fought hard to get out from under its power.

Samson, whom we might call the "Superman of the Old Testament," emerged as one of God's chosen deliverers/judges during this dark period of human history. Unlike the comic-book character, Samson and his story are real, but he was vulnerable nonetheless. The secret of his great strength didn't lie in his biceps or his hair. It lay in his dedication to God through a Nazirite vow, indicated by his uncut hair, an ancient sign of humiliation.

Samson ripped up lions, fought enemies with the jawbone of a donkey, ran thirty-eight miles carrying two doors, and eventually brought down the temple of Dagon by pushing against its two weight-bearing pillars.

But all these natural and supernatural advantages were no guarantee of success. Morally, Samson was a wimp. Like Superman's vulnerability to kryptonite, Samson was vulnerable to lust, and eventually it became his master. When it did, this biblical "Superman" fell super hard!

Paul warned the Corinthians, "If you think you are standing strong, be careful not to fall" (1 Corinthians 10:12). We all are vulnerable to something. One principle that may help us to stay strong is that of "walking in the Spirit." It denotes moving forward, making spiritual progress. Paul wrote, "Let the Holy Spirit guide your lives. Then you won't be doing what your sinful nature craves" (Galatians 5:16). Make sure that you aren't just "lounging in the Spirit" or "kicking back in the Spirit" but rather are *walking in the Spirit.* A moving target is much harder to hit than one that is standing still!

Lust at First Sight

One day when Samson was in Timnah, one of the Philistine women caught his eye. JUDGES 14:1

A news story once told of some three hundred whales found marooned on a beach. Scientists speculated that the creatures had been attracted by a school of sardines and then became trapped in the shallow water when the tide went out. In today's reading, Samson became "beached" through his pursuit of sexual pleasure. He could overcome lions and the strength of his enemies, but he was helpless against the power of his own lust.

Samson noticed a pretty Philistine woman in Timnah and demanded to have her (see vv. 1-2). He spent the night with a prostitute (see Judges 16:1). Later still, he set his sights on a woman named Delilah. Over time Samson's conscience became numb, and then Samson was attracted to anything that would give him pleasure. When it came to pretty women, it was *lust at first sight!*

When Satan wants to destroy someone, he often knocks at this particular door. More men—ministers included—have been tripped up in this area than in perhaps any other. Airbrushed photos in magazines and portrayals of unrealistic women on the movie screen can lead men to become obsessed with an ideal that doesn't exist. The result is that many men are looking for a virtual woman, one who exists only in their imaginations.

If you're a man, learn to notice and appreciate beauty that is deeper and more lasting than what you see on the surface. "Charm is deceptive, and beauty does not last; but a woman who fears the LORD will be greatly praised," says Proverbs 31:30.

If you're a woman, learn to cultivate the beauty of a godly character. God is not opposed to physical beauty, but we make a mistake when we judge a book solely by its cover and fail to take time to find out what's on the inside. Whether you're a man or a woman, ask God to give you eyes that seek out and appreciate the inner beauty of godliness.

Inward Strength for Outward Pressure

The Spirit of the LORD came powerfully upon [Samson].   JUDGES 14:19

Even the most sophisticated machines have limitations. Our nation experienced a painful reminder of that truth in 1963. The USS *Thresher* nuclear submarine was touted as one of the most advanced vessels in the United States Navy. But in a deepwater test under the arctic ice, the water pressure exceeded the sub's ability to withstand it, and the thick steel hull imploded. There had been too much pressure and not enough counterpressure. Yet certain species of fish can survive those murky ocean depths even though their skins and scales are amazingly thin, because they are able to withstand the pressure being exerted from the outside.

Samson had great potential to become a powerful vessel in God's hands, but his life was cut short because his inward spiritual character wasn't great enough to withstand the outer pressure of temptation. Samson didn't fall because the temptations were worse than those of other people. They were the same ones common to all human beings: "The temptations in your life are no different from what others experience. And God is faithful. He will not allow the temptation to be more than you can stand. When you are tempted, he will show you a way out so that you can endure" (1 Corinthians 10:13). Samson fell because he didn't rely on God, who moved mightily in him to destroy *outward* enemies and to control him enough to fight *inward* enemies.

When we face the allurements and enticements of this world, we need to be pressurized! Our inward strength must match the outward pressure. We need to fortify our spiritual walls. A person who struggles in the area of purity, for example, might have all his Internet activity monitored by an older, godly mentor who can hold him accountable. They can then talk and pray through these issues regularly.

A Spirit-controlled life will have sufficient inner force to withstand the wickedness of our culture.

Fallen Hero

*Then [Delilah] cried out, "Samson! The Philistines have come to capture
you!" When he woke up, he thought, "I will do as before and shake
myself free." But he didn't realize the LORD had left him.* JUDGES 16:20

A piano usually makes music when its strings are struck by little felt-tipped
hammers tucked away inside. But a person can also produce tones by lift-
ing the piano lid, depressing the sustain pedal, and singing a tone. The
strings that are tuned to that tone will vibrate in response. It's an interesting phenomenon. And there's nothing wrong with producing a tone that
way, except that the piano strings were designed to respond to those little
hammers, not to your voice.

That's how temptation works. Satan calls out, and you begin to vibrate.
Your human nature has the desire to respond to the impulse. So how
should you respond when Satan calls? If you were a piano, the solution
would be simple: Close the lid! As a child of God, you should close off the
opportunity.

That's where Samson failed. Rather than walk away from temptation, he
allowed himself to be lured into the devil's trap: a woman named Delilah.
She was the bait, and Samson took it! Samson could have "closed the lid,"
but instead he chose to let the song linger.

Because Samson repeatedly gave in to temptation, he lost the power of
God's Holy Spirit and was rendered weak and was defeated.

As children of God we're made to respond to the Lord's voice: "My sheep
listen to my voice; I know them, and they follow me" (John 10:27). But we
still have a powerful human nature (the Bible calls it the old nature or fleshly
nature), and it has been accustomed to responding to the devil's melodies.
So daily we have a choice: to please ourselves by letting Satan's song get to
us, or to close the lid on temptation and please our Shepherd. You may hear
many different songs today; to which ones will you respond?

As Bad As It Gets

When [the Levite] got home, he took a knife and cut his concubine's body into twelve pieces. Then he sent one piece to each tribe throughout all the territory of Israel.   JUDGES 19:29

The book of Judges demonstrates how wickedness has a way of growing. The end of the book says the people of Israel had become so distant from God that whole families and whole tribes were sold on idolatry. The last verse of the book sums up the entire 350-year period of the Judges: "In those days Israel had no king; all the people did whatever seemed right in their own eyes" (Judges 21:25). The absence of authority eventually led to national anarchy!

A gruesome account in Judges 19 shows just how bad things were. A man from the priestly tribe of Levi took his mistress (something he wasn't supposed to have) to Bethlehem. They stayed the night in the Benjamite town of Gibeah. When the men of the city told the host to send out the Levite so they could have sex with him, the Levite did a surprising thing: He pushed his concubine out the door, where these lust-filled men abused her all night long. In the morning, the Levite found her dead on the doorstep of the house. Filled with moral outrage, he cut up her body and sent a piece to each of the twelve tribes of Israel, hoping they would rise up against such immorality.

The irony is that this religious man, a member of the tribe of Levi, was supposed to be dedicated to God. Levites were to have been the moral gatekeepers of their society. But the nation had moved so far from God that its moral compass was broken.

As our culture swims in a sewer of immorality and permissiveness, make sure your own moral compass is connected to the guiding principles of God's Word. If it's not, you will be doing only what is right in your own eyes.

The Superglue of Friendship

Ruth replied, "Don't ask me to leave you and turn back. Wherever you go, I will go; wherever you live, I will live. Your people will be my people, and your God will be my God." RUTH 1:16

Love stories always draw great interest, and the eighty-five-verse story of Ruth is no exception. It's the only book in the Bible named after an ancestor of Jesus Christ who also was a Gentile. It is also a story of *providence*: how God sovereignly moves human events to accomplish his will. It is a story of *conversion*: how an unknown foreigner came to know the covenant God of Israel. And it is a story of *redemption*: how one person secured another's freedom and in doing so, foreshadowed Jesus Christ, the Kinsman Redeemer of humankind.

In today's reading, after a series of family tragedies, a parting of the ways between a bereaved widow and her two daughters-in-law, also widowed, is imminent. Naomi tells her young daughters-in-law to return home to Moab. Orpah leaves, but Ruth makes a steadfast commitment of friendship: "Don't ask me to leave you!" It has been said that there is a huge difference between involvement and commitment: A cow giving milk is involved; a pig giving ham and bacon is committed! In today's verse we can see Ruth burning all her bridges.

Ruth also made a spiritual commitment: "Your God will be my God." Ruth was willing to turn her back on everything she had been raised to believe in Moab and to follow the God of Israel. Someone once said, "If your religion hasn't changed you, maybe it's time to change your religion!" Ruth did exactly that. If she hadn't, the magi would not have made the trip to Bethlehem years later, because no Messiah would have been born there! Jesus was born in the city of David because David, the great-grandson of Ruth and Boaz, made the right choices. Think of the choices you will make today, of the impact they might have on others, and of how they might further the plan of God.

March 1 READ RUTH 2:1-23

Divine Setups

*Ruth went out to gather grain behind the harvesters. And as it happened,
she found herself working in a field that belonged to Boaz, the relative of
her father-in-law, Elimelech.* RUTH 2:3

One of the greatest truths we can learn is that of God's providence. Providence refers to the way God arranges the circumstances of our lives for his purpose, working supernaturally—naturally. The word *providence* comes from a Latin word that means "to see beforehand." God sees the scenes and events of our lives before they happen. He's what theologians call *omniscient*, or all-knowing.

The story of Ruth is really the story of Ruth's God. More than just a love story about a Moabite woman and a Jewish man, the book of Ruth shines the spotlight on God as the Master Editor of life, who providentially directs circumstances and people so that the right events happen at the right time.

Ruth could have gleaned in many of the fields around Bethlehem, but she found herself working in the field of Boaz, one of Bethlehem's most eligible bachelors and one who could marry her and restore the family heritage. While Ruth was gleaning, Boaz could have been away traveling. But he "happened" to be in the right place at the right time, and so did Ruth. It was all a divine setup!

When Ruth set foot on that field in Bethlehem, she had no idea that she would marry the owner and land a spot in the genealogy of both King David and the Messiah! Instead of looking for miracles from God (although he's perfectly capable of working that way), why not enjoy his providence more? Today's events will form part of the tapestry of your life. You will meet people, have conversations, and make decisions—all very natural. But behind the scenes will be our great God, who is arranging, editing, and moving all those elements into place to accomplish his purpose—all very *super*natural. God is behind the scenes, but he moves all the scenes he is behind!

The First Sadie Hawkins

"Who are you?" [Boaz] asked. "I am your servant Ruth," she replied.
"Spread the corner of your covering over me, for you are my family
redeemer."   RUTH 3:9

Sadie Hawkins Day began in the 1930s with Al Capp's syndicated comic strip, "L'il Abner." The mayor of Dogpatch, desperate to marry off his ugly daughter, created the holiday to give the women of Dogpatch a fighting chance at getting a man. The single men were given a short head start; then the women chased them. If a woman caught her man, he had to marry her!

Ancient Israel's laws of redemption allowed a somewhat similar practice. Since Boaz was related to Naomi, Ruth's mother-in-law, he could, if he was willing, marry Ruth and continue the family name by raising up offspring. When Ruth came to the threshing floor of Boaz on the night of today's reading, she had put on perfume and her best dress and was ready to propose! She requested that Boaz affirm his intent to marry her by placing part of his garment over her to symbolize his protection.

Ruth was hardly a stranger to taking the initiative. When her mother-in-law, Naomi, was preparing to return home from Moab, Ruth was the one who reached out and insisted they go together: "Don't ask me to leave you and turn back. Wherever you go, I will go; wherever you live, I will live" (Ruth 1:16). Now, following Naomi's direction, she was doing the same thing with Boaz.

Jonathan would take the initiative with David (see 1 Samuel 18), and a lifelong friendship would blossom. Solomon declared, "A man who has friends must himself be friendly" (Proverbs 18:24, NKJV).

Are there people in your life who could benefit from your overture of friendship? You can't choose to *have* a friend, but you *can* choose to *be* a friend. When you decide to reach out to people on the basis of meeting their needs rather than getting your own needs met, something wonderful happens. People see that you're willing to invest in them, and they will reciprocate. God can use your decision in amazing ways!

A Tale of Two Redeemers

[Boaz said,] "With the land I have acquired Ruth, the Moabite widow of Mahlon, to be my wife. This way she can have a son to carry on the family name of her dead husband and to inherit the family property here in his hometown." RUTH 4:10

If you need a home mortgage, lenders offer many options. And the process can be so complex that if you make a poor selection and interest rates rise, you could lose your property. During the days of Ruth, property transactions were less complicated. Jewish families that lost their property knew the loss wasn't permanent because of the "redemption clause," which gave them protection and the possibility of restoration.

There were several steps in this process. First, whoever bought the land must be related to the family, in other words, a *kinsman* redeemer. Second, this person needed the financial resources to pay for the land. Finally, the redeemer had to be willing to make the purchase.

Ruth's first possible redeemer was already married with children and was unwilling to become the kinsman redeemer. Once this relative had given his decision, Boaz was free to redeem the land and marry Ruth as the kinsman redeemer.

If you're seeing a connection between this story and the story of Jesus Christ, you're right. The story of Ruth presents a clear picture of Jesus Christ, who came to Earth to redeem the world. In Revelation 5:2, John saw the angel with a scroll saying, "Who is worthy to break the seals on this scroll and open it?" They were waiting for someone to pay the redemption price for humanity. When Jesus, the Worthy One, stepped forward, heaven erupted in praise.

As Boaz willingly redeemed his bride, Ruth, Jesus Christ willingly endured the cross to save us from eternal death. The Redeemer, Jesus, approached the world with a love so amazing that it's difficult—if not impossible—to understand. As George Beverly Shea sings, "O, the wonder of it all! The wonder of it all! Just to think that God loves me."

Dedicating Your Children

*[Hannah said,] "Now I am giving him to the LORD, and he will belong to
the LORD his whole life." And they worshiped the LORD there.*

1 SAMUEL 1:28

In the Old Testament, one word marked the burning desire of every Jewish
couple: *children.* Parents believed that through the lives of their children,
they had an opportunity to shape the world's future, so they should have
as many children as possible. Psalm 127:3, 5 declares, "Children are a gift
from the LORD; they are a reward from him. . . . How joyful is the man whose
quiver is full of them!"

In today's reading, Elkanah had two wives. Peninnah had a number of
children, but Hannah was barren. Peninnah taunted Hannah and made fun
of her lack of children. This weighed heavily on Hannah, and she cried out
to God, "If you will look upon my sorrow and answer my prayer and give
me a son, then I will give him back to you. He will be yours for his entire
lifetime" (1 Samuel 1:11). Hannah could never reclaim her gift of her son to
God. And Hannah's desire for her son wasn't that he go to the best schools
or make a lot of money. Her greatest desire was that he serve God.

If you have children, you may not always "feel" they are a gift from the
Lord. You may even wonder what sort of heritage you are leaving for the
future. If so, consider the long-term desires you have for your children.

Our world needs children whose hearts burn with a desire to follow God.
Psalm 127:4 says, "Children born to a young man are like arrows in a warrior's hands." Take a few minutes today to actively consider how you are
launching your children into the world. Make a point to briefly pray with
your children before you send them off to school, or read a short Bible story
at bedtime to actively build their spiritual heritage. And pray daily that your
children will serve God.

Are You Listening?

*The LORD came and called as before, "Samuel! Samuel!" And Samuel
replied, "Speak, your servant is listening."*   1 SAMUEL 3:10

How does God speak to us today? Sometimes it's easy to long for the days
of the Bible when God spoke directly to people. Hebrews 1:1 says, "Long
ago God spoke many times and in many ways to our ancestors through the
prophets." In the Old Testament, the Lord frequently spoke to the people
through his prophets, but there was a bigger question: Who was *listening*?
During the days of Samuel, it was unusual for anyone to receive a message
from God: "Messages from the LORD were very rare, and visions were quite
uncommon" (1 Samuel 3:1). That may help to explain why young Samuel
responded as he did when God called him. In the days of Eli, young Samuel
heard God's voice three times. And each time, he ran to Eli because he
thought it was the priest who had called him.

Notice that God called Samuel three times but never revealed his will
until Samuel responded to him unconditionally. Often, people today ask
God for direction but then place conditions on whether they will respond,
as if to say, "Lord, tell me your will first, and then I'll decide whether to
follow your direction. If I don't like it, I'll take my marbles and go home." We
can't respond to the Lord of the universe in this manner and expect him to
direct us. If you have placed conditions on the way God speaks to you, ask
his forgiveness. Then follow the example of Samuel. Present your body as
a "living sacrifice," and ask God to speak through you to the world around
you—in whatever way he decides is best.

A King! Give Us a King!

"Look," they told [Samuel], "you are now old, and your sons are not like you. Give us a king to judge us like all the other nations have."

1 SAMUEL 8:5

The rudder, one of the smallest parts of a boat, is also one of the most important. When a boat loses its rudder, it begins to drift and can end up far off course. The same is true spiritually.

From the days of Moses, the Jewish people had always had a leader to guide them. Samuel was the last of the judges who guided the Israelites. When Samuel appointed his sons as judges, the people recognized that these sons were corrupt and greedy and didn't follow God's laws. So they came to Samuel and demanded a king "like all the other nations have." This chapter marks a transition in Israel to the period of monarchy with Saul, David, and Solomon. Called the era of the United Kingdom, it lasted about 120 years.

When the people asked for a king, Samuel warned them about the demands a king would place on them and how life would change if they got what they wanted. But the people insisted, and their request raises this question: Was it God's will for Israel to have a king?

When Jacob was blessing his sons in Genesis 49:10, he used the word *scepter*, which refers to royal rule. So it was always in God's plan for a king to someday rule in Israel. In fact, Deuteronomy 17:14-20 includes guidelines for the king. So the question was not whether Israel would have a king someday but whether in today's story "someday" had arrived.

In the New Testament, we learn that God establishes governments. But although we want to acknowledge God's hand in establishing the government, problems come when we begin to trust government more than we trust God. We have to answer the same question the Jewish people did: Whom do we serve? Our faith for finding answers has to be in God, not in humanity.

Off to a Great Start

[Kish's] son Saul was the most handsome man in Israel—head and shoulders taller than anyone else in the land. 1 SAMUEL 9:2

The beginning of almost any new endeavor is full of hope and expectation. Strung together like pearls, our experiences and choices form our personalities and direct our lives. King Saul's rule was off to a great start. And it could have ended well if Saul hadn't squandered his choices.

A couple things were wrong with Saul's becoming king: First, he was from the tribe of Benjamin, and Jacob had named Judah as the kingly tribe. And second, Saul was selected because of his outward appearance, not because of his relationship with God.

King Saul stood out from others. His father, Kish, was a wealthy and influential man. And Saul was tall in a culture where height was admired and respected. The Philistines were the primary enemies of Israel at that time, and we know from the story of David and Goliath that they had a few "big guys" of their own. So the people of Israel valued Saul's height and appearance as a leader.

It's also possible that Saul's handsome appearance was a source of his pride. The people's appreciation may have raised Saul's sense of his own importance, which ultimately became a detriment to his kingdom. What a tragedy it is when people who have squandered God's call on their lives must say, "I could have been a powerful instrument in God's hands, but I blew it!"

Our culture makes a great deal of outward appearance—what we wear or how we look. But Scripture is clear that our spiritual natures, our hearts, are more important to God. The Lord wants to use us, but only when we are yielded to his direction. As we turn to God for his direction and enabling, we move beyond the starting point to a life of hope and expectation.

Fool!

Saul admitted to Samuel, ". . . I have disobeyed your instructions and the LORD's *command, for I was afraid of the people and did what they demanded."*   1 SAMUEL 15:24

"Everybody plays the fool," says a popular song from the 1980s. But coming to the point at which you understand that you've been a fool requires serious self-examination.

Although Saul began his reign in a humble manner, his humility didn't last long. In 1 Samuel 13, he mobilized Israel's troops with a trumpet. He took the credit for his son Jonathan's leadership. Pride is one of the easiest traps to fall into. The Lord begins to use people, and they inflate themselves with pride.

Saul was also indifferent. In 1 Samuel 14, Saul's army had been reduced to six hundred men, but Saul was sitting under a tree and watching. Jonathan was not a "sitter." Confident that God could use him and his armor bearer to defeat the enemy, he sneaked near the enemy camp. Saul ordered that no one eat until the army had taken revenge on their enemies. But Jonathan wasn't there to hear the order, so when they found some honey, they ate it, then rallied the men, and won the battle. In doing so, they signed their own death warrants—and Saul, indifferent to the fact that Jonathan had disobeyed out of ignorance, would have taken his son's life if others hadn't objected.

In 1 Samuel 15, Saul played the fool through disobedience. The prophet Samuel had told Saul to completely destroy the Amalekites. But Saul spared the king and the best of the sheep and cattle. Instead of following God, Saul followed his own rules.

When doctors find an aggressive cancer, they use strong measures to deal with it. God took the same action with Saul. The king would remain in power, but God would give the kingdom to another man. That didn't have to happen. It was a consequence of Saul's poor choices.

How will your choices today determine whether you are following God or your own rules?

March 9 READ 1 SAMUEL 16:1-13

God's Glasses

*The LORD said to Samuel, "Don't judge by his appearance or height, for
I have rejected him. The LORD doesn't see things the way you see them.
People judge by outward appearance, but the LORD looks at the heart."*

1 SAMUEL 16:7

If the spiritual part of your life has grown fuzzy, you may need a new set
of "glasses." God's perspective of the world is different from ours, and his
values are distinct from the standards of this world.

Like it or not, we are appearance oriented. God had rejected Saul and
sent Samuel on a mission to find a new king. Of course, God had already
chosen the next ruler, because he is never without a plan, but Samuel was
searching for "king material." Maybe someone Schwarzenegger-esque,
someone who fit Samuel's idea of what a king should be. But the Lord told
Samuel not to worry about the new king's appearance. God was looking at
the king's heart. It was the inside view that mattered most.

An article I read some time ago reported that some manufacturers are
using the same size package to hold less product. For example, a box of
detergent that once held sixty-one ounces now holds only fifty-five ounces.
If you want to get the same amount of detergent as before, you need to
focus on more than the outer package and check out what is on the inside.
In the same way, God is much more concerned with our hearts than with
our outward appearances.

As you look at your world, use God's lenses instead of the world's lenses.
With a new perspective, you will be surprised how different the people in
your life will appear. The world expects us to use its standard. As followers of
Jesus, we are expected to look at the heart and not at the outward package.
Make a conscious choice to wear God's glasses throughout your day.

The Giant-Killer

[David said,] "Today the LORD will conquer you, and I will kill you and cut off your head. And then I will give the dead bodies of your men to the birds and wild animals, and the whole world will know that there is a God in Israel!" 1 SAMUEL 17:46

Some people compare Goliath to a character in Greek mythology and wonder whether he ever really existed.

Even today, there are occasional accounts of giants. Robert Wadlow was the world's tallest man. At his birth in 1918 he weighed eight pounds five ounces. On his thirteenth birthday, Wadlow stood seven feet eight inches tall, and when he was fully grown, he had reached eight feet eleven inches. At Wadlow's death, it took twelve men to carry the ten-foot-nine-inch casket.

Goliath was a real Philistine giant who challenged Israel's army twice a day for forty days. David heard Goliath taunt the Jewish people and knew the attack wasn't just on the army but on all the people of God. God took that seriously: "Anyone who harms you harms my most precious possession" (Zechariah 2:8).

With Goliath, David saw the giant's taunting as a personal challenge, and that perspective gave him the courage to face Goliath in battle. David's faith was strong, and he knew that as he fought in the name of the living God, he would be protected. As he took on the giant, David understood the truth that the apostle John would later proclaim: "The Spirit who lives in you is greater than the spirit who lives in the world" (1 John 4:4). In faith, David stepped out to meet Goliath and defeated him.

Although we don't have to face physical giants, as the Israelites did, in a sense, each of us faces giant difficulties and decisions. But if we follow David's example and put our faith in the living God, we can face today's battles with courage.

Bull's-Eye on Your Back

This was their song: "Saul has killed his thousands, and David his ten thousands!"   1 SAMUEL 18:7

When someone else is successful, do you celebrate with that person, or are you intimidated? Insecure people are threatened by the success of others no matter where it happens—at home, at work, or in the church.

Dr. Seuss wrote about the Grinch, who couldn't stand to see the "Whos down in Whoville" enjoying themselves. Their celebration made the Grinch so mad that he bit himself.

In today's reading, Saul's hatred for David had become so strong that David might as well have had a bull's-eye painted on his back. At one point Saul tried to pin David to the wall with a spear. Fortunately for David, the king's aim was bad. But notice how David responded to the attack: Instead of fighting back, David ducked and ran.

When the spears of life fly your way, whether they are envy, anger, or jealousy, learn the lessons of David. First, duck and get out of the way. Judging from David's accuracy with a sling when he fought Goliath, we can assume he easily had the skills to retaliate. But he chose not to.

Second, notice that David continued going into battle and behaving wisely. He didn't allow Saul's attack to rob him of his enthusiasm for his work. Don't allow jealousy to diminish your effectiveness or performance. Plato said, "If people speak ill of you, live so no one will believe them."

The third way David reacted to Saul's attack was to stay close to his friends. First Samuel 18:1 says, "There was an immediate bond between [Jonathan and David], for Jonathan loved David."

You may feel under attack and think you are walking around with a bull's-eye painted on your back. Take a moment for a deep breath, and follow the three lessons from David in his reaction to Saul's attack. They will give you godly examples for your own response.

Beauty and the Beast

David replied to Abigail, "Praise the LORD, the God of Israel, who has sent you to meet me today!" 1 SAMUEL 25:32

Long before Disney ever released *Beauty and the Beast*, the Bible included a story about a beauty and a beast. Abigail was the "beauty" who had married a "beast" named Nabal. In Hebrew, *Nabal* means "fool," and this man made some foolish decisions. David and his men were near Nabal's property and had been protecting Nabal's flocks.

One day during shearing time, David sent ten men to Nabal with a request for provisions. Because David's army had been protecting Nabal's flocks, he expected a positive response to the request. Instead, Nabal called David an outlaw and sent away the men empty-handed. When the men recounted Nabal's response, David overreacted and decided to destroy Nabal and all the other men in Nabal's household. David's response was similar to deciding to use nuclear weapons to kill rats in the New York subway. These two men were about to collide, and Abigail knew it.

Loading a donkey with two hundred loaves of bread, two skins of wine, five dressed sheep, nearly a bushel of roasted grain, one hundred raisin cakes, and two hundred fig cakes, she sent food with a couple of servants to David. Without a word to her husband she came to meet David personally to try to avoid the looming bloodshed and regret. When Abigail returned home, Nabal was drunk, so she waited until the next morning to tell him what she had done. When Nabal learned how Abigail had saved his life, he had a stroke and died soon after. Aware of the world around her, Abigail took matters into her own hands.

Is there a situation you are avoiding? Like the priest in the parable of the Good Samaritan, you can keep walking and do nothing. Or, like Abigail, you can step into the situation to change it. How will you be known?

Suicide

Saul groaned to his armor bearer, "Take your sword and kill me before these pagan Philistines come to run me through and taunt and torture me." But his armor bearer was afraid and would not do it. So Saul took his own sword and fell on it. 1 SAMUEL 31:4

"Looking good," the man said to his sharply dressed friend. Many people focus on image as a key part of how other people see them.

King Saul was always concerned about his image. Even in his death, he was focused on looking good. Saul did not want the pagan Philistines to kill him, so he committed suicide. Even at the point of death, he was still acting in his own strength.

There is a key distinction between reputation and character. Your reputation is based on what people think you are. Your character is what you are when no one else is looking. The tragedy of Saul's death is that his reign could have ended well.

First, Saul could have taken his sin more seriously. Saul treated his sin lightly, made excuses for it, blamed others, and never dealt with it. Twice a prophet confronted Saul, and twice he admitted, "I have sinned."

Second, Saul could have chosen character over reputation. He could have stood for righteousness no matter what others thought about his decision. Instead he focused on what others thought of him. In each situation, Saul was too focused on looking good in the eyes of others.

Finally, Saul's life could have ended well if Saul had taken advantage of friendship. First Samuel describes the deep friendship between Jonathan and David. Saul didn't have that kind of friendship with anyone, yet he isolated himself and sought his own desires. Saul's stubbornness had lasting consequences. He settled for second best, and his life ended in tragedy.

Are you being stubborn in an area of your life? You may need to go through the school of hard knocks to break that attitude.

When a Friend Dies

> *How I weep for you, my brother Jonathan!*
> *Oh, how much I loved you!*
> *And your love for me was deep,*
> *deeper than the love of women!*

2 SAMUEL 1:26

The way you handle a personal crisis will reveal whether your life is one of substance or superficiality. David's reaction upon hearing of the deaths of his friend Jonathan and of King Saul showed the depth of his character. Although Saul had hounded David for ten years, David didn't rejoice at Saul's death.

But when David lost Jonathan, it was a much greater blow. Today's verse expresses the depth of pain David felt at the death of his dearest friend. Proverbs 18:24 gives us an idea of their friendship, saying, "A man who has friends must himself be friendly, but there is a friend who sticks closer than a brother" (NKJV). It takes initiative to have friends. Jonathan didn't choose to *have* a friend. He chose to *be* a friend to David, and there is a big difference. Jonathan did not operate from a basis of personal need and demand David's attention. He operated from the basis of supply and offered himself to meet David's need. He was a friend that "sticks closer than a brother."

Henry Drummond asked, "How many prodigals are kept out of the Kingdom of God by the unlovely characters of those who profess to be inside?" Each of us has overheard one Christian tear down another in conversation with a third. When Christians are in trouble, they learn who their real friends are, because those are the ones who stay with them no matter what happens. That takes involvement, getting close, being vulnerable, and getting hurt. What words would other people use to describe you as a friend? How would others miss you if you were to die unexpectedly?

March 15

Conflict and Chaos

They went into the house and found Ishbosheth sleeping on his bed. They struck and killed him and cut off his head. Then, taking his head with them, they fled across the Jordan Valley through the night. 2 SAMUEL 4:7

The Bible is an honest historical document with no embellishment of the facts. The first civil war had erupted between the house of David and the house of Saul. David was fighting with Ishbosheth. Twelve men from Abner and the tribe of Benjamin had a fierce battle with twelve of Joab's men from the tribe of Judah.

Next there was conflict inside the kings' house. Ishbosheth lost to Abner because he was weak and had no protection. Then two rogue soldiers, Recab and Baanah, broke into Ishbosheth's home, murdered him, and took Ishbosheth's head because they thought David would like it!

In a matter of days, the kingdom was in chaos. Murder, intrigue, and revenge were in operation as people took matters into their own hands and acted with a total disregard for God's laws. When Recab and Baanah, expecting to be praised for their deed, showed David Ishbosheth's head, they were executed, and David cut off their hands and feet.

We can read about these conflicts in the Bible and our history books, but the church is no stranger to conflict. We are supposed to be a family of believers, yet as brothers and sisters in Christ, we often have greater difficulty getting along with one another than we do with unbelievers. As Noah and his family might have said, "If not for the storm on the outside, we could not stand the stench on the inside."

As Christians, we have a responsibility to understand conflicts and work toward finding ways to resolve them. Jesus said, "God blesses those who work for peace, for they will be called the children of God" (Matthew 5:9).

The Right Thing in the Wrong Way

They placed the Ark of God on a new cart and brought it from Abinadab's house, which was on a hill. Uzzah and Ahio, Abinadab's sons, were guiding the cart as it left the house. 2 SAMUEL 6:3

The Israelites wanted to do the right thing in bringing the Ark of the Covenant back to Jerusalem. Not just another treasure chest or storage trunk, the Ark was holy, and holy things must be treated in a special way. The Bible includes specific instructions for moving the Ark. Each corner of the base of the Ark had a golden ring to accommodate long poles. The Ark of the Covenant had to be carried in a certain way. Only certain members of the priestly tribe of Levi could carry these poles, which were to rest on their shoulders.

In addition, moving the Ark from Abinadab's house to Jerusalem would require carrying it uphill for nine miles. Goal-oriented King David wanted to move the Ark into Jerusalem as quickly as possible, so it was placed on a new cart instead of being carried. Although David had the right motive, he was acting in the wrong way. David's sincerity wasn't enough.

When one of the oxen pulling the cart stumbled, Uzzah reached out to steady the Ark, and God struck him dead. Uzzah's action was sincerely practical, but it was wrong because it didn't follow God's instructions. Uzzah's sincerity wasn't enough.

Sincerity isn't enough for us either. Just ask a patient whose treatment has been botched by a sincere but incompetent physician. It's tempting to think that details don't matter as long as we reach the goal God has given us. But the end doesn't always justify the means. Sincerity isn't enough. God wants our sincere *obedience*.

The Covenant God

The LORD declares that he will make a house for you—a dynasty of kings! For when you die and are buried with your ancestors, I will raise up one of your descendants, your own offspring, and I will make his kingdom strong. 2 SAMUEL 7:11-12

Today's reading records a pivotal moment in God's plan to establish his Kingdom here on Earth—his promise that a descendant of David would always sit on the throne of Israel, culminating in the eternal reign of Jesus Christ.

The fulfillment of this promise is recorded in the opening chapter of Matthew's Gospel, which begins, "This is a record of the ancestors of Jesus the Messiah, a descendant of David" (1:1). The angel Gabriel confirms the fulfillment of the promise when he appears to Mary: "You will conceive and give birth to a son, and you will name him Jesus. He will be very great and will be called the Son of the Most High. The Lord God will give him the throne of his ancestor David" (Luke 1:31-32). And Revelation 22:16 closes the New Testament with similar words: "I, Jesus, have sent my angel to give you this message for the churches. I am both the source of David and the heir to his throne. I am the bright morning star."

The Gospels include two genealogies: Matthew's traces Joseph's lineage, and Luke's records Mary's line. Though Jesus was not Joseph's physical son, he was his legal heir and thus had a dynastic right to rule by virtue of Joseph's line, which extended back to Solomon, David's direct descendant on the throne of Israel.

Though David wanted to build a fancy temple to honor God, God was looking ahead to the fulfillment of his covenant with Abraham, when through the reign of Jesus Christ, David's throne would be established forever.

Consider what God has done for you through Jesus Christ in making you a part of his Kingdom, not only right now, but also for the future.

The Kind King

One day David asked, "Is anyone in Saul's family still alive—anyone to whom I can show kindness for Jonathan's sake?"   2 SAMUEL 9:1

Sometimes receiving an unexpected act of kindness can be almost jarring because we live in an unkind world. But living in that world also means we have unlimited opportunities to show unexpected kindness to others.

In David's time, when a new king came to the throne, it was customary for him to execute the heirs from the previous dynasty in order to eliminate any potential threats to the throne. King David was different. He wondered if anyone from Saul's family—his enemy's family—was still alive so that he could show kindness to that person. David wanted to fulfill his promise to his friend Jonathan, King Saul's son.

David's actions illustrate God's kindness to us. Although Jonathan's son Mephibosheth was a member of Saul's family, David treated him like one of his own sons because of his covenant with Jonathan. In addition, Mephibosheth was lame. Because of the sin of Adam (see Romans 5:12), in a sense everyone who has lived since has been crippled. We may attempt to please God through our self-efforts or good works, but they will never save us.

Mephibosheth was completely dependent on David's kindness. Similarly, it's only because Christ came to Earth to seek us that we are not lost forever. Because David reached out to Mephibosheth, the onetime enemy had his needs met and received royal treatment. Does any of this sound familiar? Romans 5:6 says, "When we were utterly helpless, Christ came at just the right time and died for us sinners." For the sake of Jesus Christ, God made us his sons and daughters.

Seize every opportunity to show kindness to others. As you do so, your actions will seem extraordinary.

Mind Your Own Business

Late one afternoon, after his midday rest, David got out of bed and was walking on the roof of the palace. As he looked out over the city, he noticed a woman of unusual beauty taking a bath.   2 SAMUEL 11:2

The story is told of a wealthy contractor who built what was called "The Tombs" in New York City. Soon after the prison was completed, the contractor was convicted of forgery and sentenced to several years in the prison he had built. As the man was escorted to his cell, he said, "I never dreamed when I built this prison that one day I would be an inmate." No one plans this sort of self-destruction.

King David had brought the nation of Israel to its pinnacle. As a celebrated musician and warrior, and now king, he had reached a place where he may have thought he couldn't blow it.

But even before 2 Samuel 11, we see that David had a weakness in a particular area. In 2 Samuel 5:13, we learn that he had many wives. As his harem grew, his lust seemed to grow as well. This king's weak spot was the opposite sex. And an unchecked weakness can destroy.

Besides his weakness for women, David had grown lazy. After the rainy season, armies went to battle, but David decided not to go with his troops. The greatest spiritual battles don't come when our hands are busy. Rather, they come when we are bored from a lack of activity.

When David saw a beautiful woman from his rooftop, he could have turned away and gone inside, but he didn't. That was a mistake. Remember that Jesus said, "Anyone who even looks at a woman with lust has already committed adultery with her in his heart" (Matthew 5:28).

Don't be lured, as David was, into laziness and lust. The apostle Paul warned the Christians in Corinth, "If you think you are standing strong, be careful not to fall" (1 Corinthians 10:12). If you don't think you need to run from temptation, you will fall.

Confrontation

Nathan said to David, "You are that man! The LORD, the God of Israel, says: I anointed you king of Israel and saved you from the power of Saul."

2 SAMUEL 12:7

If your car's check-engine light flashes, you can take the car to the shop, or you can break the light with a hammer. If you choose the first option, you fix the problem. If you choose the second option, you fix only the symptom of the problem, and eventually your car will break down.

It has been said that "secret sin on Earth is open scandal in heaven." Initially, David didn't deal with his "secret" sin with Bathsheba, and he felt miserable, empty, and spiritually sick. Although David tried to take a hammer to the "guilt light" on his internal dashboard and run and hide, God waited patiently for him. God is persistent. Nineteenth-century English poet Francis Thompson even wrote a poem about God's pursuit of those who try to run from him. "The Hound of Heaven" compares God to a hunting dog that never stops pursuing its object.

If our consciences aren't sufficient, God will get our attention in some other way. When David still wouldn't come to God, the Lord sent his prophet Nathan.

Nathan told David a parable about a rich man (David), a poor man (Uriah, Bathsheba's husband), and a lamb (Bathsheba). In the parable, the rich man, who needed nothing, stole the poor man's one treasured possession. Through the parable, Nathan held up a mirror so David could take a good look at himself. When Nathan identified "the rich man" as David himself, David immediately repented.

When the finger of God points out a fault in you, how well do you listen to your conscience and the Holy Spirit?

Absalom the Usurper

Absalom would say, "You've really got a strong case here! It's too bad the king doesn't have anyone to hear it. I wish I were the judge. Then everyone could bring their cases to me for judgment, and I would give them justice!" 2 SAMUEL 15:3-4

There is an expression that says, "The chickens have come home to roost." The truth of these words was borne out in the life of David. Because of David's adultery with Bathsheba and his murder of Uriah, God brought consequences to bear in David's life: "Because of what you have done, I will cause your own household to rebel against you" (2 Samuel 12:11). Among other things, David's son Absalom organized a rebellion against his father.

Absalom based his rebellion in Hebron, where he was out of David's sight and mind. Away from the watchful eye of his father, he had more freedom to do as he pleased and gather supporters for his attempt to usurp his father's throne.

How did Absalom get to this point? Consider the modeling he had received: From King David he learned to use his position to manipulate people, as David did with Bathsheba and Uriah. Absalom learned that power can be intoxicating, and he used it to rule armies and give others orders. Absalom put into practice what he learned from his father and turned it back on him. It's the classic example of a father who provoked his child to anger and then reaped the consequences (see Ephesians 6:4).

A busy nineteenth-century politician named Charles Francis Adams kept a diary in which one of his entries read, "Went fishing with my son today—a day wasted." Adams's son, Brook, also kept a diary, and his entry for the same day read, "Went fishing with my father—most wonderful day of my life!" If we see our children as intrusions, we need to remember the lessons from King David's life with Absalom and think about what behavior we are modeling for them.

When Words Come Too Late

The king was overcome with emotion. He went up to the room over the gateway and burst into tears. And as he went, he cried, "O my son Absalom! My son, my son Absalom! If only I had died instead of you! O Absalom, my son, my son." 2 SAMUEL 18:33

A simple poster with a photograph of a child contains these words by Forest Witcraft: "One hundred years from now, it will not matter what my bank account was, how big my house was, or what kind of car I drove. But the world may be a little better, because I was important in the life of a child."

Today's reading records a battle between David's men and Absalom's followers. David's men were skilled warriors with years of military experience, so Joab, the leader of David's army, divided his men into three companies to attack Absalom's troops. During the battle, Absalom unexpectedly came upon some of David's men and turned his mule to ride away. But his hair got caught in the branches of an oak tree, and he was left dangling in the air.

When one of the warriors told Joab of Absalom's plight, Joab replied, "What? You didn't kill him?" And in spite of David's order to take Absalom alive, Joab plunged three daggers into Absalom's heart and killed him. Absalom's death marked a sad ending to a father-son relationship, and David's words in today's verse express the anguish of a father's heart at losing a child who was estranged from him.

In the emergency rooms of hospitals, I've witnessed firsthand the deaths of relatives before there was time for words of reconciliation. If you have a broken relationship with a friend or a relative, reach out to that person. Regardless of who was wrong or right, don't lose the opportunity to speak words of healing, love, and forgiveness.

March 23

A Royal Sunset

These are the last words of David:

> *"David, the son of Jesse, speaks—*
> *David, the man who was raised up so high,*
> *David, the man anointed by the God of Jacob,*
> *David, the sweet psalmist of Israel."*

2 SAMUEL 23:1

Most babies say the same first words in English—"Mama" or "Da-Da." At the other end of our lives, our last words differ dramatically. I've seen firsthand how people die differently because they have lived differently. Some people face death with hope and sometimes even a sense of anticipation. I once watched a dying woman I know from church, who sat up, smiled, and said, "I'm ready to go!"

Others know only hopelessness and despair as death approaches. Scottish philosopher David Hume's last words were, "I am in flames." The philosopher Voltaire cried throughout the night, "I am abandoned by God and man. . . . I shall go to hell! Oh Christ, Oh, Jesus Christ." Gandhi said, "All about me is darkness. I am praying for light."

In today's reading, we find King David's last formal words before his death. David's life can be captured in a one-sentence biographical sketch: God took a peasant and made him into royalty. If you are a Christian, God has done the same for you. Peter wrote, "You are a chosen people. You are royal priests, a holy nation, God's very own possession" (1 Peter 2:9). Be careful how you use your relationship with God. Each day through the things you do, you are writing a chapter of your life story.

Although David was called a man after God's heart, his life was imperfect, full of sin and forgiveness, transgression and mercy. That's a lot like your life and mine. Aren't you glad God has a big eraser? No matter what you have done, you can celebrate the truth of 1 John 1:9: "If we confess our sins to him, he is faithful and just to forgive us our sins and to cleanse us from all wickedness."

Long Live the King!

David was now very old, and no matter how many blankets covered him, he could not keep warm. 1 KINGS 1:1

A nation's transition from one ruler to the next is always interesting. In today's reading we see Israel beginning the transition from King David to King Solomon. Solomon's reign gave Israel some of the most beautiful songs and words of wisdom. In addition, King Solomon built a global empire. His navy and merchant marine spread his reputation to the ends of the known world. In spite of Israel's physical growth and strength during Solomon's reign, however, the spiritual condition of the Jewish people declined.

We are uncertain who wrote the books of 1 and 2 Kings. Jewish tradition holds that the prophet Jeremiah was the author. In general, 1 Kings is divided into two sections: 1 Kings 1–11 is a record of the kingdom during Solomon's reign, and 1 Kings 12 through 2 Kings 25 is a record of the northern and southern kingdoms, Israel and Judah. Although 1 and 2 Kings present a history lesson, they also offer a spiritual lesson that has practical implications for our lives. The nation of Israel declined because of the spiritual decline of its leaders. David had many wives; Solomon had many more wives and concubines. These marriages divided Solomon's heart, and his legacy was a divided nation. Neither Solomon nor his father faithfully followed God throughout their lives.

Near the end of Paul's life, the apostle wrote, "I have fought the good fight, I have finished the race, and I have remained faithful. And now the prize awaits me—the crown of righteousness, which the Lord, the righteous Judge, will give me on the day of his return. And the prize is not just for me but for all who eagerly look forward to his appearing" (2 Timothy 4:7-8). Consider these words as you reflect on your own life today. How well are you running the race, fighting the good fight, and remaining faithful? Are you keeping your eye on the prize?

A Rebel Heart

David's son Adonijah, whose mother was Haggith, began boasting, "I will make myself king." So he provided himself with chariots and charioteers and recruited fifty men to run in front of him.   1 KINGS 1:5

Have you ever heard someone say, "God has no grandchildren"? We can see the truth of this saying in the rebellion of countless children of Christian leaders and pastors. Franklin Graham, the oldest son of Billy and Ruth Graham, and a friend of mine, is just one example. Some of Franklin's story is told in his book *Rebel with a Cause*. Parents' involvement in ministry is no guarantee that their children will follow in their footsteps spiritually. Today's reading emphasizes a similar lesson.

Although David was an able leader of Israel, he failed to discipline his own children, even by asking, "Why are you doing that?" Adonijah, Solomon's brother, tried to take the throne from David. When the prophet Nathan learned that Adonijah was planning to take over, he quickly informed Bathsheba, who told King David. Having already decreed that Solomon would succeed him as king, David moved quickly to anoint Solomon. In the midst of Adonijah's self-coronation, he heard celebration in the streets and learned that Solomon had been made the king, whereupon Adonijah's guests ran for the door in a panic.

The book of Proverbs contains a great deal of teaching about the importance of parental discipline: "Those who spare the rod of discipline hate their children. Those who love their children care enough to discipline them" (Proverbs 13:24). And we see the consequences of a lack of discipline in Proverbs 29:15: "To discipline a child produces wisdom, but a mother is disgraced by an undisciplined child."

If your children are still under your roof, make sure you are faithfully teaching them God's ways, setting a godly example yourself. If your children are already in rebellion, keep the door open for their return. We cannot predict which children will rebel, but like the father of the Prodigal Son, we can be prepared to welcome them home.

Blank Check from Heaven

The LORD appeared to Solomon in a dream, and God said, "What do you want? Ask, and I will give it to you!" 1 KINGS 3:5

In the 1994 Disney movie *Blank Check*, eleven-year-old Preston Waters receives a blank check from the crook who ran over his bike. Preston, seeing the opportunity to make a killing, promptly fills out the check in the amount of one million dollars. But as Preston spends his windfall without restraint, he learns a lesson about the value of relationships.

In today's reading, God essentially handed Solomon a blank check: "What do you want? Ask, and I will give it to you!" What would you have asked for?

Solomon was feeling the weight of his responsibility as king over Israel. He recognized his need for wisdom to govern the people. Because Solomon didn't ask God for long life or riches or the death of his enemies, God was pleased with his request and gave him great riches and honor in addition to the wisdom Solomon had asked for.

Each day has its own challenges. As we ask God for wisdom and an understanding heart and remain sensitive to the Holy Spirit's direction, we will be able to handle whatever challenges or difficulties come our way. In 1 Thessalonians 5:17-18, Paul gave us the prescription for staying close to God: "Never stop praying. Be thankful in all circumstances, for this is God's will for you who belong to Christ Jesus." Keep praying, maintain a heart of gratitude in all circumstances, and faithfully follow God's will for your life.

March 27 READ 1 KINGS 5:1-18

Where Does God Live?

At the king's command, they quarried large blocks of high-quality stone and shaped them to make the foundation of the Temple.   1 KINGS 5:17

Only a single wall of Solomon's Temple still stands today. Known as the Wailing Wall, this massive structure is only a shell of the former glory of this Temple, which represented the zenith of Solomon's glory and is a major topic of Kings and Chronicles. For years the Temple was the centerpiece of Jewish life and was considered the heart of Judaism. King David drew up the plans for the Temple, the vestibule, and the Holy of Holies and then gave the plans to his son. Hiram, the king of Tyre, agreed to supply the wood and skillful men to do the work. For this service, Solomon paid the king of Tyre 100,000 bushels of wheat and 110,000 gallons of olive oil each year.

Building the Temple was a massive undertaking, using a workforce in excess of 183,000 people. As the Jewish commentary Midrash says, "The land of Israel is at the center of the world; Jerusalem is at the center of the land of Israel; the Temple is at the center of Jerusalem."

God doesn't live in material temples today (see Acts 17:24). Even Solomon's prayer of dedication for the completed Temple acknowledged, "Even the highest heavens cannot contain you. How much less this Temple I have built!" (1 Kings 8:27). Although I've seen the lofty cathedrals of Europe, the huts of worship in Sudan, and the fields of worship in Thailand, I know these are just places to meet God, whose Spirit resides in the hearts of his people: "All of you together are the temple of God and . . . the Spirit of God lives in you" (1 Corinthians 3:16). If you have put your faith in Christ, you can live with the awareness that God's Spirit lives in you.

Magnetic Wisdom

When the queen of Sheba heard of Solomon's fame, which brought honor to the name of the LORD, she came to test him with hard questions.

1 KINGS 10:1

I would love to ask Solomon some hard questions because there are many things that puzzle me. For example, why do 7-Eleven stores have locks on the doors if they are open 24 hours a day, 365 days a year? Why do dogs hate it when you blow on their faces but love to ride with their heads hanging out of an open car window? King Solomon, the wisest man who ever walked the earth, might have offered some remarkable answers to these puzzles from our modern culture.

During Solomon's lifetime, people came to him with their puzzles, riddles, and conundrums, and he had answers. He was even able to determine which of two women was the mother of the baby they both claimed—long before anyone had heard of DNA testing!

In spite of King Solomon's wisdom, however, his life was not without problems or concerns, one of which was the issue of heavy taxes imposed to finance the construction of Solomon's palace and the Temple. After Solomon's death, what had already been oppressive taxation grew even worse during the reign of his son Rehoboam.

Whatever concerns you face, you will daily need God's wisdom and direction. It's available for the asking: "If you need wisdom, ask our generous God, and he will give it to you" (James 1:5). The same source from which Solomon received his wisdom is available to you, and it's only a prayer away.

A Heart Divided

[Solomon] had 700 wives of royal birth and 300 concubines. And in fact, they did turn his heart away from the LORD. 1 KINGS 11:3

The Associated Press once included a story from San Jose about Luke Goodrich. Luke was busy burning trash in his backyard, which is against the law. The fire burned out of control, spreading over one hundred acres and requiring the use of six helicopters and four hundred firefighters to extinguish it. The irony is that Goodrich was the captain of the San Jose Fire Department. He knew the law, but he chose not to obey it.

King Solomon built the Temple and reshaped Jerusalem with new streets and a gorgeous palace and other new construction. Because of his wisdom, he reveled in literature, botany, and zoology. But although King Solomon was gifted intellectually and creatively, he was weak in other ways. His mind and his morals were not on the same level. As the verse above tells us, his weakness for women turned him away from God, and his legacy was a divided kingdom.

Ecclesiastes 9:9 says, "Live happily with the woman you love through all the meaningless days of life that God has given you under the sun. The wife God gives you is your reward for all your earthly toil." How can one man "enjoy" seven hundred wives and three hundred concubines? For all of Solomon's wisdom, he disobeyed God's wise precepts.

The books of 1 and 2 Kings tell us that Solomon was a man of prayer. In fact, Psalm 72, by Solomon, is one of the most beautiful prayers in the Bible. And yet, in spite of all of Solomon's head knowledge about God, he acted like a fool because he didn't practice what he taught. If I don't live what I teach, then I'm a fool. And if you sit in church on Sunday and respond with an "amen" to what you hear but don't live the truth the other six days of the week, so are you.

A Kingdom Divided

When all Israel realized that the king had refused to listen to them, they responded,

> *"Down with the dynasty of David!*
> *We have no interest in the son of Jesse.*
> *Back to your homes, O Israel!*
> *Look out for your own house, O David!"*

So the people of Israel returned home. 1 KINGS 12:16

Where do you seek wisdom and insight? Maybe you turn to older men and women. If you are a young person, you might be unlikely to ask your peers.

When Rehoboam took over the kingdom of Israel after Solomon's death, the older men advised him to lower the oppressive tax burden imposed by his father. But Rehoboam didn't accept the counsel from the older men. He turned instead to his peers, who arrogantly advised the new king not to lower taxes but to increase them. The discontent that resulted provided Jeroboam the opportunity he needed to rebel and gain leadership. After succeeding at the rebellion, Jeroboam was smart enough to understand that Jerusalem was the people's emotional center of gravity and would always have a hold on them. So Jeroboam set up rival centers in Dan to the north and Bethel to the south. This pulled the ten northern tribes away from God and toward idolatry.

King Solomon gave Israel beautiful words of wisdom and songs, yet in the midst of the kingdom's physical growth, there was spiritual decline, and God pulled the kingdom away from Solomon's heir Rehoboam because of it. The disobedience of one person, Solomon, affected a host of others.

From the Scriptures, we know sin can affect otherwise innocent people—even unbelievers! But God can use even this kind of stupid blunder and hurt for his glory. God wants each of us to turn to him in faith and not follow the gods of this world, no matter how loudly they may call to us.

Simple but Powerful

*Elijah, who was from Tishbe in Gilead, told King Ahab, "As surely as the
LORD, the God of Israel, lives—the God I serve—there will be no dew or
rain during the next few years until I give the word!"* 1 KINGS 17:1

Ahab, one of Israel's worst kings, was a man of the world. Through his wife,
Jezebel, Ahab introduced the worship of Baal to the Israelites. In stark contrast, Elijah was a fiery, articulate prophet who was also a miracle worker.
When the nation of Israel was wandering away from God and becoming
embroiled in big problems, God raised up Elijah, who was perfect for this
situation.

The prophet warned Ahab that it would not rain again until Elijah gave
the word. And just like that, Elijah suspended rain and dew for three and
a half years!

For part of this time, Elijah hid from King Ahab at a place east of the
Jordan River. The prophet could drink from the brook and eat the food God
sent by ravens. When the brook dried up, the Lord sent Elijah to a widow
who had only enough oil and flour for one more meal. But when the prophet
asked her for it, she gave it to him. As a result, the widow, her son, and Elijah
were able to eat for many days, and miraculously, there was always enough
even though the drought continued.

James 5:16-17 says, "The earnest prayer of a righteous person has great
power and produces wonderful results. Elijah was as human as we are, and
yet when he prayed earnestly that no rain would fall, none fell for three and
a half years!" There is great power in simple prayer. As evangelist Charles
Spurgeon said, "Prayer pulls the rope down below and the great bell rings
above in the ears of God." We need to have this type of commitment to
prayer and righteous living. In addition to theology, let's be committed to
"knee-ology"—kneeling before God in prayer.

God's Troublemaker!

When Ahab saw [Elijah], he exclaimed, "So, is it really you, you troublemaker of Israel?" 1 KINGS 18:17

God had a troublemaker—at least according to Israel's King Ahab. Elijah had told Ahab there would be no rain—and then promptly disappeared. No wonder the king called Elijah a troublemaker. In his view, Elijah was the enemy. The king had no clue that Elijah was the solution to Israel's problem.

The ongoing drought culminated in a contest between Elijah and the priests of Baal. The priests of Baal built an altar, but despite their best efforts, nothing happened to their sacrifice. Elijah taunted, "You'll have to shout louder. . . . Perhaps he is daydreaming, or is relieving himself. Or maybe he is away on a trip, or is asleep and needs to be wakened!" (1 Kings 18:27). The priests redoubled their efforts, even cutting themselves in a frenzy, and still nothing happened.

Finally, it was Elijah's turn. He repaired the altar and the sacrifice, and then asked the people to pour water over the sacrifice and the wood, which made success seem even more impossible.

Elijah prayed a prayer of just fifty-seven words: "O Lord, God of Abraham, Isaac, and Jacob, prove today that you are God in Israel and that I am your servant. Prove that I have done all this at your command. O Lord, answer me! Answer me so these people will know that you, O Lord, are God and that you have brought them back to yourself" (1 Kings 18:36-37). Instantly fire fell from heaven and consumed the sacrifice, the wood, the stones of the altar, and even the water poured around it. Then Elijah had the priests of Baal seized and killed.

Elijah's faith in the midst of these difficulties and challenges should stir us to seek God's creative resources in accomplishing his purpose in our lives. Like Elijah, we can have faith that whatever God commands us to do, he will provide what we need to carry it through.

A Woman Scorned

Jezebel sent this message to Elijah: "May the gods strike me and even kill me if by this time tomorrow I have not killed you just as you killed them."

1 KINGS 19:2

An old adage says, "Hell hath no fury like a woman scorned," and Jezebel was certainly that. How do you handle that kind of anger? In response to Jezebel's threat on Elijah's life, the prophet, suffering from the "Elijah complex," fled. "I have had enough, LORD," he said. "Take my life" (1 Kings 19:4). Elijah was drained and ready to quit. The only solution he could see to his problem was to die before Jezebel could get to him and kill him, so he voiced a death wish. (That strikes me as ironic because Elijah never did die. At the end of his life, a chariot came down from heaven and carried him away.)

Elijah must have felt that his life was nothing but chaos and everyone was out to get him. But although he was the target of God's enemies, the idea of chaos implies that everything is completely out of control, and that wasn't the case. God was in control, and he saw Elijah's "whining" as selfish.

When we face turbulence, weariness, and uncertainty in our lives and want nothing more than to quit, we can turn to the one unfailing Source of resolution—Jesus Christ. He came into the fallen cosmos and brought relief. By his death and resurrection, he restored sinners to God and promised life forever in heaven. Our attitude for such an indescribable gift should be an outpouring of gratitude—even when the world seems to be spinning out of control and we feel as if we are spinning with it.

Rejoice at God's control over the turbulence of this world. Even a "woman scorned" is no threat to God. Take some moments to express your thankfulness.

A Tale of Two Kingdoms

*The angel of the L*ORD *told Elijah, who was from Tishbe, "Go and confront the messengers of the king of Samaria and ask them, 'Is there no God in Israel? Why are you going to Baal-zebub, the god of Ekron, to ask whether the king will recover?'"* 2 KINGS 1:3

The book of 2 Kings holds as much conflict and drama as a good novel, but it's not fiction. Second Kings is a tale of two kingdoms, both on a collision course with captivity. First Kings describes the rule of Solomon and how Israel split into the northern kingdom (Israel) and the southern kingdom (Judah). Second Kings describes the major events in the collapse of those kingdoms.

As the leaders of each kingdom turned away from God, their disobedience became a stumbling block to the entire nation. Instead of seeking the God who had brought them into the "land of plenty," they turned to other gods.

Our God is a pursuing God, constantly reaching out to people until he is forced to judge them. During the Last Supper, Jesus Christ was still reaching out to Judas, fully knowing that Judas was about to betray him. In Revelation, Jesus Christ said of the church at Thyatira, "I gave her time to repent, but she does not want to turn away from her immorality" (2:21).

God sent the prophets Elijah and Elisha to lead the people back to the Lord. But despite their best efforts to provide CPR to the heart of a nation, it was too late. The books of 1 and 2 Kings were completed during the Babylonian captivity.

In many ways the entire Bible is a tale of two kingdoms: the Kingdom of God and the kingdom of humanity. In the kingdom of humanity, the devil, whose mission is to do anything he can to hinder God's Kingdom, never stops working to lure people away from God.

Take a moment to consider these two kingdoms. What is your course of action for guiding people toward God's Kingdom? Be on the lookout for opportunities—they're everywhere.

Is Elijah Coming?

They replied, "He was a hairy man, and he wore a leather belt around
his waist."
  "Elijah from Tishbe!" the king exclaimed.

2 KINGS 1:8

Elijah was one of the most important people in ancient Jewish history. Even today, at every Passover meal, an extra place is prepared in case Elijah shows up. Small children in Jewish households conduct a search to see if Elijah has come.

Second Kings opens with the end of Elijah's ministry. King Ahaziah has fallen through the latticework of an upper room in his palace. To learn if he will recover, he sends messengers to the temple of Baal-zelub, the god of Ekron. God sends Elijah to the messengers with a pointed question for the king: "Why did you send messengers to Baal-zebub, the god of Ekron? Is there no God in Israel to answer your question?" Then Elijah delivers the news that Ahaziah will surely die. The messengers return sooner than expected and deliver the information. When the king hears a description of the one who has given the message, he instantly recognizes him as Elijah.

During the days of Jesus Christ, the Jewish people continued searching for Elijah. In a sense, John the Baptist was a type of Elijah, yet Jesus predicted that Elijah was yet to come (see Matthew 17:11). Is it possible that Elijah will still show up before Jesus returns? Some think it's not only possible but probable.

When Jesus was transfigured on a high mountain, Moses and Elijah were also there, and the three talked together about the future Kingdom. Could Moses and Elijah show up again? Elijah never died because a chariot of fire took him to heaven. Moses died, but his body was never found.

No one knows when or if Moses and Elijah will return. But each of us needs to be faithful to Jesus Christ and daily prepare for his return, which is a certainty.

Elisha's Confidant

When she came to the man of God at the mountain, she fell to the ground before him and caught hold of his feet. Gehazi began to push her away, but the man of God said, "Leave her alone. She is deeply troubled, but the LORD has not told me what it is." 2 KINGS 4:27

In 2 Kings 4, we meet a woman whose husband had also been one of God's prophets. But he had died, and she was financially strapped. The creditors were coming to take her sons and sell them as slaves.

When the widow appealed to Elisha for help, he asked her, "What do you have in your house?" (see v. 2).

She had only a single flask of olive oil. Elisha told her to borrow as many empty jars from her friends and neighbors as she could. Next the prophet told her to go into her house with her sons, shut the door behind them, and pour oil from her flask into the jars. The oil flowed until every jar was full. Elisha told her to sell the oil and pay off her debts, and she and her sons could live off the money that remained.

Late in the chapter, we meet a wealthy couple from Shunem who made a guest room for Elisha to use whenever he was in the area. As a reward for their generosity, Elisha prophesied that the childless couple would have a son within a year. The son was born, and some years later he died unexpectedly. The woman laid her son on Elisha's bed and then hurried to the prophet and gripped his feet, refusing to return home until Elisha agreed to accompany her. When they arrived home, Elisha shut himself in his room, prayed, and followed God's leading. Soon after, the boy was restored to life.

We should expect God to speak to us by his Spirit and understand that the Lord does reveal his plans for us when the time is right. As we read our Bibles, we should expect God to speak, and we should anticipate the Spirit's revelation with eagerness.

The "Nazareth Principle"

"Aren't the rivers of Damascus, the Abana and the Pharpar, better than any of the rivers of Israel? Why shouldn't I wash in them and be healed?" So Naaman turned and went away in a rage.   2 KINGS 5:12

We tend to have preconceived ideas about how God does or should work in our lives. Often, we're wrong. Consider Naaman, a great warrior in the king of Aram's army, who contracted leprosy. His wife's Israelite servant girl suggested that Naaman visit the prophet Elisha so he could heal Naaman's leprosy.

When Naaman told his king that he wanted to visit the prophet, the king sent a letter of introduction and money to the king of Israel. When the king of Israel received them, he tore his clothing in despair. How could *he* possibly heal a leper? Elisha had a different reaction and asked that Naaman be sent to him. But before the great general could see Elisha, he was given a message telling him that, if he washed seven times in the Jordan River, his body would be restored. Naaman could not imagine how that would help, and besides, the idea of washing in a muddy river was humiliating.

I call this the "Nazareth principle." God sent his Son into the world to be raised in one of the most insignificant towns in the Middle East. Nathanael asked Philip, "Can anything good come from Nazareth?" Of course, not only did something good come out of Nazareth; the very *best* came out of Nazareth.

Naaman expected to receive Elisha's personal attention; what he got was a message from him. At first, Naaman was going to reject the advice. Then his officers said, "Sir, if the prophet had told you to do something very difficult, wouldn't you have done it? So you should certainly obey him when he says simply, 'Go and wash and be cured!'" (2 Kings 5:13).

It is the same for us. We should not despise days of small beginnings, meager means, or insignificant circumstances. These are divine ingredients for great things.

The Invisible War

When Athaliah, the mother of King Ahaziah of Judah, learned that her son was dead, she began to destroy the rest of the royal family. But Ahaziah's sister Jehosheba, the daughter of King Jehoram, took Ahaziah's infant son, Joash, and stole him away from among the rest of the king's children, who were about to be killed. 2 KINGS 11:1-2

Are you aware that the circumstances of our lives have a physical dimension and a spiritual dimension? There is an unseen battle raging behind the scenes of every political setting and every military strategy.

This invisible war has continued since the beginning, when God revealed that he would destroy Satan's kingdom through the seed of a woman, or a child: "I will cause hostility between you [Satan] and the woman, and between your offspring and her offspring. He [Jesus] will strike your head, and you will strike his heel" (Genesis 3:15). Satan was forewarned that One was coming who would crush him.

On the human side of the battle, David's royal line was at stake. On the spiritual side, God had promised that the Messiah would be an heir of David.

Here's some outward evidence of this invisible conflict: Cain killed Abel, the righteous son, in Genesis 4. In an attempt to weaken the Jews, Pharaoh ordered the Hebrew midwives to kill the male babies. King Saul tried to kill David, which would have ended David's line, through which the Messiah was to come, but he didn't succeed. In today's verse, Athaliah tried to kill the entire royal line of Judah and almost succeeded except for one boy, Joash, who was preserved. Even after Jesus was born, the devil tried to destroy him through Herod's decree against the boy babies of Bethlehem and later, through the Crucifixion. The devil wants to make God a liar who can't fulfill his promises. Yet God has fulfilled his plan through Jesus Christ. Pause and thank God for his unfailing promises.

A Mentor Becomes a Menace

Joash began to rule over Judah in the seventh year of King Jehu's reign in Israel. He reigned in Jerusalem forty years. His mother was Zibiah from Beersheba. All his life Joash did what was pleasing in the LORD's sight because Jehoiada the priest instructed him.   2 KINGS 12:1-2

Over the years, we've changed what we call someone who guides us. Some call that person a teacher; others use the word *mentor* or *coach*. Whatever you call it, King Joash was fortunate to have a godly mentor in the priest Jehoiada. Now the young king could become a leader with a spiritual heart, and he became just that. But what happened when that mentor was no longer around?

One task of mentors is to wean their pupils from dependence on them and lead their pupils into greater dependence on God. During the early years of Joash's reign, the priests had allowed the Temple to deteriorate. They took the money designated for ministry and Temple maintenance and used it for other things. When we have no love for God, we neglect what's important to him.

King Joash followed God because of his mentor, Jehoiada, and "did what was pleasing in the LORD's sight" (2 Kings 12:2). But when Jehoiada died, the king turned to sin: "After Jehoiada's death, the leaders of Judah came and bowed before King Joash and persuaded him to listen to their advice. They decided to abandon the Temple of the LORD, the God of their ancestors, and they worshiped Asherah poles and idols instead!" (2 Chronicles 24:17-18).

If others are the props for your faith, what will you do when those props are gone? You may be looking to a mentor, a pastor, or some other leader to validate your faith. Will you be shaken to the core if you learn of some inconstancy in that person or you find a flaw in him or her? Look to Jesus, the one who initiates and perfects your faith.

Jesus never said, "Follow my people." He said, "Follow me!"

Jonah: Man, Myth, or Legend?

Jeroboam II recovered the territories of Israel between Lebo-hamath and the Dead Sea, just as the LORD, the God of Israel, had promised through Jonah son of Amittai, the prophet from Gath-hepher.   2 KINGS 14:25

If someone wants to make fun of the Bible, the story of Jonah is a convenient target. It seems outlandish that a great fish could swallow a man and the man could survive being spit on the shore and live to tell about it. People who struggle with the story of Jonah try to deny that he ever existed, much less lived inside a fish for three days and three nights. Some fishermen are prone to exaggerating. Yet the story of Jonah isn't an exaggeration. It shows up in the annals of the nation of Israel. Moreover, Jesus referred to the historical Jonah as a prophetic validation of his own resurrection: "As Jonah was in the belly of the great fish for three days and three nights, so will the Son of Man be in the heart of the earth for three days and three nights" (Matthew 12:40).

The historical reference in today's verse confirms that Jonah was a real person and a prophet. He was from Gath-hepher, a village about five miles from Nazareth in Galilee. Today the place is known as el-Meshed.

Why is this detail significant? The Pharisees tried to discredit Jesus because he was from Galilee. They attempted to argue from precedence, saying, "There has never been a prophet who has come from Galilee." Yet they were wrong, perhaps because they didn't study their Bibles enough or because they willingly passed over Jonah, who *was* a prophet from Galilee.

The story of Jonah is more than a fish tale. It's rooted in truth and historical fact. God is trustworthy and has ensured that what you find between the Bible's covers is trustworthy as well and something he wants you to know.

Strong Start, Weak Ending

Uzziah son of Amaziah began to rule over Judah in the twenty-seventh year of the reign of King Jeroboam II of Israel.   2 KINGS 15:1

At every Olympic track competition, the runners start exactly the same way. Their bodies are cocked, their minds focused, waiting for the sound of the gun. Yet not everyone finishes the same. That's what makes it a competition.

The kings of Judah had successfully executed a series of campaigns against their enemies and had expanded the borders of their nation. But one of the last great kings of Judah rebelled at the end of his life.

Uzziah committed a sin similar to King Saul's in making an unlawful sacrifice: "He sinned against the LORD his God by entering the sanctuary of the LORD's Temple and personally burning incense on the incense altar" (2 Chronicles 26:16). The Jewish historian Josephus claims there was an earthquake when Uzziah tried to act like a priest. The king had no business entering the Temple and doing what he did. Azariah the high priest took eighty other priests with him and went to confront Uzziah. When the king became furious at the confrontation and raged at the priests, God struck him with leprosy. For the rest of Uzziah's life, he had to live in isolation and remain outside the Temple.

Turn to a friend, your spouse, or someone else who knows you well, and ask that person to help you honestly identify your strengths and weaknesses. Then look to God to help you deal wisely with what you learn so that you don't rebel late in life, as Uzziah did.

Worshiping the Past

[Hezekiah] removed the pagan shrines, smashed the sacred pillars, and cut down the Asherah poles. He broke up the bronze serpent that Moses had made, because the people of Israel had been offering sacrifices to it. The bronze serpent was called Nehushtan.   2 KINGS 18:4

There is a danger in holding on to relics from our past. The relic might be an object, a person, a particular way of doing something, or even a spiritual movement. If we hold on to those too tightly, they can replace God in our priorities.

At one time in the history of Israel, the Israelites were traveling from Mount Hor when they began to complain to Moses (and to God): "Why have you brought us out of Egypt to die here in the wilderness? . . . There is nothing to eat here and nothing to drink. And we hate this horrible manna!" (Numbers 21:5).

In response to their complaints, the Lord sent poisonous snakes among the people. Many of the Israelites who were bitten died. These snakes quickly got the people's attention, and Moses made a bronze snake and hung it from a pole. When the people who had been bitten looked up at it, they were healed. God was the one who had healed them as they looked up in obedience to him, but the people gradually placed so much value on the snake itself that it became an object of worship and sacrifice until King Hezekiah broke it up.

It is great to look back and reminisce about the things God has done. These recollections are important reference points in our lives, but we cannot remain at those points. We must move on. Vital faith requires fresh experiences to keep growing; without them, spiritual entropy sets in. Celebrate what God has done in your past, but keep stretching your faith and trust into new areas of growth and learning. Our past should be a guidepost, but never a hitching post.

April 12

The Beginning of the End

On January 15, during the ninth year of Zedekiah's reign, King Nebuchadnezzar of Babylon led his entire army against Jerusalem. They surrounded the city and built siege ramps against its walls.

2 KINGS 25:1

The heart of ancient Israel was Jerusalem, and at the heart of Jerusalem was the Temple. Although initially the nation seemed to have a few heart murmurs, it finally succumbed to a devastating heart attack in the form of the Babylonian onslaught in 586 BC.

A previous attack years earlier had marked the beginning of the end for Israel. In a sense, God had fired a shot over the bow to warn the nation to correct course spiritually.

The ancient Annals of Sennacherib record that the Assyrians came against the fortified cities of Judah. The first time was in 713 BC, after Sennacherib had already conquered most of Judah.

During Sennacherib's second attack on Jerusalem in 701 BC, God intervened and destroyed 185,000 Assyrians, an event recorded in the book of Isaiah. But although this bought Judah some time, the final blow eventually came through the Babylonian king Nebuchadnezzar. In 605 BC, Babylon began the first of a series of expulsions of the Jews from Jerusalem. Daniel was in the first group taken to Babylon.

Jehoahaz, the son of King Josiah, succeeded him as king, but he did evil in the sight of the Lord and was deposed after just three months. The king of Egypt, Pharaoh Neco, replaced Jehoahaz with his brother Eliakim and changed his name to Jehoiakim. This king did evil also and was replaced after eleven years. His son Jehoiachin replaced him, but he rebelled after only three months and ten days and was replaced by Zedekiah, the final king of Judah.

With so many different kings in such a relatively short time, Judah saw a lot of change and struggle as they tried to survive. What made the crucial difference? Which king was on the throne. That will make a difference for you, too. Who is the king of your heart and life?

The Value of a Journal

These are their genealogical records. 1 CHRONICLES 1:29

Since ancient times, people have been recording the events, values, and ideas of their age.

Before the existence of cameras, CDs, and MP3 devices, there were chroniclers, people who sat in a ruler's throne room and recorded the events of the day. Today we see the word *chronicle* in the names of newspapers, such as the *San Francisco Chronicle* or the *Houston Chronicle*. If you read Chronicles, you catch a glimpse of the events of the day through the eyes of the writer. Originally 1 and 2 Chronicles were called *Dibre Hayyamim*, or the "words of the days." These records are far more than newspapers chronicling events. They cover the same ground as some other books in the Bible, such as 2 Samuel or 2 Kings, but also give the spiritual perspective of Israel's history.

We aren't certain about the author of Chronicles, but the writing style is similar to that of the priest Ezra, and Bible scholars believe these books capture his perspective. The closing verses of 2 Chronicles 36:22-23 appear with only minor changes in Ezra 1:1-3. The identification of Ezra as the writer makes sense because of the priestly emphasis on the Temple, priests, and rulers directed by divine guidance. The book of 1 Chronicles is divided into two major parts. First Chronicles 1–9 covers three thousand years and the period from Adam to David. First Chronicles 10–29 covers David's thirty-year reign and three key themes: blessing, judgment, and covenant.

Let me encourage you to keep a journal in which you note observations about your life and record things God is teaching you. Doing so helps you organize your feelings as you spill them onto the paper and allows you to determine what's important and to set priorities. Second, it allows you to reread your entries later and see how a sovereign God has been piecing your life together. Finally, your journal can pass along a wonderful spiritual heritage to children or grandchildren in the years to come.

What's in a Name?

These are the sons of David who were born in Hebron: The oldest was Amnon, whose mother was Ahinoam from Jezreel. The second was Daniel, whose mother was Abigail from Carmel.   1 CHRONICLES 3:1

If you begin reading aloud at 1 Chronicles 1:1, you will likely stumble a bit on the names. Before long, your eyes will glaze over as you try to cover three thousand years of genealogy in three chapters. This list, the most comprehensive genealogical record in the Bible, highlights the names of David, Judah, and Benjamin. Why?

The main concern of Chronicles is David's dynasty and the city of Jerusalem. As the genealogy traces David's ancestry from the dawn of humanity through the end of captivity, it proves that from the beginning of human history, God has been selecting and preserving his people.

The names of the people on this list might not seem important to us, but they were important to those people because they helped prove family heritage, which was important for land allotments. And in David's case, they traced the royal lineage.

It has always been interesting to me that the New Testament opens with a genealogy as well, which doesn't seem like a great way to capture someone's attention. Yet among the Jews, lineage was a top priority. The Gospel of Matthew reveals Jesus Christ as coming from the royal line of David, and it was natural to ask anyone claiming to be the Messiah, "What tribe did you come from? Who were your parents?"

This information proved helpful to me years ago when a man came into my office and told me he was Jesus. I squinted and then asked, "What tribe of Israel are you from?" He stared at me blankly. Then I asked, "Where were you born?" When he answered that he was from Pittsburgh, I had to laugh before asking him to leave!

If you are a Christian, your name is on a list far longer than the one in 1 Chronicles. Luke 10:20 says, "Rejoice because your names are registered in heaven."

Long Live the King!

At Hebron, David made a covenant before the LORD with all the elders of Israel. And they anointed him king of Israel, just as the LORD had promised through Samuel.   1 CHRONICLES 11:3

There was a reason Saul was rejected as king and David was anointed as his replacement, and it turned on a matter of the heart. David certainly had his flaws, but his heart was sensitive toward the Lord. Samuel's words to Saul confirm this: "Now your kingdom must end, for the LORD has sought out a man after his own heart. The LORD has already appointed him to be the leader of his people, because you have not kept the LORD's command" (1 Samuel 13:14). David wasn't perfect, but he became the most influential king in all of Israel's history. In fact, the reign of King David will be acknowledged forever through the eternal reign of David's greatest son, the Lord Jesus Christ.

There is an old recipe for rabbit stew that begins with these words: "First, catch the rabbit." That probably seems like a restatement of the obvious, but don't miss the significance of such simple instruction. The recipe for spiritual influence requires, first, that you have spiritual priorities.

Each of the three doors at the front of the Milan Cathedral has a caption. One says, "All that which pleases is but for a moment." Another says, "All that which troubles us is but for a moment." The central entrance to the main aisle has this inscription: "That only is important which is eternal." Your day and life are filled with many unspiritual influences, but where are your priorities, and what is your central focus? If you keep your mind and heart on what is eternal and recall these three truths, you will be a person with a heart that runs after God.

Divine Editorial

David became more and more powerful, because the LORD of Heaven's Armies was with him.   1 CHRONICLES 11:9

If you listen to two different people tell the same story, you will get two different perspectives. It's the same with Chronicles. If you compare the account in 1 Chronicles to 2 Samuel, you will see two views, each of which portrays King David in a different light: Although 1 Chronicles includes David's sin of moving the Ark in the wrong manner, it completely omits David's struggle with Saul, his sin with Bathsheba, and Absalom's rebellion.

Why the difference? In 1 Chronicles, the audience is living after the Captivity, and the writer knows the people will need encouragement to come back to the land and rebuild. Also, this writer shows that God is merciful. Even though the past is often dark, there is a glorious future. This book is written with a divine editorial. The writer understands that history is one thing but God's story is another.

When Samuel was seeking out Saul's replacement, God told him, "The LORD doesn't see things the way you see them. People judge by outward appearance, but the LORD looks at the heart" (1 Samuel 16:7).

About one hundred years ago in Portsmouth, England, a man who was blind in one eye and had only one arm was walking down the street. This man couldn't walk on the deck of a ship without becoming seasick, but he was a sailor. In fact, he was the foremost sailor in the world and none other than Lord Nelson, England's greatest admiral. You can't judge a book by its cover—or an admiral by his appearance.

King David committed adultery and had serious family troubles. In the eyes of many people, David was a loser. Yet to God, David was a king in the royal line that led to Jesus Christ, King of the world. This is amazing reconciliation on God's part.

Listen to how God describes your life in 2 Corinthians 5:19: "God was in Christ, reconciling the world to himself, no longer counting people's sins against them." Ours, too, is an amazing reconciliation.

Bringing God to the Battle

David asked God, "Should I go out to fight the Philistines? Will you hand them over to me?"
  The LORD replied, "Yes, go ahead. I will hand them over to you."

1 CHRONICLES 14:10

Charles Spurgeon once said, "It does not matter how heavy troubles are, if you can cast them on the Lord. The heavier they are, so much the better, for the more you have got rid of, and the more there is laid upon the Rock." God wants us to unburden our hearts with our pleasures, our pains, our likes, and our dislikes. We can tell God about our temptations, the wounds of our past, and our dreams for the future.

This section of 1 Chronicles recounts the Philistine battles and gives insight into David's prayer life. David was a man after God's own heart who prayed much, and at this point, he prayed about which battles to fight.

Philippians 4:6 says, "Don't worry about anything; instead, pray about everything. Tell God what you need, and thank him for all he has done." We're prone to pray about the big things in life, yet we forget the so-called little things until they have grown and become big things, and then our anxiety levels peak.

A widow came to the great preacher G. Campbell Morgan and said, "Dr. Morgan, do you think we should pray about the little things in our lives?"

Dr. Morgan, in his characteristically British manner, said, "Madam, can you mention anything in your life that is big to God?" It's all little stuff to the Lord, and he wants nothing excluded.

In Luke 18:1, Jesus Christ "told his disciples a story to show that they should always pray and never give up." He told about a widow who repeatedly brought her request before a judge until she wore him down and received satisfaction. We can learn about our need for persistence in prayer from this widow's example.

Bible commentator and great Bible scholar F. B. Meyer said, "The great tragedy of life is not unanswered prayer, but unoffered prayer."

Does God Need a House?

"Look," David said, "I am living in a beautiful cedar palace, but the Ark of the LORD's Covenant is out there under a tent!"   1 CHRONICLES 17:1

The Jewish people were used to worshiping God in a specific place. But King David grew concerned that he had a lavish palace and the Lord of the universe was living in a tent. This tent was the Tabernacle created during the Israelites' forty years in the wilderness after they had left Egypt. David wanted to build something more than a tent for God. He literally wanted to build a house, but God wanted to build David's house into a lasting dynasty.

As David made plans to construct the Temple, God told Nathan the prophet, "Tell him that I have plans for him." You can never outgive God when you want to give something to him, and the truth is, God doesn't really need anything from us. Acts 17:25 says, "Human hands can't serve his needs—for he has no needs. He himself gives life and breath to everything, and he satisfies every need."

When Jesus walked the earth, he used simple things: a donkey for a ride, a boat as a pulpit, and a mountainside as a sanctuary for preaching. When Jesus wanted to feed the crowd that had gathered, he used a few loaves of bread and some fish to provide food for the multitude. When Jesus was crucified, he was buried in a borrowed tomb. The stories in the Bible teach us that God can use anything for his glory. If you have property or a talent or money, God can use it. Whatever you place in God's hands, he will bless and use for his work.

Instead of speaking in an audible voice from heaven, the Lord has chosen to use us. As amazing as it sounds, God wants us to partner with him in the work of his Kingdom. Paul wrote, "God chose things the world considers foolish" (1 Corinthians 1:27). His work in our lives happens no matter where we are.

The Covenant

I will confirm [David] as king over my house and my kingdom for all time, and his throne will be secure forever. 1 CHRONICLES 17:14

Today's reading covers the affirmation of the Davidic covenant, in which the Lord promised David that his dynasty would last forever. Whom was he talking about in this promise?

Part of the fulfillment of this promise came through David's son Solomon. But the lasting fulfillment for David's throne could come only through Jesus Christ. This chapter shows the scarlet thread of redemption.

Earlier in chapter 17, David had told the prophet Nathan, in essence, "I've got some nice digs, but God is homeless in a tent."

Nathan responded by giving David the go-ahead to build the Temple. But that night, God spoke to Nathan and told him he had spoken too soon. It wasn't God's plan for David to build the Temple.

Then God made a covenant with David. The first part of the covenant promised that David's son Solomon would build the Temple. In addition, David's throne would be established forever. And although as a son of David, Solomon was an archetype of the greater Son of David, the second part of the covenant was fulfilled when Jesus Christ came to conquer sin and provide salvation for the world. It is hard to understand the prophets, the ministry of Jesus Christ, and the future events of the Bible unless you know 1 Chronicles 17.

When the angel Gabriel appeared to Mary, he told her that God would give her son "the throne of his ancestor David" (Luke 1:32). On the day of Pentecost, Peter included in his sermon what we know as 2 Samuel 7, saying, "Dear brothers, think about this! You can be sure that the patriarch David wasn't referring to himself, for he died and was buried, and his tomb is still here among us. . . . David was looking into the future and speaking of the Messiah's resurrection" (Acts 2:29, 31).

Let's celebrate God's faithful fulfillment of his promise to David through Jesus Christ.

The End of David?

[David] died at a ripe old age.　1 CHRONICLES 29:28

Earlier in 1 Chronicles 29, David offered praise for God's abundant provision for the building of the Temple. He acknowledged that he and the people were giving to God only what they had received from him. And he was quick to thank God for his blessing, particularly in light of the brevity of life: "We are here for only a moment. . . . Our days on earth are like a passing shadow, gone so soon without a trace" (1 Chronicles 29:15). As if to cement that truth, by the end of chapter 29 we have read of David's death "at a ripe old age" after a forty-year reign.

If you've ever seen the 1964 film *Mary Poppins*, starring Julie Andrews and Dick Van Dyke, you may remember a comment Mary Poppins made to the children in her care: "That's a piecrust promise—easily made and easily broken."

All of the promises we make have boundaries. They have starting points. They may last for only a short time or be in force for years. We may even keep some promises for a lifetime (think marriage vows). But when we die, our death marks the end of those promises. King David died, but unlike a human promise, God's promise to him did not end because the promises of God are not bound by time. They last forever.

The apostle James understood that God's promise to David was an eternal one. Addressing the elders at Jerusalem, he quoted God's words to the prophet Amos: "I will restore the fallen house of David. . . . From the ruins I will rebuild it and restore its former glory" (Amos 9:11). In other words, God promised to restore David's dynasty. And this came to pass in Jesus Christ, the Son of David, who sits on the throne and reigns forever.

How wonderful it is to serve a God who is faithful to his promises!

Promotion!

Solomon son of David took firm control of his kingdom, for the LORD his
God was with him and made him very powerful. 2 CHRONICLES 1:1

Most people love a promotion. It's a vote of confidence from a company or
a leader about the capability of a worker. A promotion is often accompanied by a pay increase, additional responsibilities, or greater authority. As
we move from 1 Chronicles to 2 Chronicles, the theme shifts from quality
to captivity, or from the excellence of Solomon to the exile of the southern
kingdom. Second Chronicles shows God's continued faithfulness to the
house of David through the forty-year reign of Solomon, from 971 BC to
931 BC. That reign marked the golden age of peace and prosperity, with a
united kingdom and the expansion of its territory. This period in the life of
Israel was something like life in the United States after World War II, when
prosperity was on the upswing and the future of the country looked bright.
Why was there such prosperity during this period for King Solomon?

God's presence in Solomon's life made Solomon a powerful person. The
Lord gave him the wisdom and abilities to handle his promotion to the
throne of the kingdom of Israel. Because of the Lord's presence, Solomon's
leadership had a lasting impact on the kingdom, and Solomon's wisdom
continues today through books such as Proverbs, Ecclesiastes, and Song of
Songs. God's presence made the difference.

Is God's presence in your life noticeable to those around you, or do you
lack spiritual power because you're not seeking God's presence? Make it a
point to increase your focus on God in your daily life. Ask him to fill your
mind, your thoughts, and your actions.

April 22 READ 2 CHRONICLES 3:1-17

Under Construction

Solomon began to build the Temple of the LORD in Jerusalem on Mount Moriah, where the LORD had appeared to David, his father. The Temple was built on the threshing floor of Araunah the Jebusite, the site that David had selected.   2 CHRONICLES 3:1

The orange sign with black letters screams the information: Construction Zone. Whenever you see these words, you know a building is in process and not yet completed. The most prominent theme in the first nine chapters of 2 Chronicles is the building of the Temple. These chapters give details about the Temple construction, the supplies, and the workers. The theme of Temple construction continues throughout the entire book. In chapters 10–36, the text emphasizes the kings of Judah who restored the Temple and omits a list of the northern kings because they don't have ties to the Temple. The final portion of 2 Chronicles closes with the proclamation of Cyrus to return and rebuild the Temple.

King Solomon and his workers took seven and a half years to build the Temple. It was dedicated in the seventh month and timed to coincide with the Festival of Tabernacles. The Temple was built on Mount Moriah, the same place where Abraham offered his son Isaac. Notice that the worship center was built where a father gave his son. The Temple was elaborate. It was ninety feet long, thirty feet wide, and forty-five feet high. It had a front porch area and was decorated with gold and jewels. People came from across the known world to see its beauty.

In the New Testament, those who belong to Christ are called the temple of God. The Lord wants you to become a place where his worship is carried on consistently. Having a regular time to read God's Word, to pray, and to share what you're learning with others is a good starting point. In this world, the temple of the Lord is still a work in progress, because to become effective, we must be growing in our faith and remain "under construction."

The Power of Humility

When the LORD saw their change of heart, he gave this message to Shemaiah: "Since the people have humbled themselves, I will not completely destroy them and will soon give them some relief. I will not use Shishak to pour out my anger on Jerusalem." 2 CHRONICLES 12:7

God's Kingdom is an upside-down Kingdom because the Lord's values are different from ours. Jesus said in Luke 16:15, "What this world honors is detestable in the sight of God." Our world exalts the proud and self-sufficient, those who know what they want and will stop at nothing to get it. But these aren't God's values. The Lord honors humility.

King Rehoboam inherited the leadership of Israel from his father, King Solomon. Rehoboam experienced God's blessing during the first three years of his reign; then, in the fourth year, he rebelled, and in the fifth year, he suffered God's judgment. King Rehoboam forsook the Lord, and as a result, Egypt invaded Israel.

The prophet Micah said, "The LORD has told you what is good: . . . to do what is right, to love mercy, and to walk humbly with your God" (Micah 6:8). God considers humility a good thing, but what exactly is humility?

Humility begins with an honest and accurate self-awareness and continues with a proper God-awareness—that is, that the Lord is in charge and he is merciful: "God blesses those who are poor and realize their need for him" (Matthew 5:3).

The author of *Roots*, Alex Haley, kept a picture of a turtle sitting on top of a fence. Haley explained, "If you see a turtle on a fence post, you know he had some help! Any time I start thinking, *Wow isn't that marvelous what I've done!* I look at that picture and remember how this turtle—me—got up on that post."

Take a moment and consider how you come across to others. Do you owe someone an apology? If so, make a specific plan to take care of this. God will honor your commitment to living in humility.

What God Sees

Asa did what was pleasing and good in the sight of the LORD his God.

2 CHRONICLES 14:2

Nothing escapes God's view. He sees everything. Solomon declared, "The LORD sees clearly what a man does, examining every path he takes" (Proverbs 5:21). We wonder how much of this truth King Solomon was able to pass on to the kings who reigned after him.

Unfortunately, the reformation efforts of a few good kings didn't stop the downward spiral of the Jewish people toward captivity. About 70 percent of 2 Chronicles 10–36 deals with the good kings, and 30 percent of these chapters covers the bad ones. Each king is presented with his relationship to the Temple as a pivotal factor. The reign of King Asa (see chapters 14–16) encouraged revival and destroyed the pagan altars, yet he did it in his own strength. Chapters 17–21 tell about King Jehoshaphat, who continued the revival but also sent priests throughout the land to teach God's law to the people.

God dealt with the Israelites corporately, but he also dealt with each king as an individual. David declared, "O LORD, you have examined my heart and know everything about me. You know when I sit down or stand up. You know my thoughts even when I'm far away. You see me when I travel and when I rest at home. You know everything I do" (Psalm 139:1-3). What is the ever-seeing eye of the Lord seeing as he looks at the details of your life? What do your efforts for him reveal?

Jumpin' Jehoshaphat!

[Jehoshaphat] sought his father's God and obeyed his commands instead of following the evil practices of the kingdom of Israel.

2 CHRONICLES 17:4

A copywriter applying for a job at a newspaper was asked, "Are you good at condensing material?"

"Sure," he replied.

"Okay, do a rewrite on this and really cut it short," said the editor, tongue in cheek, as he handed the applicant a copy of the Ten Commandments.

In a few minutes the applicant returned with the rewrite—and was hired on the spot. His rewrite contained just one word: *Don't.* Not all of the Ten Commandments are negative, but many fall into that category.

2 Chronicles 17–21 describes the reign of King Jehoshaphat, who could have been the man described in Psalm 1:1-3 because he is marked by what he did not do, the company he did not keep, and the places he did not rest. While there is a great deal written about the power of a positive attitude, there is also power in "negative" thinking. An athlete chooses *not* to eat Snickers or stay up late. The king makes choices to avoid things that will hinder his relationship with God. The righteous person understands that saying no enables him to say yes to the things of the Lord.

Unfortunately, Jehoshaphat also made some wrong choices. He married the wrong woman, chose the wrong allies, and fought the wrong war. He aligned his kingdom with Ahab, one of the bad kings of Israel, and Ahab talked him into going into battle wearing his royal robes.

Ahab knew these robes would make Jehoshaphat an easy target, so he wore a disguise into battle. The Syrian army attacked Jehoshaphat in his royal robes, assuming it was Ahab. But Jehoshaphat called on God and was delivered.

Consider the choices you are making for your life. Something simple may be keeping you from following God. Make a concrete plan today to say no to the things that will hurt your relationship with him.

Turning Up the Tunes

At the very moment they began to sing and give praise, the LORD caused the armies of Ammon, Moab, and Mount Seir to start fighting among themselves.   2 CHRONICLES 20:22

Music fills our lives. We drive to it, work to it, and work out to it. Christians also worship with music. Music is central to our experience of worship. In today's story, music was a key factor in the military victory of Judah.

In the face of the armies of Ammon, Moab, and Mount Seir, Jehoshaphat commanded the people, "Believe in the LORD your God, and you will be able to stand firm. Believe in his prophets, and you will succeed" (2 Chronicles 20:20). The king commanded this action before anything had happened on the battlefield. Belief was the first step in their preparation for battle, and the belief was further communicated in the words of praise the singers proclaimed.

Part of the preparation for spiritual warfare is understanding our position in Christ and being willing to wait on the Lord for victory. In doing so, you will have a faith-based perspective and will be able to march forward in praise and thanksgiving. (Notice that it was the singers, not the soldiers, who led God's people into battle.)

Why is praise so important? First, it elevates our view. Too often, we look at the size of the problem rather than at the greatness of God. Second, praise eradicates our fear. Songs of joy and praise are declarations that we trust confidently in God's power and that we are not afraid. Third, songs of praise anticipate our victory. Worship music is an acknowledgment that we are waiting for God to work. And that's essentially what God told the king: Don't worry; don't even fight. Just watch me work!

You may need God to intervene in a particular situation. Take the first step and believe that he will undertake for you; then praise him in anticipation of the victory he will bring about.

The King of Encouragement

[Hezekiah said,] "Don't be afraid or discouraged because of the king of Assyria or his might army, for there is a power far greater on our side! He may have a great army, but they are merely men. We have the LORD our God to help us and to fight our battles for us!"   2 CHRONICLES 32:7-8

Once I went to India with a group whose self-proclaimed ministry was to cast out demons from Christian leaders. Now, India has many Christian leaders who have sacrificed to the point of poverty, persecution, and even death for the gospel of Jesus Christ. So I was shocked to hear one American speaker say to the audience, "I see demons around you right now."

I thought, *How cruel to shame these godly men with such a large dose of false teaching.* Even more shocking was the response from the audience, which was grinning, clapping, and in some cases, even laughing. Later I learned that the translator was not only translating the message but was also correcting the faulty theology. Instead of saying exactly what the speaker had said, the translator was saying, "Right now the angels of the Lord are surrounding you." Encouragement is one of the strongest tools in the Christian's tool bag.

King Hezekiah was a great encourager. During his reign, he restored the Temple and proper worship. He also destroyed the idols and high places of idol worship. When Sennacherib of Assyria came to attack Jerusalem, King Hezekiah prayed and spoke to the prophet Isaiah about it. Together the prophet and king prayed and asked for God's protection.

Encouragement is the grease in the gears of relationships. Each of us has overheard Christians tear down other people, and it is discouraging. Evangelist Dwight L. Moody said, "The measure of a man isn't how many servants he has but how many men he serves." How are you using encouragement to serve others? Remember that, although a pat on the back is only a few vertebrae removed from a kick in the pants, it is miles ahead in results.

When Hope Is but a Glimmer

King Cyrus of Persia says: "The LORD, the God of heaven, has given me all the kingdoms of the earth. He has appointed me to build him a Temple at Jerusalem, which is in Judah. Any of you who are the LORD's people may go there for this task."   2 CHRONICLES 36:23

Today's reading shows the rapid turnover of the throne in Judah. King Jehoahaz ruled for only three months before Pharaoh Neco of Egypt took him away as a prisoner and appointed Jehoahaz's brother Jehoiakim as king. Jehoiakim's evil rule lasted for eleven years, until Nebuchadnezzar took him to Babylon. When Jehoiakim's son Jehoiachin took over, he lasted only three months and ten days before being replaced by his uncle Zedekiah, the last king of Judah.

Notice this sober warning in 2 Chronicles 36:15-16: "The LORD, the God of their ancestors, repeatedly sent his prophets to warn them, for he had compassion on his people and his Temple. But the people mocked these messengers of God and despised their words. They scoffed at the prophets until the LORD's anger could no longer be restrained and nothing could be done."

Second Chronicles ends with a glimmer of hope, but only a glimmer. The Babylonian army had destroyed the Temple, and the children of Israel had been taken captive. Before the candle of national identity was extinguished, the very last breath of prophecy was about another Temple. What hope would have filled the hearts of the exiles more than five hundred miles away! The chronicler (whom we believe to be Ezra) ended optimistically, and King Cyrus of Persia allowed the Jews to return to Jerusalem.

Through the image of the Temple, 2 Chronicles points ahead to Jesus Christ. When Jesus came to earth, it was better than having the Jerusalem Temple with God's presence. In Matthew 12:6, Jesus said, "I tell you, there is one here who is even greater than the Temple!" Our hope rests in Jesus Christ, in whom "lives all the fullness of God in a human body" (Colossians 2:9).

Sluggishness

A total of 42,360 people returned to Judah, in addition to 7,337 servants and 200 singers, both men and women. EZRA 2:64-65

Many people know about the first Exodus, in which the Jewish people escaped Egypt and eventually came to the Promised Land. The story is told in the first five books of the Old Testament. But the opening pages of the book of Ezra tell about a second exodus, when after seventy years in Babylon, the Jewish people returned to Israel. Ezra tells of two returns. The first was led by Zerubbabel, and the second by Ezra. Chapters 1–6 of Ezra mark the national restoration, and chapters 7–10 detail the spiritual reformation.

Ezra, a direct descendant of Aaron through Eleazar, Phinehas, and Zadok, was an educated scribe who taught God's law to the people. Tradition says that Ezra was the founder of the great synagogue where the Old Testament was formulated and canonized.

The first two chapters of Ezra cover the Israelites' return to the land from which the Babylonians had removed them seventy years earlier. The Medo-Persian Empire was in charge, and the Jews were allowed to return home. You might think a groundswell of enthusiasm would have driven them back to Israel en masse, but that didn't happen. Only about fifty thousand returned, because Babylon had become their home and they felt comfortable raising families there. But they became *too* settled. During the time of Jesus Christ, a million Jews were still living in Babylon.

Take a lesson from that fact: Are you too comfortable in this world? Does the comfort of your surroundings work against your spiritual fervor? Think about how you respond when you hear of a need for volunteers at church or a financial need for a godly cause. Ask God to touch your heart and keep you from becoming too settled. When you begin to feel a little too comfortable where you are, ask the Lord to fill you with increased spiritual passion.

It's My Party, and I'll Cry If I Want To

Many of the older priests, Levites, and other leaders who had seen the first Temple wept aloud when they saw the new Temple's foundation. The others, however, were shouting for joy.   EZRA 3:12

Ezra writes about the Jews' return to Jerusalem to rebuild the Temple. When the foundation of the new Temple had been completed, the people celebrated and praised the Lord, but not everyone was ecstatic. Some of the older priests, who remembered the first Temple, cried at this holy party.

It is hard to move forward when you are looking backward. If you want to be miserable, try looking over your shoulder as you walk forward. Paul wrote in Philippians 3:13, "I focus on this one thing: forgetting the past and looking forward to what lies ahead." It is easy to see why the Jewish people were disappointed with Zerubbabel's Temple compared to Solomon's. According to the Babylonian Talmud, it lacked five things: the Ark of the Covenant, the holy fire, the shekinah glory, the Spirit of Prophecy or the Holy Spirit, and the Urim and Thummim (which the priests used to learn God's will regarding certain decisions). Despite these missing things, God promised to be present in this new Temple.

Most families (including most church families) have members who see only the negative side of a situation. Their "songs" are usually in a minor key. Sometimes it's irritating to be around those people.

How do we handle them? We should learn from the crowd in Jerusalem to sing louder. Our songs of joy can drown out others' negativity. Instead of seeing the smudges on a white shirt, look at how much white there is left. It's all a matter of perspective. Look for the positive in a situation, and help others to focus on it. Ask God to help you see the glass as half-full rather than half-empty. He is able to move your day and thoughts in the right direction.

Preach It!

At that time the prophets Haggai and Zechariah son of Iddo prophesied to the Jews in Judah and Jerusalem. They prophesied in the name of the God of Israel who was over them. EZRA 5:1

Ezra squeezes sixteen years into chapters 4 and 5. While the Jewish people had returned to Israel and had begun rebuilding the Temple, the enemies of the Jews forced them to stop work on the Temple.

But during this period, God sent two prophets, Haggai and Zechariah. Haggai preached four messages directed to Zerubbabel, the political leader, and Jeshua. As the Word of God was proclaimed, it made a deep impact on the town mayor. In Ezra 5:2, we read, "Zerubbabel son of Shealtiel and Jeshua son of Jehozadak responded by starting again to rebuild the Temple of God in Jerusalem. And the prophets of God were with them and helped them." The ministry of preaching inspired the people to resume the task of rebuilding the Temple.

At 211 degrees, water is hot enough to make a cup of coffee. If you heat the water one more degree, it boils and begins to change to steam, which can power a locomotive or propel a steamship. That one little degree means the difference between a hot beverage and the ability to generate fuel with immense power.

Ask God to give you that one extra degree in your endeavors. As you give direction, admonition, or instruction using the Word of God, you might bring one of God's servants to the "tipping point" between failure and success. What work has God called you to do with your life? Have you started but not finished it? Do you feel like giving up? Choose to put in one extra degree of effort. Give to God's servants that one extra degree, and you'll be cheering them on to continue the work of God.

Favor with God and People

Ezra was a scribe who was well versed in the Law of Moses, which the LORD, the God of Israel, had given to the people of Israel. He came up to Jerusalem from Babylon, and the king gave him everything he asked for, because the gracious hand of the LORD his God was on him.   EZRA 7:6

Occasionally in a novel, the narrator is also a character in the story. This device is used in the book of Ezra. Chapters 1–6 cover the rebuilding of the Temple. Between chapters 6 and 7, there is a fifty-nine-year gap. Ezra, a teacher of the Law and a scribe, received favor from the king, who gave Ezra not only permission to journey to Jerusalem but also an expense account from the treasury to help him accomplish a program of religious education.

The words in Ezra 7:6 remind us of one of the earliest descriptions of Jesus in the New Testament: "Jesus grew in wisdom and in stature and *in favor with God and all the people*" (Luke 2:52, emphasis added).

The key principle to think about today is found in the words the apostle Paul wrote to the Romans: "If God is for us, who can ever be against us?" (Romans 8:31). This doesn't mean that if we belong to Christ, we will never face opposition from others. In fact, the world, the flesh, demons, and unbelievers are all against us, and at times that can feel overwhelming. But it does mean that if God decides something needs to happen, no one—not even a king—can thwart that plan.

When a young preacher who was a candidate for a pastoral position learned that the congregation had turned him down, he e-mailed his father, "Rejected." Immediately, his father wrote back, "Rejected on earth / accepted in heaven." The same God who created the Milky Way created you. As you go into the world today, ask God to guide your every move; then go out in the confidence that comes from knowing that he can grant you favor in your endeavors.

Good Tears

While Ezra prayed and made this confession, weeping and lying face down on the ground in front of the Temple of God, a very large crowd of people from Israel—men, women, and children—gathered and wept bitterly with him. EZRA 10:1

When Ezra came before the Lord in heartfelt prayer and confession, God immediately answered Ezra's prayer and convicted the people of sin. Some of the people offered to make a covenant with God and divorce their pagan wives. This should not have been necessary, because Deuteronomy 7:3-4 strictly forbade the Jewish people to intermarry with those from pagan nations, but even the priests and Levites had been disobedient to the law.

It took from December until April to straighten out this intermarriage problem, which began with the priests and then included more of God's people. And how long did this recommitment to be faithful to God's law last? Ironically, within twenty-five years, Nehemiah faced the same problem Ezra had. The repeated sin required repeated confession and repentance. History does repeat itself.

Jesus encouraged our sensitivity and serious attention to the reality of sin: "God blesses those who mourn, for they will be comforted" (Matthew 5:4). Perhaps the greatest need in the church today is for genuine mourning, for tears of confession, and for repentance over our sins.

Robert Browning Hamilton wrote,

> I walked a mile with Pleasure,
> She chattered all the way;
> But left me none the wiser,
> For all she had to say.
>
> I walked a mile with Sorrow,
> And ne'er a word said she;
> But, oh, the things I learned from her
> When Sorrow walked with me!

Learn to cultivate godly sorrow over your sin, and respond accordingly to the Spirit's prompting to turn from it.

Movers and Shakers

[Nehemiah recorded,] "Hanani, one of my brothers, came to visit me with some other men who had just arrived from Judah. I asked them about the Jews who had returned there from captivity and about how things were going in Jerusalem." NEHEMIAH 1:2

There are two kinds of people in the world: those who make things happen and those who watch things happen. Nehemiah belonged to the first group. He was a mover and a shaker who made things happen because God had directed him to move to Jerusalem and rebuild the city. He changed "careers" from being a king's cup-bearer to being a construction engineer. This contemporary of Ezra led a third and final return of the exiles to Jerusalem. Nehemiah's God-given vision was bold, and in spite of intense opposition, he oversaw the rebuilding of Jerusalem's wall in just fifty-two days.

The name *Nehemyah* means "comfort of Yahweh," and Nehemiah must have been a comfort to God's people as he stood with and encouraged the builders in the face of opposition.

It has been said that a Jew never forgets Jerusalem. The psalmist wrote, "If I forget you, O Jerusalem, let my right hand forget how to play the harp" (Psalm 137:5); in other words, if he forgot Jerusalem, he might as well have forgotten the thing that was most natural to do—play the harp. Notice how, in today's reading, Nehemiah asked the right questions, felt the right emotions, and had the right reaction. You never know how God will use a conversation in your life.

Whatever you are facing today, you can be a mover and shaker. You have to ask the right questions, feel the right emotion, and then have the right reaction. Some people never care enough to ask questions. Do you? Are you asking the right questions and then seeking God for the answers and for the way he wants you to respond?

Popcorn Prayers

The king asked, "Well, how can I help you?" With a prayer to the God of heaven, I replied. NEHEMIAH 2:4-5

My wife calls them popcorn prayers: short, pointed prayers that express a single thought. Praying this way can be a lot of fun—and also powerful. In my experience, sometimes the shortest prayers can be the most effective, especially when they come at an opportune time. James tells us that it's the heartfelt intensity of prayer that matters: "The earnest prayer of a righteous person has great power and produces wonderful results" (James 5:16).

In Nehemiah's day, when servants were in the presence of the monarch, they were expected to look happy. Kings were to be protected from sadness, and servants who did not seem happy in their positions could be banished or killed. It was four months before Nehemiah's unhappiness became evident to the king he served, and Nehemiah's sad countenance led the king to ask Nehemiah what he could do to help him.

Nehemiah was well aware that the king's power came from God: "The king's heart is like a stream of water directed by the LORD; he guides it wherever he pleases" (Proverbs 21:1). So the king's question presented Nehemiah with the possibility of an open door, and Nehemiah seized the opportunity—but not before first praying a "popcorn prayer." We know the prayer was quick because if Nehemiah had stood and worshiped in silence for too long, the king might have suspected treason. After praying, Nehemiah made his bold request to the king: "If it please the king, and if you are pleased with me, your servant, send me to Judah to rebuild the city where my ancestors are buried" (Nehemiah 2:5). And—bingo!—the king granted Nehemiah's request.

As you move through your days, be ready to let your heart kneel before the King of heaven and express popcorn prayers. And learn to live in expectancy for what God will do.

Extreme Makeover: Jerusalem Edition

Eliashib the high priest and the other priests started to rebuild at the Sheep Gate. They dedicated it and set up its doors, building the wall as far as the Tower of the Hundred, which they dedicated, and the Tower of Hananel. People from the town of Jericho worked next to them, and beyond them was Zaccur son of Imri. NEHEMIAH 3:1-2

If you had lived during the time of Nehemiah and had been in Jerusalem before its walls had been rebuilt, you would likely have felt vulnerable, because a city's walls provided protection for its residents. But the priests and others listed in Nehemiah 3 had something going for them—God's promises. The Lord had said concerning Jerusalem, "My name will be honored forever in this Temple and in Jerusalem—the city I have chosen from among all the tribes of Israel" (2 Kings 21:7).

Nehemiah contains a full list of "next tos" to describe how the people pitched in to complete the task of rebuilding Jerusalem's walls. It takes just a bit of imagination to see this chapter as an ancient version of *Extreme Makeover*, as the people worked together to rebuild the wall from a pile of rubble in record time while also fighting off their enemies.

The work wasn't done by one man or one small group. In fact, Nehemiah's name doesn't even occur in Nehemiah 3, but the text does mention thirty-eight individuals by name and identifies forty-two different groups. In 1 Corinthians 12:12, Paul compares the church to a human body: "The human body has many parts, but the many parts make up one whole body. So it is with the body of Christ." As Moses learned in the Old Testament, one person cannot accomplish ministry alone.

Some people attend church as spectators, but being a Christian is not a spectator sport. So take your place "next to" your brothers and sisters, and get involved in the work of God's Kingdom.

Some Walls Are Harder to Build

Sanballat was very angry when he learned that we were rebuilding the wall. He flew into a rage and mocked the Jews.   NEHEMIAH 4:1

Murphy's Law says, "Anything that *can* go wrong *will* go wrong," but from today's story, you can begin to understand a phenomenon that I call Lucifer's Law: If you are doing God's will, *you can expect an attack.*

As the cup-bearer for the king, Nehemiah could have gone anywhere else in the empire to build a wall and would not have had half the hassle that he found in Jerusalem. That's because Jerusalem was God's city and represented the epicenter of God's program for the future. Whenever you undertake God's work, you will be a target and should be prepared to pay a price.

Consider David, a shepherd who might have had a relatively hassle-free life. But after the prophet Samuel anointed David, a man after God's own heart, as Saul's successor, life would never be simple again.

Nehemiah 4–5 focuses on the opposition to restoring the walls of Jerusalem. The builders experienced ridicule (see 4:1-5); they experienced discouragement (see 4:10); and they faced financial difficulties because of greed on the part of Jewish nobles (see chapter 5). Ultimately, in spite of the constant opposition, the people completed the rebuilding of the wall, as recorded in chapter 6.

If you are serving the Lord, nothing excites the devil more than taking the wind out of your sails, and he will see to it that you encounter opposition, so be prepared for battle. When you become God's friend, you become an enemy of the world and of Satan, the prince of this world. Paul encouraged Timothy, "Endure suffering along with me, as a good soldier of Christ Jesus" (2 Timothy 2:3); "I have fought the good fight, I have finished the race, and I have remained faithful" (2 Timothy 4:7).

As you face each day, be aware of the opposition you face, but be aware as well of the greater power inside you through Jesus Christ.

Water-Gate Revival

They read from the Book of the Law of God and clearly explained the
meaning of what was being read, helping the people understand each
passage.   NEHEMIAH 8:8

Even if you're too young to remember the Watergate scandal, you have
probably heard about the 1972 break-in at Democratic National Committee headquarters at the Watergate Hotel in Washington, D.C. A cover-up by
President Richard Nixon and his administration of who had ordered the
break-in led to the president's impeachment and resignation from office.

Today's reading talks about a different Water Gate, and what happened
there in Jerusalem in the fifth century BC had nothing to do with a scandal.
After the rebuilding of the wall around Jerusalem and the consecration of
the people, Ezra read the Book of the Law before the people gathered just
inside the Water Gate.

As the people heard the Law read, God's Spirit sparked a spiritual revival,
and the people experienced deep remorse over their sins. History has never
seen a genuine revival that did not have the Word of God at its core. One
day on the streets in India, a man was explaining to his friend that God was
sending a revival, but with his pronunciation, his words came out, "We are
having a great re-bible!" I think this man's pronunciation hit the nail on
the head. The Spirit empowers God's Word and brings revival, and revival
causes people to have a renewed interest in the Bible. You could call it a
re-Bible.

Today's reading says the people continued to gather and listen to the
Law. So the centerpiece of the Water Gate revival was teaching from the
Scriptures.

In 2 Timothy 4:2, Paul mentors Timothy, saying, "Preach the word of God.
Be prepared, whether the time is favorable or not. Patiently correct, rebuke,
and encourage your people with good teaching." Be aware of opportunities
to sprinkle God's Word into your conversations.

Epiphany!

[Mordecai told Esther,] "If you keep quiet at a time like this, deliverance and relief for the Jews will arise from some other place, but you and your relatives will die. Who knows if perhaps you were made queen for just such a time as this?" ESTHER 4:14

Many Christians ask, "What am I doing here?" "What is my purpose and significance?" "What am I doing in sales or plumbing or engineering or law or hairstyling? I want my life to count." One of the definitions for *epiphany* is a moment of revelation or insight. An epiphany can be the defining moment in which things become crystal clear or one's purpose becomes unmistakable.

In today's reading, Esther, a young Jewish woman in Persia (modern-day Iran), experienced such a moment. Haman, a member of the king's court, had hatched a plot to exterminate all the Jews in the empire. Esther's uncle Mordecai revealed the plot to Queen Esther and told her, "Who knows if perhaps you were made queen for just such a time as this?" (Esther 4:14). It was no accident that Esther became queen. God had worked behind the scenes to put Esther in a position to save her people.

The book of Esther has alarmed some critics because it makes no mention of God. But rather than focus on what isn't in the book, I'd encourage you to focus on what is there: a beautiful picture of God's providence. John Nelson Darby, an Anglo-Irish evangelist from the 1800s, said, "God's ways are behind the scenes, but he moves all the scenes which he is behind."

At times, God overrides natural law, as when Jesus and Peter walked on the water. But most of the time he orchestrates the ordinary and non-miraculous to bring about a predetermined outcome, and his provision is right in front of us. The next time you find yourself wondering, *Why am I here?* ask God to increase your awareness of how he is working in your life.

At the Bottom, Looking Up

Job stood up and tore his robe in grief. Then he shaved his head and fell to the ground to worship.   JOB 1:20

A comedian once quipped, "You can tell you're going to have a rotten day when a team from *60 Minutes* is in your office." Job knew firsthand about having a rotten day. He lost his seven sons and three daughters, seven thousand sheep, three thousand camels, five hundred oxen, and five hundred donkeys. Now that is a rotten day.

As we read this section of the Bible, we are unnerved because Job was godly. After all, if someone such as Job was that vulnerable, what can we expect? It's true that a relationship with God brings no guarantee of an easy life.

Job responded to what happened in two ways. First, in the midst of his pain, Job did what we would expect and expressed his grief. He wasn't stoic or hyperspiritual. He sorrowed openly. Second, Job acted in an unexpected way—he worshiped God.

Our suffering reveals our true feelings about God because pain strips away any superficial religious veneer. Pain moves us in one of two directions: toward God or away from God. Anyone can say that the Lord gives or takes away. But only genuine faith can respond, with Job, "The LORD gave me what I had, and the LORD has taken it away. Praise the name of the LORD!" (Job 1:21).

The lyrics to a song by Scott Krippayne say, "Sometimes He calms the storm, and other times He calms His child" in the midst of the storm. In whichever situation you find yourself today, follow Job's example: Don't be afraid to grieve, and don't forget to worship God in the midst of your pain.

Lurking in the Shadows

The LORD asked Satan, "Have you noticed my servant Job? He is the finest man in all the earth. He is blameless—a man of complete integrity. He fears God and stays away from evil. And he has maintained his integrity, even though you urged me to harm him without cause." JOB 2:3

Reading the book of Job is like watching a movie. Job is the main character, and the director takes the audience backstage and gives them some inside information. The camera pans from one scene to the next, and we learn an interesting fact about Satan. We often think of Satan, whom the Bible calls "the god of this world" (2 Corinthians 4:4), as residing in hell. The Bible tells us that Satan will end up there, but until then, he is busy causing trouble.

What is Satan doing? He is people watching. In the key verse above, God says, "Have you noticed . . . ?" This word *noticed* is a military word that refers to studying a town's defenses before laying siege to it. Satan has been studying Job, looking for his weak points. In other words, it's overt spiritual warfare.

Peter gives this warning: "Stay alert! Watch out for your great enemy, the devil. He prowls around like a roaring lion, looking for someone to devour" (1 Peter 5:8). Yet notice that Satan can operate only by divine permission. In the New Testament, the demons ask Jesus for permission to enter a herd of pigs (see Matthew 8:30-31). The devil is on a leash, though I sometimes wonder why the leash is so long.

If God allows us to go through the fire of Satan's attack, he will still have his eye on us and his finger on the thermostat.

Today, when Satan comes knocking on your door, let Jesus answer it. And since the devil lurks in the shadows, be sure you live in the light of God's presence.

Miserable Comforters

[Job responded,] "I have heard all this before. What miserable comforters you are!"   JOB 16:2

Life is full of unanswered questions. When Job was reduced to nothing, he first worshiped, and then he poured out his questions and grievances to God in the company of his friends, who each offered a different explanation for Job's difficulties. Eliphaz said that Job had sinned and God was punishing him. Bildad's take was that Job needed to repent. Zophar didn't have anything original to say, so he repeated Bildad's message. If Job's physical difficulties weren't enough, he now had the added mental agony of the advice from these "friends," and he began to think, *With friends like these, who needs enemies?*

These friends did some "Monday-morning quarterbacking" and only added to Job's unimaginable grief by reducing his sufferings to a cut-and-dried philosophy of laws and formulas.

Some of the best advice I ever received about counseling people was to "walk softly around a broken heart," but Job's friends analyzed his suffering in front of him and tried to explain it. If someone in your life is suffering, don't be quick to offer advice. Rather, listen patiently. Become an unshockable listener and a walking, breathing, emotional intensive-care unit. Advice can wait for another day.

When Lazarus died, his grieving sister Martha vented to Jesus, "Lord, if only you had been here, my brother would not have died" (John 11:21). Jesus' response teaches us a valuable lesson. He didn't rebuke Martha or give her a one-minute theology lesson. Instead, Jesus listened and loved.

As you comfort someone, be prepared to hear many emotions—denial, anger, bargaining, depression, acceptance, and hope. You can also expect outbursts of tears. But if you want to be a genuine and effective comforter, be less like Job's "friends" and more like Jesus.

God Has the Last Word

[God said to Job,]

> *"Brace yourself like a man,*
> *because I have some questions for you,*
> *and you must answer them.*
>
> *Where were you when I laid the foundations of the earth?*
> *Tell me, if you know so much."*

JOB 38:3-4

Job had been listening to his "comforters'" cheap philosophy about why there is suffering in the world. Finally, Elihu, a fourth friend, rebuked Job and the others for trying to be God's spokesmen. But in the end, neither Job nor his four friends had the final word on the subject of suffering.

Instead, God spoke on his own behalf. In chapters 38–39, he said, in essence, "Look, I'm God, the Creator and Maintainer of the entire physical world. My ability to create is so fast and detailed that you'll never figure it out. If you can't understand my ways in the physical realm, why would you think you can understand the spiritual realm?" Here is the key to this passage: Don't let your inability to understand God's ways shake your faith in God's love.

Professor Peter Kreeft of Yale used this illustration: A hunter caught a bear in a trap in order to relocate the animal to a more remote area where it wouldn't be in danger from other hunters. But the bear couldn't know that. So when the hunter took aim and shot the bear with a tranquilizer dart, the bear, unaware of the motive of compassion behind the hunter's action, would believe the hunter was trying to kill him. In the same way, God often does things that are for our good, despite the fact that we don't understand the reason for the pain we experience at the time.

When children beg to go out and play before finishing their homework, parents often say, "Not now. Later." When a fourteen-year-old asks, "Can I drive?" the same response is given: "Not now. Later." Perhaps that's what God is saying to us when we don't see the reason for our suffering: *Not now, dear child, but later.*

Prescription for a Prune Face

> *Oh, the joys of those who do not*
> *follow the advice of the wicked,*
> *or stand around with sinners,*
> *or join in with mockers.*

PSALM 1:1

"Remedy for a Prune Face," proclaimed an article in the *Detroit Free Press*: "Ladies, do you want to stay young? Then join a church choir. Women who sing stay younger-looking. A singer's cheek muscles are so well developed by exercise that her face will not wrinkle as soon as the non-singer!"

If that's true, then the perfect cure for a prune face is the book of Psalms, which was the hymnal of ancient Israel. On the surface, Psalms is the longest Old Testament book, but it is actually a compilation of five different songbooks by at least seven different composers, with King David responsible for the largest number of psalms.

Psalm 1 sets the stage and tells us how to obtain something many people are chasing: happiness, which the Bible often translates as "blessed." God has a great deal to say about true happiness. How do we find it? The psalmist answers, through a holy life. According to David, the happy person declines some things and delights in others. First, the happy person declines ungodly advice and unrighteous companions but delights in God's truth.

It's not enough to not do certain things; you need to pursue things that will make you more like Christ. Many have enough religion to make them decent but not enough holiness to make them dynamic. What steps are you taking to follow the counsel in Psalm 1:2-3? "They delight in the law of the LORD, meditating on it day and night. They are like trees planted along the riverbank, bearing fruit each season. Their leaves never wither, and they prosper in all they do." As you follow this prescription, it will do more than help you inwardly. It will help your external appearance. How's your face lately?

When God Laughs

The one who rules in heaven laughs.
The Lord scoffs at them.

PSALM 2:4

The second psalm is a stark contrast to the first one. David wrote the first psalm from a human perspective. The second psalm is written from God's perspective, or about God's response to people's rebellion. The second psalm is also one of many messianic psalms. Referring to Psalm 2, the ancient Rabbi Rashi conceded, "Our rabbis expound it as relating to King Messiah."

The psalmist paints a picture of a rebel force that rules the world and rejects the God of creation. More than just a generic rebellion, the psalm rejects the idea of God as an abstract being. The rulers of the earth plot "against the LORD and *against his anointed one*" (Psalm 2:2, italics added). The Hebrew word for "anointed" is *Meshiach,* and the Greek equivalent is *Christos.*

In our contemporary culture, many consider it acceptable to be "spiritual," whether New Age or Buddhist or something else. Yet two words form a dividing line between what is generally acceptable and what is not. Those two words are *Jesus Christ.* As soon as you mention this singular name, the tone of a conversation will usually change.

Notice that when people swear, they don't say, "Oh, Buddha!" or "Oh, Muhammad!" No, they use the name of God's Son, Jesus. In today's psalm, we learn not to treat the Lord's name that way and how God responds to those who do. Does he cringe in terror? Does he tremble or hide behind heaven's walls? No. According to the psalmist, God laughs because that rebellion will be vain and futile. The sovereign Lord remains in control.

Voltaire, the eighteenth-century French philosopher, and an atheist, once boasted, "In twenty years Christianity will be no more. My single hand shall destroy [it]." Shortly after Voltaire died, the house where he wrote became a depot for the Geneva Bible Society. Would you agree that God has a sense of humor?

How to Get Sheep to Snore

The LORD is my shepherd;
I have all that I need.

PSALM 23:1

Known as the Shepherd's Psalm, Psalm 23 is one of the most familiar parts of the Bible. Many people have memorized it and can quote the entire psalm. Nineteenth-century English preacher Charles Spurgeon said of Psalm 23, "This is the pearl of psalms, whose soft and pure radiance delights every eye."

Sometimes this psalm is read at funerals because it refers to the "darkest valley" (some Bible translations say "valley of the shadow of death"). But this psalm is much more for the living than for the dead. The psalmist is celebrating his living relationship with the Good Shepherd.

The Bible often uses the image of a shepherd as a comforting and familiar illustration of God's relationship with us. By implication, then, if the Lord is our Shepherd, we are the sheep. And depending on what you know about sheep, you could view this comparison as somewhat insulting because sheep are not known for their intelligence.

But as I consider the Shepherd's Psalm, I see it as a statement of dignity. David grew up taking care of sheep. He knew that the quality of life for sheep was completely dependent on the characteristics of the shepherd. With a sense of distinction and pride, David is saying, "Hey, look who my Shepherd is! It's none other than the God of the universe!" It's the equivalent of a kid who brags to the other kids in his school, "My dad is the greatest dad in the whole world."

The psalmist tells us that his Shepherd "lets me rest in green meadows; he leads me beside peaceful streams. He renews my strength. He guides me along right paths, bringing honor to his name" (Psalm 23:2-3). As you assume this type of trust in your Shepherd, you, too, will have peace and rest.

The Confessional

Against you, and you alone, have I sinned;
  I have done what is evil in your sight.

PSALM 51:4

I heard about a taxpayer who wrote a letter to the IRS. It read, "Gentlemen: Enclosed you will find a check for $150. Last year I cheated on my tax return, and I have not been able to sleep since. If I still have trouble sleeping, I will send you the rest!" Clearly, that man's guilt and sense of responsibility didn't run deep enough!

Both of the psalms in today's reading talk about the importance of confession. David wrote Psalm 51 after his sin with Bathsheba. The king had arranged the death of Bathsheba's husband, Uriah, and then, in an attempt to appear noble, had married the new widow. For almost a year, David had tried to cover up his sin. But he was not enjoying relaxing evenings with his newest wife. On the contrary, he wrote, his sin weighed heavily on his soul: "I recognize my rebellion; it haunts me day and night" (Psalm 51:3).

Not only does unconfessed sin haunt you emotionally; it also affects your physical health by adding to your load of fear, stress, and worry. Beyond this, you feel ashamed and far from God. As Longfellow wrote, "The mills of God grind slowly, yet they grind exceeding small."

Confession is more than merely admitting in a general way that you've sinned or temporarily feeling bad about something you've done or failed to do. It involves agreeing with what God says about the sin and then making a conscious choice not to repeat that sin in the future. Find a few quiet moments to search your heart and ask God to reveal the sin in your life. Then confess that sin to God and turn from it. David's words are a great place to start: "Create in me a clean heart, O God. Renew a loyal spirit within me" (Psalm 51:10).

I Can See Clearly Now

> *I tried to understand why the wicked prosper.*
>   *But what a difficult task it is!*
> *Then I went into your sanctuary, O God,*
>   *and I finally understood the destiny of the wicked.*

PSALM 73:16-17

Life is filled with difficult questions. Asaph, one of King David's chief musicians, honestly acknowledges a theological struggle he's having. As he has observed the ways of the world, he has had his belief system challenged by the fact that often, it's the wicked who enjoy material or professional success.

Asaph is asking, "How can God be both all-loving and all-powerful and yet allow evil not only to exist but also to prosper?" Asaph's question is honest, but what he sees is not an accurate picture. There *are* pains in the lives of unbelievers, and they do have trouble. Asaph has become envious and must be thinking, *What good does it do to turn to God if it's the wicked who get blessed?* Then, just as Asaph is about to get swept down the path of the wrong attitude, he walks into God's Temple and begins to see things from an eternal perspective. Perhaps he sees the altar of sacrifice or the priests or God's people worshiping. Whatever he sees causes him to think about how the wicked are going to end up—with nothing and without God. That brings Asaph up short and causes him to think more clearly about what is really important.

Imagine you are holding a handful of sand that contains some iron particles. How do you locate the iron? You can run your fingers through the sand and find a few of the particles, or you can sweep a magnet through the sand, and suddenly, millions of iron particles will appear. Trying to find iron particles by running your fingers through the sand is like going through the day with an ungrateful heart. You will find few mercies in life with that attitude. A grateful heart, however, acts like a magnet, making the particles of God's blessings easier to see.

Life Is Short; Make It Count

Teach us to realize the brevity of life,
so that we may grow in wisdom.

PSALM 90:12

Psalm 90 is the only recorded psalm written by Moses. In order to understand and appreciate the psalm, you need to know some of Moses' background from Numbers 20. His sister, Miriam, the leading female figure in the Exodus, had died, a terrible loss for Moses and the people of Israel. At one point, God had told Moses to speak to a rock to get water. Instead, in a display of anger and impatience, Moses struck the rock with his staff, and he was forbidden by God to enter the Promised Land. For the past thirty-eight years, Moses had looked forward to finally entering Canaan, and suddenly his dream had come to an end. Then Moses' brother, Aaron, died, and the entire nation mourned for a month.

In light of all these things, Moses wrote, "Teach us to realize the brevity of life, so that we may grow in wisdom." Or to paraphrase, "Time flies, so it is up to you, Lord, to be our navigator."

If you are thirty-five, you have the equivalent of five hundred days left to live. When you subtract the time spent sleeping, working, eating, traveling, and other miscellaneous activities, over the next thirty-five years you'll have the equivalent of only five hundred days to spend time however you want. There is great wisdom in remembering that counting each day isn't as important as making each day count.

How do you make each day count for God? First, recognize that life is short and you are not guaranteed a long life. You may have twenty more years, or you may have one more day. Second, focus on smaller periods of time. It's easier to maintain an ongoing awareness of hours or days than of months or years. Focus on how you will make the most of this day. Third, live each day for God. If today were the last day of your life, how would you use it to make a difference?

Make Some Noise

Praise him with a clash of cymbals;
*   praise him with loud clanging cymbals.*
Let everything that breathes sing praises to the LORD!

PSALM 150:5-6

It's easy to figure out the theme of the final psalm. The word *praise* occurs thirteen times in just six verses, and the phrase "Praise the LORD" begins and ends the psalm. This short psalm is a primer on how to praise the Lord.

Psalm 149:4 tells us, "The LORD delights in his people." What better reason to offer praise than that? For what should we praise God? For who he is and what he does.

Verse 1 of Psalm 150 instructs us to "praise God in his sanctuary" and in heaven. Of course, we aren't there, but those who are there praise him unceasingly. Other words in this psalm indicate that those on earth are to praise God as well, because we read a listing of various musical instruments that we recognize. In fact, verse 6 tells "everything that breathes" to sing praises. In other words, praise God with the breath he gives you, whether you play an instrument or sing. This would apply to other creatures that breathe as well—sea creatures, birds, monkeys, horses, and a list of creatures far too long to recount. If horses, birds, monkeys, and other voices all offer praise, that's a loud symphony to the living God.

Have you ever heard little children singing off-key at the top of their lungs in a Sunday school program? Depending on how "bad" it sounded, you may have been waiting for it to be over. But although it may be hard on *our* ears, sincere, heartfelt praise, whether spoken, shouted, whispered, or banged out on "clanging cymbals," is always music to God's ears. Praise the Lord!

Wise Up

Fear of the LORD is the foundation of true knowledge,
but fools despise wisdom and discipline.

PROVERBS 1:7

Science-fiction writer Isaac Asimov said, "Based on the rate at which knowledge is growing, it can be speculated that by the time today's child reaches 50 years of age, 97 percent of everything known in the world at that time will have been learned since his birth."

We live in a remarkable period of history when knowledge has never been more readily available. The advancements in technology enable almost anyone anywhere to click a mouse and get information. Yet, in spite of this wealth of knowledge, wisdom seems to be in short supply.

The book of Proverbs can help you wise up. Its wisdom has nothing to do with IQs or SAT scores, but if you study and apply it, you will become an expert in godly living, because the wisdom of Proverbs runs the gamut of life's experiences from the home to the office to your innermost thoughts.

Proverbs are short statements in a poetic form that help you remember the nuggets of truth they contain. I like to think of them as little "truth bombs" that detonate in your brain. Each time you read them, they strike the walls of your memory with maximum impact. Because the statements are simple and subtle, they stick in your mind.

Today's proverb says that true knowledge begins with the fear of the Lord, a deep and reverential awe that produces humble submission to a loving God. When we have this reverential "fear" of God, we begin to live wisely and well.

The Bible calls the person who rejects the knowledge of God and refuses to be directed through God's wisdom a fool. Are you foolish, or are you seeking wisdom through the knowledge of God?

Pursuing God with Passion

> *Cry out for insight,*
> *and ask for understanding.*
> *Search for them as you would for silver;*
> *seek them like hidden treasures.*
> *Then you will understand what it means to fear the LORD,*
> *and you will gain knowledge of God.*

PROVERBS 2:3-5

For a time when I was a boy, I wanted more than anything else to be a fireman. That lasted a few months, and then I wanted to become a policeman—then an American spy, an astronaut, a doctor, a musician, and finally, a photographer.

As an adult, I've interacted with some of the finest surgeons and spent time with NASA's chief photographer and various musicians. What made the difference between my childhood dreams and the professionals' achievements? Passion. The professionals had a passion that drove them to achieve, while I had a fascination that dribbled away. Passion is what separates the dreamers from the doers.

In today's verses from Proverbs, Solomon describes a passionate desire to understand life, to know God's will, and to live well. Notice the use of the words *cry out*. The writer didn't say, "Mention it in passing or casually inquire about it or window-shop for it."

Jesus said, "God blesses those who hunger and thirst for justice, for they will be satisfied" (Matthew 5:6). The ones who hungered and thirsted for justice weren't looking for an occasional "snack." They had a passionate desire for justice. Charles Spurgeon said, "No prayer ever reaches God's heart that does not come from our hearts. Nine out of ten prayers that you listen to . . . have so little zeal in them that, if they obtained a blessing, it would be a miracle of miracles indeed."

Look for passion in your pursuit of God.

In God We Trust?

Trust in the LORD with all your heart;
do not depend on your own understanding.

PROVERBS 3:5

Through an act of Congress passed in 1956, our currency was stamped with the motto "In God we trust." Some may dispute whether this motto is really true on a national level, but each of us as individuals needs to decide where we place our own trust.

François Fénelon wrote, "The wind of God is always blowing . . . but you must hoist your sail." Trust in God is our sail.

A Bible translator who was working on John 3:16 could translate every word except trust. Yet he knew the concept of trust was the key to understanding the meaning. As the translator was discussing the concept with the local people, one of them ran into the tent, muttered something, and threw himself down on a cot.

"What did he say?" the translator asked.

One of the people answered, "He said, 'I will throw my whole weight on this cot.'"

With joy the translator said, "That's it!" Then he translated John 3:16 this way: "God so loved the world . . . that whoever throws his or her whole weight on Him [believes in God] will not perish but have everlasting life."

Many times when we ask God to direct our steps, we are like the people who hired an architect to design a home for them. Later, the architect discovered the couple had already designed their home. They only wanted him to sanction their plans and draw on paper what they had already conceived in their minds. In the same way, we ask God for his guidance, but we've already planned out in our minds how God should build our lives. This type of prayer for guidance requires no trust.

A Jewish proverb says, "It is better to ask the way ten times than to take the wrong road once." Throw your wholehearted weight or trust on God, and do not depend on your own understanding.

What Makes a Good Parent?

My child, listen to me and do as I say,
and you will have a long, good life.

PROVERBS 4:10

Throughout the book of Proverbs, the word *son* or *child* appears frequently. King Solomon wrote these words as a parent to his children.

After God had created the earth and then Adam, he said it was not good for Adam to be alone, and he created Eve. The idea of family is marked with a divine origin. A family is the place with the greatest potential for joy and sorrow and the place where much of our lives is molded. Socrates used to say he wondered how men who were so careful in training a colt could be so indifferent to the training of their own children. Scripture tells us, "Children are a gift from the LORD" (Psalm 127:3), but these men were placing a higher priority on their work than on their families.

Parenting is serious business. I believe parents are in partnership with God to make disciples of their children. Yet no one has the job of parenting down pat. Parents learn parenting skills while rearing their children or as members of the PTA (Poor Tired Adults). One of the challenges of parenting is that by the time you gain sufficient experience in it, your children have grown up. At that point, your time of influence is limited.

King Solomon's method was for parents to train their children with both instruction and practical living (see Proverbs 4:10-11). The wisest man on earth taught us to find a balance between using words and personal examples.

My friend Josh McDowell puts it this way: "Rules without relationship lead to rebellion." If you're a parent, take a few moments and plan some practical ways to find a balance between words and examples. They could be significant moments for the life of your child. If you're not a parent, commit to praying for young parents you know. They need it!

Are You a Great Worker?

A little extra sleep, a little more slumber,
* a little folding of the hands to rest—*
then poverty will pounce on you like a bandit.

PROVERBS 6:10-11

When we meet someone new, one of the first questions we ask is, "What do you do?" Our work helps define us as human beings. But the Bible is less concerned with your specific work than with how you do your work. Someone once quipped, "I like work, and it fascinates me. I can sit and look at it for hours." So the question is, are you a worker or just a watcher?

The book of Proverbs contains a great deal of sound biblical counsel about work. In fact, work is a megatheme of Proverbs.

Some people think that work is part of God's curse after Adam and Eve sinned, but it's not. It's the sweat on our brows that is a result of the curse. From the beginning, God gave us work to do: "The LORD God placed the man in the Garden of Eden *to tend and watch over it*" (Genesis 2:15, emphasis added). God gave Adam the position of gardener.

Various proverbs praise the loyal, wise, and hardworking man or woman. God could operate alone on the earth, but he has chosen to use people. One of the ways our lives can reflect the Lord whom we serve is to let excellence be the hallmark of our work.

The name *Stradivarius* is synonymous with fine violins. Antonius Stradivarius insisted no instrument in his shop could be sold unless it had been made as nearly perfect as humanly possible. He observed, "God needs violins to send his music into the world. If any violins are defective, God's music will be spoiled." He summarized his work philosophy this way: "Other men will make other violins, but no man shall make a better one."

As Christians, we have an obligation to strive for excellence in anything we do because it reflects our loving service to the Lord.

The Weight of Our Words

Kind words are like honey—
sweet to the soul and healthy for the body.

PROVERBS 16:24

Statisticians say that on average, we spend a fifth of our lives talking. During a single day, we speak enough words to fill a fifty-page book. After one year, we've spoken enough words to fill 132 volumes containing four hundred pages each.

Words contain incredible power to delight or to destroy, to poison or to praise. I clearly recall the night I asked my wife to marry me and how I used many disjointed words to express my love. On the day I responded to the Good News about Jesus Christ, I listened to the words of Billy Graham. We worship by singing words of praise and hearing the pastor speak words from God's Word.

In the book of Proverbs, the words *tongue, lips,* or *mouth* appear almost 150 times, which says a lot about the power of speech. Proverbs 18:21 says, "The tongue can bring death or life; those who love to talk will reap the consequences." Compare the words of two well-known people: Adolph Hitler and Billy Graham. For every word in Hitler's *Mein Kampf,* 125 people died during World War II. Billy Graham has spoken the Good News about Jesus Christ to more people than anyone throughout history. One person's words result in death; another's offer eternal life. How important are words, and does it really matter what I say? Mark Twain once said, "The difference between the right word and the almost right word is the difference between lightning and the lightning bug." Consider carefully the words you speak. Are your words stirring and nourishing life in those God brings across your path today?

Virtuous Woman or Virtual Woman?

Who can find a virtuous and capable wife?
She is more precious than rubies.

PROVERBS 31:10

A popular medium in the computer world is virtual reality, which uses computer technology to create an artificial but convincing environment. When you "enter" these virtual worlds, you can fly over a Martian landscape or rip along a Grand Prix racecourse at breakneck speed, and you don't even need to leave your easy chair. The graphics are so advanced that it's easy to forget they're not real. The same is true for special effects in movies and even airbrushed fashion spreads, from which our culture absorbs its ideas of the appearance of the ideal woman. Unfortunately, men end up searching for virtual women instead of virtuous women.

The American Standard Version of the Bible translates the words *virtuous woman* as "worthy woman," and the Berkeley translation uses "wife with strength of character," while the New International Version says, a woman "of noble character." The Hebrew word is *chayil*, which means "strength, ability, and [often implies] moral worth," in other words, a woman of excellence.

How does Proverbs measure the worth of a woman? "She is more precious than rubies" (Proverbs 31:10). One person translated this phrase, "The value of her life is beyond monetary calculations." The Mishnah, a rabbinical discussion of the Law, says, "The death of a good wife is for the man who loses her as great a calamity as the destruction of Jerusalem."

Notice some of the characteristics of a virtuous woman: She is trustworthy (v. 11). She is diligent (vv. 13-18). She is kindhearted (v. 26). She is well attired (vv. 22, 25). She is devoted to her husband and those in her home (vv. 12, 15, 21, 27).

A virtuous woman is far more awesome than a virtual woman. You can't even begin to compare the two. In a culture that promotes this growing separation from reality, let's say no to the virtual woman. Instead, look for the virtuous women in your life.

What's the Point?

> *"Everything is meaningless," says the Teacher,*
> *"completely meaningless!"*

ECCLESIASTES 1:2

During Elvis Presley's last engagement at the Las Vegas Hilton in 1976, he wrote, "I feel so alone sometimes. The night is quiet for me. I'd love to be able to go to sleep. I am glad that everyone is gone now. I'll probably not rest. I have no need for all of this. Help me, Lord." Elvis had discovered firsthand that life in the spotlight didn't satisfy.

At one time or another, most of us reach the place Elvis did, and we end up wondering, *What is the purpose of life, and why am I here?* Through the centuries, people from philosophers to college students have wrestled with these questions.

In Ecclesiastes, Solomon makes some general observations about the monotony of life and the various life cycles. In fact, it's hard to miss the cynicism in his voice and his fatalistic attitude as he describes the predictability and tedium of life.

For most of us, life is routine. The laundry basket keeps filling with dirty clothes. Dishes keep getting dirty. We drag ourselves out of bed, put in a long day at work, drive home, go to sleep, and do it all again the next day. After fifty weeks of work and two weeks of vacation, the annual cycle starts over.

But although Solomon is correct in his observations, his conclusions are faulty. Apart from God's Son, it's impossible to understand our existence. Christ gives deep meaning and purpose to even the most mundane activities and routines. And that *is* the point.

Talk Is Cheap

As you enter the house of God, keep your ears open and your mouth shut.
It is evil to make mindless offerings to God. . . . Talk is cheap.

ECCLESIASTES 5:1, 7

In today's short reading, Solomon turns his attention to how people worship. He had observed people entering the Temple with their lambs for sacrifice and the priests in their official robes, and he had heard people reciting prayers and musicians singing and playing instruments. All of this must have been impressive. But Solomon must have also heard people making rash vows to God and reciting prayers in a perfunctory way, without giving much thought to what they were saying or to the fact that they were in the presence of the Almighty. He perhaps also heard prayers full of eloquence but empty of any heartfelt emotion. Flowery speech may impress the person who is praying, but it makes little if any impression on God.

I've heard people say, "God doesn't seem to speak the way he used to." When I hear that, I respond, "Maybe we aren't listening the way we used to." Unfortunately, for some people, our churches today have become similar to the Temple in the days of the Old Testament, with people reciting empty prayers that sound nice but never reach God's ears. The focus in many churches is no longer the Lord.

A familiar chorus says, "I'm coming back to the heart of worship, / And it's all about You, / It's all about You, Jesus." When we're thinking only about our parking spots, where we are sitting, our levels of comfort with the music, and whether we agree with the sermon, we might as well be at home, because whatever we're doing, it's not worship.

R. A. Torrey said, "We should never utter one syllable of prayer, either in public or in private, until we are definitely conscious that we are coming into the presence of God and are actually praying to Him." The Holy Spirit can increase your sensitivity to God's presence. Ask him to do that today.

While We're Young

Don't let the excitement of youth cause you to forget your Creator. Honor him in your youth before you grow old and say, "Life is not pleasant anymore." ECCLESIASTES 12:1

I was at my mother's side as she took her last breaths on this earth before going to heaven. Those final days drove home to me the importance of preparation. Mom had prepared for her funeral in advance and had paid for all the arrangements, which made it easier on the rest of the family. But more important than that, she was spiritually ready to go because she knew she belonged to Jesus.

King Solomon concluded Ecclesiastes with some basic principles related to aging and preparing for death. First, he said we should fear God, which means to revere him or hold the Lord in the highest regard. Next, Solomon said we should obey God. Some people seek an emotional experience with God but stop short of a life-changing commitment to obedience. Finally, we should prepare before we are old to give an account of our lives to God.

Ocean water contains seven times more salt than the human body can safely ingest. If you drink seawater, you will quickly dehydrate because your kidneys demand extra water to flush the salt out of your body. The more you drink, the more your thirst increases, and the sooner you'll die of thirst.

Now, compare seawater to the life-giving water Jesus offers: "Anyone who is thirsty may come to me! Anyone who believes in me may come and drink!" (John 7:37-38). Trying to find satisfaction and meaning in what the world offers is like trying to quench your thirst by drinking seawater. And the only way to prepare for what comes after this life is to look beyond it now to the One who gives it meaning.

From his detailed observations, Solomon learned there was no lasting satisfaction to be found in anything "under the sun." Wine, women, wisdom, work, or wealth cannot satisfy. Our only real enjoyment in life can be found "in the Son," or with Jesus. H. H. Halley, a great biblical scholar, described the book of Ecclesiastes as "humanity's cry for a savior." Where are you looking for life's satisfaction?

All You Need Is Love

> *He escorts me to the banquet hall;*
> *it's obvious how much he loves me.*

SONG OF SONGS 2:4

In the 1960s, the Beatles released "All You Need Is Love," a song that became the anthem of the younger generation. But despite its popularity, this pop tune doesn't tell us much about love. True to the spirit of the sixties, the lyrics seem to define love as a loose combination of flowers, pacifism, and sexual promiscuity.

Today we are bombarded by songs, movies, and magazines with images that are even more sexual. Yet why should we forfeit God's worldview on sex (after all, he invented it) for shallow representations?

At this point in our reading, we've reached Song of Songs, a three-thousand-year-old manual that gives us God's insights into love, sex, and romance within marriage. Given its provocative language, this book is sometimes called "the most misunderstood book in the Bible."

According to Jewish tradition, King Solomon wrote this book, probably in his younger years. The key word in the book is *lover*; it appears thirty-two times. In fact, Song of Songs is organized around the story of a couple's love relationship. It begins by detailing the couple's mutual attraction and engagement (1–3:5); it then describes their marriage ceremony and honeymoon (3:6–5:1). The next section describes a period of conflict and resolution (5:2-6). The book ends with images of their deepening romance and commitment (7–8).

In today's Bible reading, the lovers' relationship has been made public. As others see them together, the couple openly demonstrate their commitment and love. What else does today's reading tell us about the signs of budding love? If you are married, how might you demonstrate love for your spouse in tangible and God-honoring ways?

How to Have a Good Fight

> *I responded,*
> *"I have taken off my robe.*
>   *Should I get dressed again?*
> *I have washed my feet.*
>   *Should I get them soiled?"*

SONG OF SONGS 5:3

No couple can be in sync 100 percent of the time. The question is, how can the inevitable conflict be resolved? The answer, according to Solomon, seems to be "with a good fight."

Song of Songs 5–6, a full 25 percent of this book, casts a disagreement between Solomon and his bride in very romantic, poetic terms. Perhaps Solomon came home late from the office. (It's hard work to run a nation!) By the time he arrived, dinner was cold, and the candles had burned out. When he came to bed, hoping to snuggle with his wife, his advances were met with resistance.

Their conflict is real but doesn't last long. By chapter 6 verse 3, the lovers are reunited. This is a beautiful picture of a couple who desire to restore their relationship rather than prove they are right. So how can you and your spouse have a "good fight"?

- Don't seek to win but to resolve the conflict.
- Don't use absolutes such as, "You never . . ." or "You always . . ."
- Don't bring up the past; instead, deal with the present issue.
- Give a quiet spouse time to think before expecting him or her to speak.
- Don't confront your lover publicly.
- Listen with your full attention.
- Forgive each other and keep short accounts.

If you remember that it's the relationship that counts, you can learn how to have a good fight!

Keep the Fire in the Fireplace!

Oh, how beautiful you are!
How pleasing, my love, how full of delights!

SONG OF SONGS 7:6

After learning about the Ten Commandments in Sunday school, a boy asked his dad, "What does it mean when it says, 'Thou shalt not commit agriculture'?" Dad's reply was classic: "Son, that means you're not supposed to plow another man's field."

Sexual passion is God's gift to man and a part of our nature. Unfortunately, whenever people pervert sex, it roars into an uncontrollable fire that burns many relationships.

Today's passage is probably set a year after Solomon and his bride's honeymoon. The fire of passion between these two lovers is still burning bright because the flame of commitment is still present. We have a tendency to bring flowers, write notes, and make frequent phone calls when we're courting. Yet for romance to stay vibrant and passion to burn brightly, we must also devote thought and effort to our marriages. So how are you dating your mate?

It's important to stay connected at other times as well. A wise person once said, "If you want to have an energized sex life, try a little tenderness during the other twenty-three and a half hours of the day." It has also been said that sex starts in the kitchen. There is some truth to the value of washing dishes and cleaning up together while talking over the details of each person's day.

Our sexual impulses are God given, and they must be God guided. Stoke your sexual passion with the fire of a loving, nurtured commitment.

Let's Make a Deal

"Come now, let's settle this,"
  says the LORD.
"Though your sins are like scarlet,
  I will make them as white as snow.
Though they are red like crimson,
  I will make them as white as wool."

ISAIAH 1:18

From 1963 to 1977 Monty Hall hosted the popular game show *Let's Make a Deal.* The audience was challenged to match wits with the host, who walked into the studio audience looking for guests anxious to make deals that could earn them prizes.

In today's reading, the prophet Isaiah proposes a deal to the nation of Judah, the southern kingdom of God's people. The Lord, he tells them, promises to take their rebellion and place it on a perfect sacrifice—his Son. They must turn only to God and trust him to save them.

Isaiah was written by one of the sixteen Old Testament prophets. Because his book is the longest and the most frequently quoted in the New Testament, Isaiah is considered the best-known prophet. He lived in Jerusalem and had access to the royal court, where he ministered and testified to God's greatness for fifty-eight years.

Isaiah is called the messianic prophet because so much of his book dwells on Christ. Psalms is the only book with more messianic predictions.

Isaiah's name means "Jehovah is salvation." Some scholars say *salvation* is the key word in the book, which highlights God's willingness to save us as long as we will receive his grace. God has made a deal with the world that is too good to pass up. Do you know someone you should talk to today to present God's offer of salvation? What a deal!

I Saw God!

It was in the year King Uzziah died that I saw the Lord. He was sitting on a lofty throne, and the train of his robe filled the Temple.   ISAIAH 6:1

In 739 BC, King Uzziah of Judah died, which shook his nation to the core. Because the people of Judah lived under the threat of foreign occupation, they wondered what would happen next. A few miles to the north, the Assyrians were overrunning Israel and creating chaos.

In the middle of this situation, Isaiah saw a vision of God's majesty, heard anthems attesting to God's holiness, and felt the angels' thunderous cries of "Holy!" shake the Temple. While the people were asking, "Who will lead us? Who will sit on the throne?" Isaiah focused his eyes on the Lord.

His experience provides a valuable lesson for us today. Think about it. Is evil abounding? Yes, of course, evil is thriving. Is Satan deceiving people? Yes, the devil is continually blinding people. Does God hate it? Yes. But as the prophet Isaiah reminds us, ultimately God is sovereign.

If we fail to see the Lord's face, then we will live in despair. We attend weekly worship services because we need a perspective adjustment. As we worship, we are able to see the Lord in the midst of drastic circumstances. We may enter church overwhelmed with a problem, but in the presence of God, we will see our difficulties with a fresh view.

Are you preoccupied with a problem, or do you need a perspective adjustment? Get a fresh vision of God. He is firmly in charge, and he is not overlooking a single detail of your life.

What the Prophets Saw

> *Out of the stump of David's family will grow a shoot—*
> *yes, a new Branch bearing fruit from the old root.*

ISAIAH 11:1

Anyone can make predictions. Psychics make them all the time, but making accurate predictions is a different thing altogether.

Some years ago *National Enquirer* ran an article detailing over sixty specific prophecies about movie stars, sports, and politics from "modern-day prophets." Guess how many predictions they got right? Were they accurate half the time? One-third of the time? No, they were not right about a single prediction.

The record of the Old Testament prophets is quite different. They were known as "seers" because they often foresaw the future. These prophets anticipated the arrival of the Messiah, who would rule and reign over the earth.

The fulfillment of Isaiah's messianic prophecies began with Christ's birth, but its completion will be spread over a long period of time. After all, Christ came first as the Suffering Servant; at his second coming, he will be the Victorious King.

In this way, the prophet's vision was similar to what we see when looking at distant mountains through a telephoto lens. The optics flatten the view so that we can't see the valleys between the ridges. From his view, Isaiah could not see the huge period of time between the first and second comings of Jesus.

When writing about Isaiah in his book *Exploring the Scriptures*, Dr. John Phillips notes, "One moment his book is black with the thunder and the darkness of the storm. The next the rainbow shines through, and he sweeps his readers on to the golden age that still lies ahead for the world." Celebrate the prophets who tell us about future events and the second coming of Jesus.

Don't Mess with Angels

That night the angel of the LORD went out to the Assyrian camp and killed 185,000 Assyrian soldiers. When the surviving Assyrians woke up the next morning, they found corpses everywhere.   ISAIAH 37:36

I once heard about a Wisconsin homemaker with a collection of 11,161 angel figurines. She's removed the doors and windows from her home to make room for more shelves with angels. Her collection is a sign that, through movies and other elements of popular culture, we've popularized angels so they've become just a form of decoration.

Yet we get a much different picture of angels from the thirty-four books of the Bible that refer to them. Rather than describing angels as tame, winged harp players, Scripture depicts them as mighty creatures who jealously guard God's holiness. They have immense, God-infused power.

In today's story, we read that the Assyrians had made it to the doorstep of Jerusalem. They came making threats and telling the Jewish people not to bother trusting in God because the great Assyrian empire would soon govern the whole world. They taunted the people of Judah about their tiny army, offering to give Judah two thousand horses if they could find that many warriors. Yet the Assyrians had spoken too soon.

As the sun rose the next day, the people of Jerusalem peered down their city walls and saw an amazing sight. The enemies they had so feared were lifeless corpses. It had taken only one of God's angels to destroy 185,000 Assyrians.

As you begin to understand the power of angels, imagine what Jesus Christ is saying to Peter: "Don't you realize that I could ask my Father for thousands of angels to protect us, and he would send them instantly?" (Matthew 26:53).

Never underestimate the power of the angels—and more important, the God whom they serve.

Crushed!

He was pierced for our rebellion,
    crushed for our sins.
He was beaten so we could be whole.
    He was whipped so we could be healed.

ISAIAH 53:5

The first time I heard the gospel was in 1973. Billy Graham was speaking on television, and he said Jesus gave himself for me. Because of his sacrifice, I could become God's child. Immediately I thought, *Why? It sounds like God is getting a bad deal.* Yet as I continued to think about it, I concluded, *But it also means that I'm getting the deal of a lifetime.*

In the eyes of the world, it looked absurd for the Messiah to be crucified on a cross. As Paul writes in 1 Corinthians 1:23, "when we preach that Christ was crucified, the Jews are offended and the Gentiles say it's all nonsense."

The prophet Isaiah foresees the coming servant Messiah as one who would be pierced and crushed. Jesus took our place. He died so we could accept God's great offer. "God made Christ, who never sinned, to be the offering for our sin, so that we could be made right with God through Christ" (2 Corinthians 5:21).

Let me spell this out: God's wrath was placed on Jesus at the Cross. He was willing to treat Jesus as if his Son were guilty of every sin ever committed by every person. Why did he do that? God the Father treated Jesus as we deserved to be treated so that the Lord could treat us as Jesus deserved to be treated. The Son of God became a man so men could become sons of God.

Take a moment to thank God for the vicarious atonement we've received through the death and resurrection of Jesus.

Just a Kid?

"O Sovereign LORD," I said, "I can't speak for you! I'm too young!"

JEREMIAH 1:6

One evening when D. L. Moody came home from an evangelistic meeting, his wife asked, "How many people were saved tonight?"

He replied, "Two and a half."

She smiled and asked, "You mean two adults and one child?"

"Two children and one adult. The adult has already wasted half his life," he said.

Moody knew the value of a young person in the Kingdom of God. Yet some people had trouble believing God could use someone young named Joseph, Samuel, Jeremiah, Daniel, or Timothy. In fact, Paul encouraged Timothy, "Don't let anyone think less of you because you are young" (1 Timothy 4:12).

Jeremiah was probably between seventeen and twenty-five years old when God called him as a prophet. He went on to minister for forty years through the reign of five Judean kings. Of course, God's call sometimes comes at the opposite end of life. Moses was eighty, and Caleb was eighty-five when God called them to lead his people. When God chooses foolish and weak things, the Lord receives glory from their accomplishments.

In a dark sky over Bethlehem, God hung a star to announce the arrival of his Son. A single sunbeam can drive away many shadows. The prophet Jeremiah was one of the brightest sunbeams in ancient Israel. Allow God's sunshine of hope to flood your life and heart today.

When Should You Cry?

If only my head were a pool of water
*   and my eyes a fountain of tears,*
I would weep day and night
*   for all my people who have been slaughtered.*

JEREMIAH 9:1

Do you know where to find your lachrymal ducts? Everyone has them. These are the ducts that produce tears, which lubricate your eyes and protect them from foreign matter and infection. These tiny ducts are also tied to the emotional centers of our brains, so our tears can also be signs of grief, sorrow, pain, or joy.

It's appropriate that Jeremiah is known as the weeping prophet. He didn't remain aloof from the conditions of his audience. He was deeply saddened by the hardness of the Jewish people. Jeremiah shed tears for the right reasons and displayed a balance between toughness and tenderness, despite being a leader who had to deliver a hard message.

The compassionate heart of Jeremiah reminds us of Jesus Christ. In fact, one of the rumors about Jesus during his earthly ministry was related to Jeremiah. So "when Jesus came to the region of Caesarea Philippi, he asked his disciples, 'Who do people say that the Son of Man is?' 'Well,' they replied, 'some say John the Baptist, some say Elijah, and others say Jeremiah or one of the other prophets'" (Matthew 16:13-14). Like Jeremiah, Jesus sometimes expressed his grief and sorrow with tears. He wept over the death of his friend Lazarus and also over the spiritual condition of Jerusalem.

What moves you to tears? Is it the spiritual condition of your neighborhood or your city or your country? We can learn from the weeping prophet, Jeremiah, how to have a heart of compassion for our world.

Prophets at Pottery Barn

[The Lord said to Jeremiah,] "Go down to the potter's shop, and I will speak to you there." JEREMIAH 18:2

In Jeremiah's day, the potter's wheel consisted of two circular stones. The clay pot was placed on the upper stone, and the potter used his foot to turn the lower stone. Both stones were connected to a wooden beam so they turned together.

As long as the clay remained moist and pliable, the potter could continue to shape it and work out any defects. If it became too rigid, however, the potter smashed it to pieces and started over. Through this image, the Lord warned his people not to cross the invisible line where they became so hard of heart that they could not repent. In today's story, Jeremiah describes the process of remaking a misshapen vessel. It's really a metaphor about Israel.

The potter can teach us today as well. Paul wrote to the church at Rome, "Don't copy the behavior and customs of this world, but let God transform you into a new person by changing the way you think" (Romans 12:2) or, as the J. B. Phillips translation reads, "Don't let the world around you squeeze you into its own mould."

Throughout the Bible, there is a call to nonconformity. We should not simply go with the flow. Early in the Old Testament, God warned the Israelites, "Do not act like the people in Egypt, where you used to live, or like the people of Canaan, where I am taking you. You must not imitate their way of life" (Leviticus 18:3).

How flexible are you to God's molding process? It may hurt for God's firm hand to push your life into shape, but it's better than being broken.

What Does God Think of You?

"I know the plans I have for you," says the LORD. *"They are plans for good and not for disaster, to give you a future and a hope."*   JEREMIAH 29:11

Does God love us simply because, as the all-powerful and all-loving Creator, he's obligated to do so? Does he truly have our best interests at heart? The Jews must have asked these questions when Nebuchadnezzar of Babylon took them captive, a move predicted by Jeremiah (see Jeremiah 25:11).

In 597 BC, when the Babylonians besieged Jerusalem for a second time, they took the religious and political leaders, as well as thousands of other Jews, captive. The people were then led on a five-hundred-mile journey to Babylon. The prophet Jeremiah quickly penned a letter of encouragement and instruction to these captives. Essentially his letter said, "Prepare for a long stay. You'll be there seventy years." Although the people were being disciplined for their rebellion, the Lord promised he would bring his people home again.

Just as Jeremiah's letter must have been a source of comfort to those displaced Jews, so Scripture is full of hope for Christians today. After all, we are also strangers in a strange land. We'll live for about seventy years with people who don't believe in our God and may even be hostile toward him.

In our moments of crisis, we need to hold on to God's Word with its promises, admonitions, and rebukes. As Jesus said, "I have told you all this so that you may have peace in me. Here on earth you will have many trials and sorrows. But take heart, because I have overcome the world" (John 16:33).

In your moments of crisis, turn to God's Word. You will be reassured that God has a plan for your life and your future. You can claim God's promise through Jeremiah 29:11.

The Death of a Nation

Does it mean nothing to you, all you who pass by?
Look around and see if there is any suffering like mine,
which the LORD brought on me
when he erupted in fierce anger.

LAMENTATIONS 1:12

It must have been painful to watch the death of a nation. Yet part of the prophet Jeremiah's calling was to observe the death of his own nation and watch many of his fellow Jews go into captivity. The Babylonians had entered his beloved Jerusalem and executed God's wrath.

The five chapters of Lamentations contain five dirges, or elegies, expressing Jeremiah's deep sorrow. Through this book, the prophet seems to invite us to express our sorrow for the sin in our world as well.

Lamentations also seems to point out the positive side of God's wrath. As the great Bible teacher G. Campbell Morgan said, "A state that cannot punish crime is doomed and a God who tolerates evil is not good. Deny me my Biblical revelation of the anger of God and I am insecure in the universe." Good can come from reading a sad book like Lamentations. It helps us focus on ultimate realities.

In this book, the prophet Jeremiah bares his soul. Consider the sadness he must have felt, since his ministry began during the reign of King Josiah. This righteous king had led a revival in Judah, yet soon after his death, the nation's passion for God fizzled, and rituals replaced revival. The people relapsed into their sinful practices.

With the help of the words of Jeremiah, take a fresh look at the world around you today, and begin to have God's view of sin and the hope that comes only through Jesus Christ.

Anthem of Hope in the Pit of Despair

> *The faithful love of the LORD never ends!*
>   *His mercies never cease.*
> *Great is his faithfulness;*
>   *his mercies begin afresh each morning.*

LAMENTATIONS 3:22-23

In 1956, *Time* magazine highlighted the findings of a Canadian school-teacher who, on his twenty-seventh time reading through the Bible, listed the 7,487 promises God makes to man in Scripture. Certainly, Jeremiah seemed to reflect on some of these as he wrote Lamentations. In the middle of his five dirges, Jeremiah included the bright anthem of hope above.

Coming across this passage is like finding a diamond in a lump of coal. Through the smoke of judgment, Jeremiah could see God's mercy and expressed his confidence that God would not utterly consume his people.

God's mercies and covenant of loyal love toward the Jews, his chosen people, are affirmed numerous times in the Old Testament. In the same way, God has made a covenant with us, believers in Jesus. He will act in love and mercy toward us as well. Jeremiah's words, "Great is his faithfulness," affirm the bedrock of our faith.

Pastor Thomas Chisholm captured the spirit of the verses while writing his classic hymn: "Great is Thy faithfulness, O God my Father. There is no shadow of turning with Thee." Chisholm, who was born in a log cabin in Franklin, Kentucky, and had limited education, once said, "I must not fail to record the unfailing faithfulness of a covenant-keeping God."

What do you do with the promises of God? As you read your Bible, underline them and then memorize them. Rejoice in God's faithfulness in your life.

What a Good Spanking Can Do

Let us test and examine our ways.
Let us turn back to the LORD.

LAMENTATIONS 3:40

Some Christians believe they should be exempt from all hardship and pain. They even invoke the theological concept of "binding," which conveniently allows them to wish away anything painful. They say things such as, "I bind all bad stuff."

Author and talk-show host Dennis Wholey cleverly points out the fallacy of this reasoning: "Expecting not to be treated badly just because you're a good person is like expecting an angry bull not to attack you just because you're a vegetarian." Job, a godly man with plenty of experience in suffering, said, "People are born for trouble as readily as sparks fly up from a fire" (Job 5:7).

The third chapter of Lamentations provides us with several lessons about affliction: First, affliction that comes from God's hand is always tempered with compassion (see v. 32). Also, God allows affliction but doesn't delight that it happens (see v. 33). Affliction in a believer's life is always under the sovereign control of a loving God (see v. 38). Finally, no matter what causes the pain, it should always turn us back to God (see v. 40).

The apostle Paul vouched for the good that could come out of difficulty: "We can rejoice, too, when we run into problems and trials, for we know that they help us develop endurance" (Romans 5:3). David noted another positive outcome of suffering: repentance. Psalm 119:67 says, "I used to wander off until you disciplined me; but now I closely follow your word."

If you are in the midst of a difficult situation, how can you, with God's help, turn your obstacle into an opportunity?

What Are You Watching?

Son of man, I have appointed you as a watchman for Israel. Whenever you receive a message from me, warn people immediately.

EZEKIEL 3:17

David Blaine, sometimes dubbed a "modern-day Houdini," has performed many daring feats of endurance. He spent sixty-three hours in a box made of ice; stood on a twenty-two-inch-wide platform at the top of a ninety-foot-high pole for thirty-five hours; and lived underwater for seven days.

In many ways, the prophet Ezekiel was the David Blaine of the Old Testament. Though Ezekiel didn't use magic, his ministry was marked with strange, attention-getting stunts, such as lying on his side or shaving his hair and beard. When Ezekiel's wife died, God told him not to mourn her death as another symbolic act. Each of Ezekiel's life experiences became a teaching point for the Jewish people.

While Jeremiah ministered to people back home, Ezekiel was led into captivity with the country's leaders. Chapters 1–24 were written before the Babylonian siege and predict the judgment of Jerusalem; chapters 25–32 were written during the siege and lay out God's judgment of surrounding enemy nations; and chapters 33–48 were written after the siege and prophesy about God's restoration of the Jews in his Kingdom.

In today's Bible reading, we see that God viewed Ezekiel as a watchman, a very important role in ancient times. Walls protected the city from invaders, and watchmen were trained with their eyes and ears to see shadows in the dark and hear faint sounds. The watchman saw critical details and issued warnings.

We still need watchmen in our world today who will cry out against the repercussions of a godless worldview. Are you watching? What are you doing to actively warn others of the repercussions of the world's choices?

You Can't Fool God!

The Spirit of the LORD came upon me, and he told me to say, "This is what the LORD says to the people of Israel: I know what you are saying, for I know every thought that comes into your minds." EZEKIEL 11:5

Someone once estimated that if man's accumulated knowledge from the beginning of recorded history until the year 1845 were represented with one inch, then what we've learned from 1845 until 1945 would be represented with three inches. The knowledge we've acquired from 1945 until 1975 would reach the height of the Washington Monument, which is over 555 feet.

As impressive as this upward curve is, all our knowledge is still only learned or accumulated. Furthermore, no single human mind can hold all this knowledge. God, on the other hand, knows everything. His knowledge is intuitive and innate. That puts us at a disadvantage if we are trying to deceive the Lord or hide something from him. As Hebrews 4:13 says, "Nothing in all creation is hidden from God. Everything is naked and exposed before his eyes."

During the days of Ezekiel, the leaders in Jerusalem thought no one knew their plans and plots. They may have kept the truth from other people, but they couldn't fool an all-knowing God. Proverbs 5:21 says, "The LORD sees clearly what a man does, examining every path he takes."

In reality, heaven has the best reception in the universe. God sees, hears, and records everything, even the inner thoughts of our hearts. He wants us to live in the open and walk in his light. Be aware of God's presence throughout your day, whether people can see you or not.

June 17

The Devil in the Details

"Son of man, sing this funeral song for the king of Tyre. Give him this message from the Sovereign LORD:

> *'You were the model of perfection,*
> *full of wisdom and exquisite in beauty.*
> *You were in Eden,*
> *the garden of God.'"*

EZEKIEL 28:12-13

Tyre played an important role throughout the history of ancient Israel. This city first became prominent during the reigns of King David and King Solomon, and it helped in the construction of the Temple.

Yet Tyre was a worldly city, filled with pride and reliant on money. Its people were particularly proud of their location. The city stood on an island known as the "holy island," according to Sanchoniathon, an ancient Phoenician writer. The surrounding region looked to Tyre as the mother city of their religion.

In chapter 28, Ezekiel begins by speaking judgment against the city's arrogant king but soon shifts to the spiritual realm. As you look at today's Bible reading, note that the descriptive language could not have referred to any earthly ruler. The king of Tyre had never been inside the Garden of Eden.

The prophet speaks of the real force behind the king's actions—Satan, who is called an "angelic guardian" (Ezekiel 28:14). Satan had been appointed to stand guard at God's throne but coveted the throne instead. Isaiah 14:12-17 records the story of Satan's expulsion from heaven, and Jesus Christ recalls Satan's fall in Luke 10:18. With this fall from heaven, Lucifer the angel became Satan.

As Christians, we can make two key mistakes regarding Satan. The first is to deny that he exists; the second is to become obsessed with him. Instead of focusing on Satan, we need to be aware of his existence but concentrate on Jesus.

Dem Bones, Dem Bones!

He said to me, "Speak a prophetic message to these bones and say, 'Dry bones, listen to the word of the LORD!'" EZEKIEL 37:4

The 1911 edition of the *Encyclopedia Britannica* included this statement: "The possibility that we can ever again recover the correct pronunciation of ancient Hebrew is as remote as the possibility that a Jewish empire will ever again be established in the Middle East." Of course, the Jewish state was reestablished in 1948, and a visit to Israel reveals two facts. First, the Jewish people have revived the Hebrew language, and second, they speak Hebrew in their ancient homeland.

Beginning with chapter 37, Ezekiel begins to shift his message to prophecy about the future restoration of Israel. The survival of the Jewish people and their return to Israel since 1948—about twenty-six hundred years after Ezekiel recorded this prophecy—is miraculous. The rebirth of Israel fulfilled the first part of Ezekiel's prophecy, since the very dry bones have been reassembled into a recognizable nation.

The survival of the Jewish people and their return to Israel since 1948 are miraculous. Today, in fact, they have a two-hundred-billion-dollar annual economy. If you ever doubt God's promises, remember the hope and restoration in this chapter of Ezekiel. God is able to revive dry bones.

Still, some of Ezekiel's events have not been fulfilled because Israel has not yet experienced a spiritual resurrection. We need the truth to restore the dry bones in our world. Ask the Holy Spirit to come and bring genuine revival, which comes from God's Spirit and belief in the Scriptures.

Daniel's Deli

Daniel was determined not to defile himself by eating the food and wine given to them by the king. He asked the chief of staff for permission not to eat these unacceptable foods.   DANIEL 1:8

The year 605 BC was a pivotal year in the history of ancient Israel. When Nebuchadnezzar conquered the Egyptian army at the Battle of Carchemish, which took place between the Euphrates and Orontes rivers, the rest of the world became easy pickings for the Babylonians. Soon after, they besieged Jerusalem for the first time. One of the captives they took to Babylon was Daniel, who was about fifteen when he was taken from his home.

Daniel, along with a number of other young men from Judah's noble families, was brought to Nebuchadnezzar's court. The Babylonians chose young people with three qualifications to serve there. First, they had to be physically healthy with a pleasing appearance. Second, each one had to be mentally sharp. Finally, since they would represent the king's court, they had to be socially poised.

Daniel and three other young men were among those chosen. They were offered food from the finest caterers in Babylon. However, some of this food was sacrificed to the Babylonian gods (Marduk, Nebo, and Ishtar). Eating it was meant to honor the deities.

Daniel did not want to defile himself with the Babylonian food, so he requested vegetables and water instead. He knew that God would see everything he did. As Proverbs 15:3 says, "The LORD is watching everywhere, keeping his eye on both the evil and the good."

Your reputation is what you are on the outside; your character is what you are when no one is looking. Who are you when no one is looking? Begin each day asking God to help you be faithful in serving him.

What a Great Fall!

That is the meaning of the rock cut from the mountain, though not by human hands, that crushed to pieces the statue of iron, bronze, clay, silver, and gold. The great God was showing the king what will happen in the future. The dream is true, and its meaning is certain.   DANIEL 2:45

In Daniel's day, King Nebuchadnezzar of Babylon was the top leader of the world. The problem with being on top, though, is that it's a long way down if you fall.

One night in a dream God warned this pagan king about the future of the world. The dream centered on a huge statue or idol. Because Babylon was a land of idolatry, King Nebuchadnezzar could relate to this image.

The statue the king saw pictured man's rule on the earth. It was made of four types of material, and each one represented a different empire. The statue had feet and legs of iron and clay, a belly and thighs of bronze, a chest and arms of silver, and a head of gold.

King Nebuchadnezzar and his empire were represented by the head of gold. Babylon was known as a city of gold because of its decorated shrines, temples, and public buildings. When King Nebuchadnezzar heard Daniel's interpretation of his dream, he must have swelled with pride. Yet when Daniel interpreted the dream, he told the king that his empire would fall. In fact, Nebuchadnezzar was overthrown in 539 BC.

Jesus Christ pointed out the danger of self-importance in Luke 20:18, saying, "Everyone who stumbles over that stone will be broken to pieces, and it will crush anyone it falls on." On the day that Jesus Christ returns, in fact, all of man's kingdoms will come to a screeching halt.

Fire Walker

"Look!" Nebuchadnezzar shouted. "I see four men, unbound, walking around in the fire unharmed! And the fourth looks like a god!"

DANIEL 3:25

Three Jews faced an ethical dilemma regarding a commandment from Nebuchadnezzar. The king had built a huge gold statue, which measured ninety feet by nine feet. These Jewish men were ordered to attend the dedication ceremony. When the musical instruments sounded, everyone was ordered to bow to the ground and worship the statue. Anyone who didn't bow to the statue faced being thrown into a blazing furnace.

Ancient brick furnaces the size of a city block have been discovered in northern Iraq. Some scholars believe each furnace was two stories high, thirty-two feet high on the outside and twenty feet high inside the chamber. When a fire was burning in one of these furnaces, it must have been an intimidating sight.

Yet Shadrach, Meshach, and Abednego refused to bow down. The fire was fed with coal and heated seven times hotter than usual, killing the executioners.

As you read the key verse for today, you'll notice the men did not try to escape the furnace. Instead, they talked and walked around inside. They didn't come out until Nebuchadnezzar called to them.

In Aramaic, the mysterious fourth person in the flames is called *Bar elahin*, which means "son of the gods." Most scholars believe this fourth person was a preincarnate appearance of Jesus Christ. Nebuchadnezzar probably thought it was one of the Babylonian gods, perhaps Bel, the supreme god.

While Nebuchadnezzar was astonished by the sight of the men walking unharmed in the furnace, this incident should inspire hope. It reminds us that while God doesn't always save us from our troubles, he walks with us in our trials.

Divine Timetable

*Seven sets of seven plus sixty-two sets of seven will pass from the time
the command is given to rebuild Jerusalem until a ruler—the Anointed
One—comes.* DANIEL 9:25

A pastor once said he didn't preach on prophecy because prophecy distracts
people from the present. One of his colleagues responded, "Then there's
certainly a lot of distraction in the Scriptures."

One of the towering prophetic chapters in the Bible is Daniel 9. This
landmark text lays out the divine timetable for some key events.

Daniel gives the exact time that the Messiah would arrive in Jerusalem—
sixty-nine "weeks" in the future. Using the Babylonian calendar of 360 days,
Sir Robert Anderson, a theologian who also served in Scotland Yard, com-
puted that 483 years would equal 173,880 days.

Artaxerxes Longimanus gave the command to rebuild the city on March
14, 445 BC. Anderson determined that 173,880 days later would be April 6,
AD 32, known to the Jewish people as the ninth day of the month of Nisan.
This date was very significant because it was the time when lambs were
selected for Passover. According to Luke 19, during the ninth day of Nisan
(April 6, AD 32), Jesus Christ entered Jerusalem on a donkey. He arrived at
the exact time of Daniel's prophecy.

Today's story reassures us that God is right on time. You can trust the
Lord with your life and rest assured that he knows the end from the beginning in all things.

Live Demonstration

When the LORD first began speaking to Israel through Hosea, he said to him, "Go and marry a prostitute, so that some of her children will be conceived in prostitution. This will illustrate how Israel has acted like a prostitute by turning against the LORD and worshiping other gods."

HOSEA 1:2

King Edward III of England was to speak to Americans during a 1936 radio broadcast. Minutes before the king was scheduled to give his remarks, a man tripped over a wire at WJZ in New York, snapping the only line of communication between the two countries. The engineer was frantic. With only a few seconds before airtime, a quick-thinking apprentice grabbed the two broken ends of the wire to bridge the gap. The king addressed the United States with his words transmitted through the man's body.

Just like that apprentice, the biblical prophets bridged a gap—this one between heaven and earth. Sometimes the prophets achieved this connection through proclamation and strong preaching. At other times they foretold future events. Still other times the prophets delivered a message from God through specific acts.

In one such situation, the Lord told Hosea to marry a harlot as a symbol of how far Israel had moved away from God. Just as Hosea's wife left him to return to prostitution, so Israel had acted like a prostitute by turning away from God and worshiping other gods. God then commanded Hosea to buy her back. This demonstrated to the Israelites that the Lord still loved Israel and would restore his wayward people.

In following God's guidance in his life, Hosea willingly accepted the pain that came from being married to an unfaithful partner. However, he also was able to demonstrate God's extravagant faithfulness and love. Be encouraged by Hosea's example. You, too, can bridge the gap, demonstrating the love of God even in difficult circumstances.

Project Restoration

Afterward the people will return and devote themselves to the LORD their God and to David's descendant, their king. In the last days, they will tremble in awe of the LORD and of his goodness.   HOSEA 3:5

When Dr. Thomas Holmes of the University of Washington researched stress, he measured it in "life-change units": marriage was assigned 50 points; divorce, 73; death of a spouse, 100; pregnancy, 40; marital separation, 65; death of a close family member, 63; major personal injury or illness, 53; vacation, 13; and Christmas, 12. People who score 300 points in twelve months will likely break down.

You have to wonder how Hosea survived the pressure of his marriage to a harlot, particularly since God had predicted the details *in advance.*

Hosea 3 has been called one of the greatest chapters in the Bible because it portrays the greatest story in the Bible. At God's command, Hosea goes to the slave market and buys back his harlot wife. In the same way, Jesus Christ redeemed our lives from the slave market of sin and made us children of God

Romans 5:20 says, "As people sinned more and more, God's wonderful grace became more abundant." Or as American pastor and theologian Donald Barnhouse paraphrased this verse, "Where sin reached the high-water mark, grace completely flooded."

Sin cannot erect a dam so high that God's grace can't overflow its walls. God loves the chance to restore a life, even one that appears completely soiled by sin.

After Jesus told his disciples how hard it is for a rich person to enter heaven, they asked, "Then who in the world can be saved?" Jesus said, "Humanly speaking, it is impossible. But with God everything is possible" (Matthew 19:26).

Can you think of anyone who seems beyond hope and God's reach? Think again, and trust the "God of All Things Possible."

Improved by Breaking

> *Return, O Israel, to the LORD your God,*
> *for your sins have brought you down.*
> *Bring your confessions, and return to the LORD.*
> *Say to him,*
> *"Forgive all our sins and graciously receive us,*
> *so that we may offer you our praises."*

HOSEA 14:1-2

Someone once said, "The only thing improved by breaking is the heart of a sinner." Hosea's ministry compelled him to deliver a heartfelt message from a heartsick prophet about a heartbroken God.

Of course, the invitation to repent is often unwelcome. But as Proverbs 28:13 says, "People who conceal their sins will not prosper, but if they confess and turn from them, they will receive mercy."

Frederick the Great once toured a Berlin prison. As he walked by the prisoners, they insisted they were innocent. All but one man, that is.

The king said to him, "I suppose you're innocent too?"

"No, sir, I am guilty and I deserve punishment." Smiling, the monarch turned to the warden and ordered, "Come release this rascal before he corrupts all these fine innocent people in here."

Just as Hosea proclaimed a weighty message, so the apostle Paul had to call the believers in Corinth to repentance in his first letter to them. Later he wrote, "I am not sorry that I sent that severe letter to you, though I was sorry at first, for I know it was painful to you for a little while. Now I am glad I sent it, not because it hurt you, but because the pain caused you to repent and change your ways. It was the kind of sorrow God wants his people to have" (2 Corinthians 7:8-9).

Does your heart need breaking? Brokenness before the Lord brings great strength.

Insects and the End of the World

> The LORD says, "I will give you back what you lost
>   to the swarming locusts, the hopping locusts,
> the stripping locusts, and the cutting locusts.
>   It was I who sent this great destroying army against you."

JOEL 2:25

In 1866, a plague of locusts invaded Algiers. The insects destroyed the crops so thoroughly that two hundred thousand people died from famine afterward.

The prophet Joel wrote his short book in the aftermath of a similar disaster in Judah. Joel explains that the plague, which destroyed all vegetation in the land, was essentially God's wake-up call to the Jewish people. He also assures the people that God will take pity on them and restore the land.

Joel doesn't focus solely on the current calamity. His prophecies look through the lens of immediate judgment and move to the ultimate judgment, which will occur at the end of the world. Joel refers to this ultimate judgment as the "Day of the Lord," a common Old Testament phrase signifying a dramatic intervention of God's judgment.

In chapter 1, Joel announces the coming of the Day of the Lord. In chapter 2, he fills in some of the details of the end of the world. Beyond the destruction, the prophet reveals God's heart to restore man. He tells of a time of physical, spiritual, and national restoration.

Maybe today you sit in the barrenness and waste of painful circumstances. May the book of Joel remind you not to give up. God is all about restoration. Remember his promise: "From there you will search again for the LORD your God. And if you search for him with all your heart and soul, you will find him" (Deuteronomy 4:29).

Famous Amos

Amos replied, "I'm not a professional prophet, and I was never trained to be one. I'm just a shepherd, and I take care of sycamore-fig trees."

AMOS 7:14

In 1957, Wally Amos enthusiastically launched the cookie business he called Famous Amos. The prophet Amos would never have used that moniker. He was a humble farmer and shepherd who lived at the edge of the Judean wilderness in Tekoa, six miles south of Bethlehem. (Centuries later, John the Baptist lived in this same region.)

While this prophet doesn't get much attention, God greatly used Amos. Because Amos was a shepherd, he had lots of time in his fields to think and pray. He was the first prophet to predict the captivity of the northern kingdom, and he emphasized God's judgment over the affairs of human government.

In fact, the Bible is filled with lowly men and women whom God used. Amos was called to leave his sheep and be a spokesman for God. God called another shepherd named Moses to tend the flocks of God's people. Jesus called Peter, inviting him to leave his nets and be a fisher of men. In fact, the Lord will use any humble person devoted to him. God's calling is more important than qualifications.

As someone once said, "You can never be too small for God to use, only too big." Rejoice in the good news that God can use anyone to proclaim the Good News of his Kingdom.

One-Hit Wonder!

The LORD *says to Edom,*
"I will cut you down to size among the nations;
   you will be greatly despised.
You have been deceived by your own pride."

OBADIAH 1:2-3

In 1977, Debbie Boone sang "You Light Up My Life." In 1995, the group Los del Rio recorded the hit "Macarena." In 2000, Baha Men topped the charts with "Who Let the Dogs Out?"

What do all these performers have in common? They were one-hit won-ders. The minor prophets have a lot in common with them. They aren't known for their inferiority but their brevity. With only twenty-one verses, Obadiah is the shortest of these minor prophets.

We know the meaning of Obadiah's name is "servant of the Lord" or "worshiper of the Lord." However, we know nothing about Obadiah's par-ents, his hometown, or his friends.

Rather than penning a hit, however, this one-hit-wonder prophet wrote on an unpopular subject: God's judgment. Specifically, he wrote about the coming judgment of Israel's neighbor, the country of Edom. The Edomites had mistreated the Jews and become full of self-reliant pride. They believed their land was impenetrable and invulnerable to attack.

God hates pride, and clearly Edom was a cocky, godless nation. The Lord didn't punish Edom immediately—in fact, the country even thrived for a while. Ever patient, God waited hundreds of years before executing his judgment.

Which tune do you sing? What message are you known for? Be consistent as you faithfully serve the living God. As you do so, you will remind people of a God who loves them but one day will intervene in human history to judge the world.

The Unprofitable Prophet

Jonah got up and went in the opposite direction to get away from the LORD. He went down to the port of Joppa, where he found a ship leaving for Tarshish. He bought a ticket and went on board, hoping to escape from the LORD by sailing to Tarshish. JONAH 1:3

I once had a springer spaniel, Toby, who acted a bit like the prophet Jonah. This dog had a bad habit. When we called for him to come, he ran in the opposite direction. In fact, one day Toby ran into a car. That's right—the car didn't run into him. Thankfully, both were fine after the collision.

Jonah was the first foreign missionary sent out to stir the biggest revival in history, yet he was also the first prodigal prophet. God had called Jonah to make the five-hundred-mile trek to Nineveh. Normally prophets complied with God's direct commands, but Jonah didn't. Rather than heading to the capital of the great Assyrian empire to call the people to repentance, Jonah decided to go on a cruise headed two thousand miles due west.

As a prophet, Jonah should have known he couldn't run from the Lord of the universe. God is everywhere, and no matter where Jonah tried to run, God would catch up with him. As David wrote in Psalm 139:7, "I can never escape from your Spirit! I can never get away from your presence!"

Is there something you're trying to hide from God? Or are you trying to escape his call? As a Christian, you should be compliant to God's will and the commands of Scripture. Are you? If not, confess your sin today. Ask God for a tender and submissive heart.

An Angry Evangelist

[Jonah] complained to the LORD . . . : "Didn't I say before I left home that you would do this, LORD? That is why I ran away to Tarshish! I knew that you are a merciful and compassionate God, slow to get angry and filled with unfailing love. You are eager to turn back from destroying people." JONAH 4:2

Jonah was one angry evangelist. What's stunning is the root of that emotion. Jonah was livid because God was so kind.

Why did Jonah try to run from God? Maybe it was because of the danger. Assyrians had a reputation for brutality, and perhaps Jonah feared their violence would extend to anyone who dared tell them to repent. That would be understandable—but that wasn't the real reason.

Jonah didn't want to go to Nineveh and preach because *he knew it would work*. He knew God was gracious and forgiving to anyone who turned from evil, and he knew the Ninevites would repent. When they did and God forgave them, Jonah was upset.

Sadly, we have something in common with Jonah. Because of our corrupt human nature, it's hard for us to see God bless others.

Paul said, "Be happy with those who are happy, and weep with those who weep" (Romans 12:15). Have you found that the second part of that command is easy while the first part is more difficult?

It's easy to encourage those who are down and out. But how do we feel when God blesses someone we've been praying for with something that we want? For example, if you have an old car that is ready to fall apart and God blesses someone else with a brand-new vehicle, are you jealous? If you are single, are you despondent when one of your single friends finds a godly mate?

Take a moment and check your attitude. Ask God to fill your life with his peace and enable you to respond with joy when he blesses others.

What Does God Want from Me?

The LORD has told you what is good,
*   and this is what he requires of you:*
to do what is right, to love mercy,
*   and to walk humbly with your God.*

MICAH 6:8

Micah 6 is the original courtroom drama. God, the plaintiff, states his case against the nation of Israel, the defendant.

During the trial, the Israelites ask God what he wants from them (see vv. 6-7). Does he require more worship or better worship? Perhaps God wants them to be like the pagans, who even sacrificed their own children to the false gods.

No! Through the prophet Micah, God tells Israel what he wants: three elements that deal with our daily lives and sum up the whole law. When we follow these, we are loving God and loving our neighbors as ourselves.

First, the people were to act justly rather than abusing power, oppressing the poor, and mocking the prophets. We need to do what is right in every aspect of our lives. Our worship should affect our "work-ship," or our businesses, social lives, and family lives.

Next, the people should love mercy. In verses 4-5, God rehearses his compassionate dealings with the Israelites throughout history, including rescuing them from slavery. Jesus said in the Sermon on the Mount, "God blesses those who are merciful, for they will be shown mercy" (Matthew 5:7). To the ancients, showing mercy was a weakness. Yet God calls us to emulate him by showing mercy to others.

Finally, God wants us to live with humility or walk humbly. We can cultivate this humility through prayers that show our dependence on God. Walking humbly may also mean being willing to take a task assigned to us, no matter what it is, and serve joyfully.

The Lord has acted compassionately to us. In gratitude, we can do what is right, love mercy, and live in humility.

Vengeance!

> The LORD is a jealous God,
>> filled with vengeance and rage.
> He takes revenge on all who oppose him
>> and continues to rage against his enemies!

NAHUM 1:2

The prophet Nahum delivered a prophecy about the destruction of Nineveh—a message the prophet Jonah would have loved to preach. Instead, a century and a half before Nahum, Jonah's message to Nineveh started the greatest revival in the history of the world when more than six hundred thousand people committed their lives to the Lord. Yet the Ninevites' changed lives lasted only for a short time, and soon they resorted to their old ways of life or worse.

God sent Nahum to deliver his message. Nahum first decreed the destruction of Nineveh and then described it. Finally, he explained why the destruction was deserved. This brief book deals with one of Christianity's most uncomfortable doctrines: the wrath of God.

Many people think of God as weak, sentimental, passive, and indulgent when in fact the Lord is strong, active, and jealous. Eight times the Bible declares that God is jealous—and not in the human sense. *Jealous* means that God wants no rivals. The Bible uses the Hebrew word *qaw-naw,* referring to a zeal for one's own property. In other words, God is telling others to keep their hands off what belongs to him.

Jesus Christ said in John 15:15, "I no longer call you slaves, because a master doesn't confide in his slaves. Now you are my friends, since I have told you everything the Father told me." As believers, we belong to God. Whenever someone comes against God's people, the Lord takes it personally.

Why would anyone consciously decide to make God an enemy? You are much better off having the whole world as an enemy and God as your friend than having the world as your friend and God as your enemy. Jesus has given you the opportunity to be called his friend. Take it with gratitude!

Jump for Joy

> *Even though the fig trees have no blossoms,*
> > *and there are no grapes on the vines;*
> *even though the olive crop fails,*
> > *and the fields lie empty and barren;*
> *even though the flocks die in the fields,*
> > *and the cattle barns are empty,*
> *yet I will rejoice in the LORD!*
> > *I will be joyful in the God of my salvation!*

HABAKKUK 3:17-18

You could call Habakkuk the "puzzled prophet." His book isn't so much of a prophecy as it is a personal struggle.

The crucial question for Habakkuk wasn't, why do bad things happen to good people? In his conversation with God, he was asking, why do bad things happen to *God's people?* This book was written after the fall of Nineveh (612 BC) and before the fall of Jerusalem (596 BC), at a time when Judah was ruled by kings who were wicked, oppressive, and violent. In this book, God gives Habakkuk a vision of the future Babylonian invasion that he would use to punish Judah. The enemy would destroy the Israelites' fig orchards, vineyards, and olive groves and would carry away their flocks.

Habakkuk eventually made a decision to rejoice in the Lord, yet he did not rejoice in the coming invasion. The prophet understood that faith does not always understand God's means but trusts God's motives. As Oswald Chambers wrote, "Faith is deliberate confidence in the character of God whose ways you may not understand at the time." Often in difficulties, we are asking the wrong question. Instead of wondering, *How can I get out of this?* we need to ask, "What can I get out of this?"

How did Habakkuk change? Through his faith in God. The prophet knew that suffering in the hands of a loving God could bring about great good. Is your life in the midst of a painful pruning? It is the mark of mature faith to rejoice even in the pain because you trust the Lord for the good results in your future.

Severe Mercy

"I will sweep away everything
from the face of the earth," says the LORD.

ZEPHANIAH 1:2

Zephaniah's great-great-grandpa, Hezekiah, pulled off a milestone revival. During his twenty-five-year reign, King Hezekiah initiated reforms that removed the high places and broke into pieces the bronze serpent that Moses had created and the people had turned into an idol. Hezekiah's grandson Josiah also started reforms during his reign, but they did not last. Often these public reforms masked a deeper need—the need for people to remove idols from both their homes and their hearts.

During a time of spiritual consecration, the prophet Zephaniah looked deeper and saw that the Israelites' hearts were shallow. They could not recover from their long history of corruption. In this book, Zephaniah writes about the forthcoming severe mercy from God. The wrath would be necessary to purge an unrepentant Judah; however, the wrath was not the whole story. The Lord would also be merciful. He would someday restore his people.

Consider this story: A screaming girl was held tightly by her mother. A man ran into the room, grabbed the screaming girl, drove her to a stark building, and carried her into a room with a single light. Another man plunged a knife into the girl's stomach.

"What a cruel story!" you exclaim. But you haven't seen the whole picture. The full story is that the girl's father took her to the hospital because she had a ruptured appendix. The doctor used his scalpel to excise the burst organ and save the girl's life. What seemed cruel was really merciful.

Zephaniah declares that God, through his day of wrath, will save Israel. Is God trying to cut anything out of your life in order to save you from something? Ask him to help you respond humbly to his sometimes severe mercy.

Put God First

Why are you living in luxurious houses while my house lies in ruins?

HAGGAI 1:4

God's Temple was lying in ruins. Under the leadership of Zerubbabel (called Sheshbazzar in the book of Ezra), fifty thousand Israelites returned to Jerusalem from captivity and began restoring the Temple. But the people grew tired of hardships, and the leaders were weary. They were working on their own houses instead of on God's house. The prophet Haggai was called to awaken the people and encourage them to finish what they had started. He called attention to their excuses.

When it comes to doing God's work or going to church, we can find many excuses. Sometimes we don't do it because we say, "The weather is too bad." Yet in that same weather we manage to shop or get to a movie. We might say, "The traffic is too much at church, and the crowds are overwhelming." Yet we don't mind waiting for hours in the long lines at Disneyland. Or we speculate, "What if the preacher goes too long today?" Yet we don't complain if our sports events go into overtime.

God's questions through the prophet Haggai reveal the people's serious priority problems. Jesus himself highlighted the importance of making God's Kingdom work a first priority. He said, "Seek the Kingdom of God above all else, and live righteously, and he [God] will give you everything you need" (Matthew 6:33). We constantly need to look at our activities and ask, "Is this what God wants?"

American evangelist J. Wilbur Chapman said, "My life is governed by this rule: Anything that dims my vision of Christ or takes away my taste for Bible study or cramps my prayer life or makes Christian work difficult is wrong for me, and I must, as a Christian, turn away from it."

Pause for a moment and evaluate where God fits in your priorities. Then seek to make him and his Kingdom your primary and daily concern.

Come Back!

Say to the people, "This is what the LORD of Heaven's Armies says: Return to me, and I will return to you, says the LORD of Heaven's Armies."

ZECHARIAH 1:3

It's common to think of the prophets as a long chain of God's messengers, but that's not always the case. Zechariah and Haggai were contemporaries yet with different messages. While Haggai challenged people to rebuild the Temple, Zechariah proclaimed a call for personal revival and social renewal. He brought the hopeful message that God was active.

In the midst of instability and change, the Jewish refugees were growing anxious. They felt small and weak compared to the great Persian Empire. Zechariah reminded the people that the Lord promised to be with them if they returned to him.

God is always waiting for people to come to him for salvation and fellowship. While he could force himself on us, God instead offers himself to us and waits for our return.

The word *repentance* means "a turning" and begins with a change of mind or heart. If you repent, you put away your evil practices and replace them with godly values. If someone deliberately turns to the Lord, then he or she cannot habitually continue to do evil. Some of the Jewish people had returned to practicing evil deeds. Through Zechariah, God called them to return to him.

When Jesus spoke to the church at Ephesus, he said, "I have this complaint against you. You don't love me or each other as you did at first! Look how far you have fallen! Turn back to me and do the works you did at first" (Revelation 2:4-5). He is always calling us back to him.

Today, is there any distance between you and God? God has never walked away from you, but if you have walked away from God, choose to return.

Altar of Tears

Here is another thing you do. You cover the LORD's altar with tears,
weeping and groaning because he pays no attention to your offerings and
doesn't accept them with pleasure.   MALACHI 2:13

The prophet Malachi delivered the final words of what we know as the Old
Testament before the four hundred silent years leading to the birth of Jesus
Christ. The name Malachi means "my messenger" in Hebrew, but nothing
else is known about the prophet.

He ministered to the restored Jewish nation a century after Haggai and
Zechariah. The Lord's Temple had been rebuilt, but the spiritual life of
the nation was decaying. What's worse, the people were unaware of their
own spiritual condition. When Malachi delivered God's Word, the people
responded with arguments.

In the name of the Lord, Malachi rebuked the priests. These clergymen
were supposed to know the will of God and teach it to the people, yet they
were divorcing their wives and entering into ungodly marriages. This was
so serious that when they offered sacrifices to the Lord, he did not receive
them.

Marriage is God's invention and not man's creation, so it is subject to
the Lord's principles and regulation. Speaking of husband and wife, Jesus
Christ said in Matthew 19:6, "Let no one split apart what God has joined
together."

A marriage between believers is not to be abandoned or taken for
granted. In Genesis 2:18, God said, "It is not good for the man to be alone.
I will make a helper who is just right for him." Speaking of Eve, Matthew
Henry wrote, "She was not made out of [Adam's] head to top him, nor out
of his feet to be trampled on by him, but out of his side to be equal to him,
under his arm to be protected and near his heart to be beloved."

Turning away from what God has ordained has serious consequences.
If you have a godly spouse, thank the Lord for that gift and ask him to keep
your marriage strong.

Women in the Line of Jesus

This is a record of the ancestors of Jesus the Messiah, a descendant of David and of Abraham. MATTHEW 1:1

The pages of the Gospels provide a fourfold picture of Jesus Christ, like a string quartet that performs in perfect harmony. Each Gospel provides a different emphasis and is written for a different audience.

Matthew was written to the Jews and emphasizes that Jesus Christ is the prophesied King. Mark was written for the Romans and reveals Jesus as an obedient servant. Dr. Luke, who wrote the books Luke and Acts, writes to Greeks about Jesus as the perfect man. Finally, the apostle John wrote his Gospel so the world would believe Jesus was God's divine Son.

Matthew begins with a genealogy. For his audience, knowing Jesus' lineage was a priority. This list of names shows that Jesus came from David's royal line—critical proof for anyone who claimed to be the Messiah.

Women were typically excluded from Hebrew genealogy, since they had few rights. So you may be surprised that Matthew includes five women in the genealogy of Christ.

The lineage of Jesus includes Tamar (see v. 3). A childless widow, she dressed as a prostitute and stood by the road until her father-in-law, Judah, came along—and from their union came twins (see Genesis 38). Also notice Rahab (see v. 5), the harlot from Jericho who hid the two Jewish spies who later spared her life. She became the great-great-grandmother of David. Ruth (see v. 5), the Gentile and Moabite, appears in the next generation. The Moabites' origins included incest between Lot and his daughters, yet Ruth followed the God of Jacob. The fourth woman is Bathsheba (see v. 6), whose firstborn son was a product of adultery with King David. She was also the mother of King Solomon. The final woman is Mary, Jesus' mother.

The genealogy of Jesus reveals the spiritual history of great sinners who needed a great Savior. Take a moment and thank God that Jesus identified with sinful people to pay the price for their sins.

Second Fiddle

The prophet Isaiah was speaking about John when he said,

> *"He is a voice shouting in the wilderness,*
> *'Prepare the way for the LORD's coming!*
> *   Clear the road for him!'"*

MATTHEW 3:3

Someone asked orchestra director Leonard Bernstein, "What is the hardest position in the orchestra for you to fill?" He quickly responded, "Second fiddle. I can always find plenty of first violinists, but to get someone to play second is tough."

John the Baptist is an example of a true minister. He did not push to be seen, and he did the duty of a slave. John was willing to play second fiddle.

He lived in the wilderness by the Dead Sea, a barren, ugly limestone desert. John was a PK, or "priest's kid." Because he came from a priestly family descended from Aaron, everyone had high expectations.

The descriptions of John the Baptist make him sound eccentric, a reclusive hippie who ate bugs and was into fur. His life in the limestone wilderness was a protest. In the hot sun with temperatures reaching 120 degrees, people came more than thirty miles to this ugly spot to listen to John (see Matthew 3:5).

Church theory teaches that a church needs to be conveniently located or it will fail. Yet John the Baptist chose the most inconvenient place as the headquarters for his ministry. John may have gone to the desert to base his life and ministry on these verses in Isaiah 40. He declared that he was the prophetic fulfillment of the Messiah's forerunner and exhorted the people to prepare the way of the Lord. In ancient times, whenever a monarch came into a province, the herald or announcer came ahead, saying, "Get ready; the king is coming." The people would be embarrassed if the king arrived and they were unprepared.

John's task was to point people to Jesus Christ. You and I today have the same task. How are you pointing people toward Jesus? And how prepared are you for the arrival of your Lord and King?

The Upside-Down Kingdom

> *God blesses those who mourn,*
> *for they will be comforted.*

MATTHEW 5:4

On a sloping hill on the shores of the Sea of Galilee, the people heard the greatest teacher who ever lived preach the Sermon on the Mount.

Jesus used the theme of the Kingdom of God, which was one of his favorite subjects. The man who Isaiah said would be King of kings gave a Kingdom manifesto. Essentially he was telling his listeners, "This is how Kingdom dwellers will live when I am their King."

If you had to describe in one word how Kingdom dwellers live and act, what would it be? *Differently*. Followers of Jesus are different from both "religious" and worldly people.

In Matthew 6:8, Jesus Christ said about the people of the world, "Don't be like them." Don't take your cues for how to act from folks who aren't followers of Jesus. In fact, Christianity is the ultimate in "counterculture." If you don't believe that, glance at the Beatitudes. Since when does the world think like that?

In *Your God Is Too Small*, Bible translator J. B. Phillips, speculating about how the world might rewrite the Beatitudes, wrote the following: "Happy are the pushers: for they get on in the world. Happy are the hard-boiled: for they never let life hurt them. Happy are they who complain: for they get their own way in the end. Happy are the blasé: for they never worry over their sins. Happy are the slave-drivers: for they get results. Happy are the knowledgeable men of the world: for they know their way around. Happy are the troublemakers: for people have to take notice of them."

That reflects the world's attitude, but we're called to something else. As the Phillips translation of Romans 12:1 says, Kingdom dwellers don't let the world squeeze them into its own mold.

Take a moment and evaluate your life. Are you living differently from the world around you? What in your actions, thoughts, and words makes you distinct? If you don't find much dissimilarity, then what steps do you need to take to increase the difference?

How to Build a House

[Jesus said,] "Anyone who listens to my teaching and follows it is wise, like a person who builds a house on solid rock."   MATTHEW 7:24

One year I learned firsthand what it takes to build a home. We had purchased five acres of land in the Rocky Mountains. The soil was hard, and the foundation—which was made of rock—was difficult to lay. However, our builder assured us that when it was finished, our home would withstand both time and weather.

When it comes to your life, what are you using for your foundation? Through his teaching, Jesus Christ has given us the Kingdom building code. He has taught us how to build a solid life filled with God's truth. Yet not everyone builds his or her life to Kingdom specifications. Some people attempt to take shortcuts, and others have used the wrong materials.

The first principle the wise builder follows is to build on the right foundation and to the right specifications. Have you submitted your life plans to the Master Builder and Architect? Think through areas of major decision such as marriage or vocation. In your decision-making processes, are you teachable and open to God's direction?

The Gospel of Luke also includes this story about the wise builder. In Luke 6:47-48, Jesus said, "I will show you what it's like when someone comes to me, listens to my teaching, and then follows it. It is like a person building a house who digs deep and lays the foundation on solid rock. When the floodwaters rise and break against that house, it stands firm because it is well built." The wise man was willing to give the maximum effort to build his life on the right foundation—the Word of God.

When we hear God's Word and don't put it into practice, we are like foolish builders whose work will be swept away. Are you allowing Jesus' teachings to impact your choices and actions? Make sure you are building your life on the right foundation of God's truth.

To the Gutter-*most!*

As Jesus was walking along, he saw a man named Matthew sitting at his tax collector's booth. "Follow me and be my disciple," Jesus said to him. So Matthew got up and followed him. MATTHEW 9:9

Hebrews 7:25 says, "[Christ] is also able to save to the uttermost those who come to God through Him, since He always lives to make intercession for them" (NKJV). William Booth, the founder of the Salvation Army, would often paraphrase this verse, saying, "God is able to save, even to the *gutter-most.*" General Booth meant that God's grace reached even to the sordid individuals who came to Christ through his street evangelism.

I suspect that of Jesus' disciples, Matthew would have been voted "the *most unlikely* to get saved." His original Jewish name was Levi, which means "priestly house" or the special place set apart for Temple service. Yet Matthew was far from serving God in the Temple. As tax collector, his occupation was right up there with robbers and murderers on the Israelites' most-hated list.

Ancient tax collectors could set their own tax amounts as long as their fees didn't lead to a revolt. A minimum amount had to be turned over to the Roman government, but anything they collected over that was theirs to keep—a circumstance that lent itself to greed and injustice.

When Jesus entered Matthew's home, the people asked him, "Why are you eating with the tax collectors and sinners?" Tax collectors were usually barred from involvement in the synagogues and would never associate with religious leaders, yet Jesus established a personal relationship with Matthew. And the result was that Matthew eventually became his devoted disciple.

Are you following Jesus' example as you tell other people about him? It's too easy for Christians to become cloistered. While our lives need to be separate and different from the world, we also need to reach the lost with God's message of hope.

Take a moment and consider your relationships. What steps are you taking to reach the "tax collectors" who cross your path?

Everyone Loves a Story

Other seeds fell on fertile soil, and they produced a crop that was thirty, sixty, and even a hundred times as much as had been planted!

MATTHEW 13:8

Jesus was a storyteller, and that distinguished his teaching from that of the other leaders of his day. Those religious leaders often used heavy-handed language and complex words. By comparison, Jesus' stories were a breath of fresh air. No wonder the Scriptures tell us, "The large crowd listened to him with great delight" (Mark 12:37).

Jesus never taught with stuffy, abstract, or heady theology. And he didn't use big words to impress others. He talked about God, using word pictures that conveyed simple, easy-to-grasp concepts. Jesus took theological images and made them available to everyone.

Jesus taught the people using parables. The word *parable* means "to place beside" or, literally, "something thrown next to something else." He told an earthly story with a heavenly meaning. These stories placed everyday, earthly situations beside the unknown, eternal, and spiritual in order to teach deep truth.

Why did Jesus use these stories? To reveal *and* to conceal. For those who cared to know the truth, Jesus revealed the meaning. For those who wanted only to trap him, Jesus concealed the truth (see Matthew 13:11-16).

Truth that awakens one person will harden another. The warm sun can melt ice, but it also hardens clay. Whether someone understood the parables depended on the condition of his or her heart.

God wants to reveal himself to you, and God wrote the Bible in human language so we could understand him and relate to him. What is your attitude toward his teaching? Do you have a soft heart ready to learn? Ask God to daily use the Scriptures to awaken truth in your life and heart.

Who Am I?

[Jesus] asked them, "But who do you say I am?" MATTHEW 16:15

Every person throughout the ages must answer one fundamental question, and Jesus asks that question in today's key verse.

Books and television contain a steady stream of the most bizarre ideas about Jesus Christ, most of which have no supporting evidence. The new theories are amazing and almost laughable. Some people say Jesus was a magician who practiced illusion and hypnosis, while other people call him a zealot, a guru, or a world traveler. A novel proclaims Jesus as the husband of Mary Magdalene and states that the couple procreated a secret lineage to rule the world. Once people have rejected the truth about Jesus, it is incredible what they will believe.

Jesus gave his twelve disciples an exam with two questions. The first was, "Who do men say that I am?" The second question is the one each of us ultimately must face: "Who do you say that I am?"

When Jesus asked the second question of his disciples, Peter passed the test. He said, "You're the long-awaited Messiah. You are the deliverer that we've been waiting for, and you're the Son of God."

Who is Jesus Christ to you? When this question is settled, you'll be settled. Possibly you've reached a point where you are ready to confront this question on a personal level. It's a great day for some spiritual soul-searching and a look at your life. Do you truly believe that Jesus is the Son of God?

A. W. Tozer said, "We do not preach Christ with a comma after his name, as though we are waiting for something else; or Christ with a dash after his name as though leading to something else; but we preach Christ period."

If Jesus Christ is a stranger to you, come to him. Let him be your friend. Not only did Jesus proclaim he was the Son of God, but he saved you from eternal death and separation from God. Surrender your life to him.

An Impossible Case

The disciples were astounded. "Then who in the world can be saved?" they asked.

Jesus looked at them intently and said, "Humanly speaking, it is impossible. But with God everything is possible."

MATTHEW 19:25-26

There are some things that I just can't do. I can't read people's minds, I can't stretch out my arms and fly through the heavens unaided, and I can't snap my fingers to create a five-course meal. These things are impossible for me. But something else falls into this impossible category: salvation. No matter what I say or how hard I work, it is impossible for me to save anyone, including myself.

The disciples were stunned when Jesus told them that it was difficult for a rich man to enter heaven. Most ancient Jews thought riches were evidence of God's blessing on their lives. They would often quote God's promise of material blessing if they obeyed God's laws as recorded in Deuteronomy 26–28. So after the disciples heard these words from Jesus, they wondered, *If a wealthy person can't be saved, what about the rest of us?*

If you think about Jesus' statement long enough, it begins to make more sense. Alongside the perfection of God, our sins become clear. No one—whether rich or poor, righteous or unrighteous—can produce the change needed to bring salvation. Jesus talked about the need to be "born again." Salvation requires a powerful work of re-creation and regeneration. No philosophy, self-help ideology, or meditation can make a soul heaven bound.

Listen, the truth is, you're an impossible case. In fact, each of us is! It is only through believing in Jesus and his sacrificial death to atone for our sins that we are saved.

Be encouraged, because there is hope for every individual. No matter how impossible someone appears to the human eye, Jesus can save him or her. Never marginalize the possibility of anyone's salvation by saying, "Oh, she'll never become a Christian." God specializes in impossible cases. Aren't you glad? Celebrate the words of Jesus that *with God*, everything is possible.

Sign, Sign, Everywhere a Sign

Jesus sat on the Mount of Olives. His disciples came to him privately and said, "Tell us, when will all this happen? What sign will signal your return and the end of the world?" MATTHEW 24:3

We read in Matthew 24 that Jesus' disciples approached him privately about the signs for the future. They knew that God is a God of signs. Signs are intended to reveal, warn, or direct. God always indicates when he is going to do something because he wants people to be aware of these future events.

Through the prophet Amos, God said, "Indeed, the Sovereign LORD never does anything until he reveals his plans to his servants the prophets" (Amos 3:7). Repeatedly in the Old Testament God warned the Israelites through the prophets and sent signs about his future actions.

The Old Testament is filled with prophecies about the coming Messiah—signs that would reveal his identity. By some counts, Jesus fulfilled 330 of these, including his birth in Bethlehem, his place in the lineage of King David, and his arrival before the Temple in Jerusalem was destroyed.

Some of the signs indicated the first coming of Jesus, while others pointed to the Second Coming. Are you waiting and watching? It's easy to be focused on the where and when of the signs, but I think we should be more focused on where the signs point—to Jesus. As one person put it, "We're not so much looking for the coming of the Lord as we are for the Lord who is coming."

When I was a kid, my mom often said to me and my brothers, "Your dad will be home soon." Depending on our actions during that particular day, the reminder about my dad's return was either great news or sobering news. How do you react when you are reminded that Jesus is coming? Are you excited or a bit insecure? Today's passage is a reminder to be watchful and ready for our Lord to return.

Marching Orders

[Jesus said,] "Go and make disciples of all the nations, baptizing them in the name of the Father and the Son and the Holy Spirit."

MATTHEW 28:19

Philadelphia radio preacher Harry Ironside (1876–1951) heard about a church that had the motto "Jesus Only" hanging over its front door. At first Pastor Ironside was impressed with the declaration, but when he learned more about this particular church, he realized it was known in the community for being self-centered and isolated. One day the wind tore away the first three letters of the sign so that it read, "us Only." The torn sign, said Pastor Ironside, was probably a more accurate description.

Are we concerned about others who aren't in our little circles? The message of the gospel needs to reach beyond current believers. Anglican Bishop J. C. Ryle (1816–1900) wrote, "The highest form of selfishness is a man content to go to heaven alone!" Or to repeat a saying I've heard, "Jesus Christ called us to be fishers of men rather than keepers of the aquarium."

Of the world's population, 33.1 percent are professed Christians, leaving 66.9 percent who are non-Christians. If you lined up all the lost people in the world side by side, this line would circle the globe thirty times, and every day it would grow twenty miles longer. How do you react to these numbers?

Before Jesus left the earth and returned to heaven, he gave marching orders to his disciples. Notice, Jesus didn't say to the world, "Come to church." Instead Jesus, through the verses known as the great commission, told the church, "Go to the world." Take a moment and consider your response to the great commission. When was the last time you told a friend, neighbor, or coworker about Jesus?

Jesus Christ came to earth "to seek and save the lost," and he returned to heaven, saying, "Go." Let's make sure we're obeying his command.

Immediately

The Spirit then compelled Jesus to go into the wilderness. . . . They left their nets at once and followed him. MARK 1:12, 18

Of the four different accounts of the life of Jesus Christ, the Gospel of Mark is the shortest and the one written first. When missionaries are trained in linguistics and Bible translation techniques, they are often encouraged to use Mark as the first Gospel in their translation work. Why? Mark uses straightforward storytelling and less imagery than the other Gospels.

According to an early tradition, Mark based the contents of his book on the testimony of the apostle Peter. He wrote it for the Gentile reader, and it contains less teaching and more action than the other three Gospels. We see this through the use of the phrases "immediately" and "at once," each appearing at least seven times in just sixteen chapters.

As we read Mark's Gospel, we gain a clear picture of who Jesus was: a servant of God who immediately did the will of his Father. Read the first chapter of Mark and consider Jesus' rapid actions. First, John baptized Jesus. Then, immediately after a voice spoke from heaven and identified Jesus as God's Son, the Holy Spirit compelled him to go into the wilderness, where he was tempted. Next, Jesus began his earthly ministry of preaching and healing, and he also began calling his disciples.

When Jesus called Peter and his brother Andrew, who were commercial fisherman, he said to them, "Come, follow me, and I will show you how to fish for people!" (Mark 1:17). There was no hesitation from Peter and Andrew. Verse 18 says, "They left their nets at once and followed him." *At once* they dropped their lifelong occupation and followed Jesus Christ.

When the Holy Spirit speaks to your heart and life, how soon should you respond? The answer is *immediately*. Follow the example of Peter, Andrew, and Jesus himself. Take a moment to ask God to speak to your heart, then listen and faithfully respond.

Unforgivable

Anyone who blasphemes the Holy Spirit will never be forgiven. This is a sin with eternal consequences.   MARK 3:29

Jesus' words sound so final and so hopeless. Why did he say them?

The convincing nature of Jesus' miracles forced the Pharisees to try to explain them away, and their explanation was blasphemous: that Jesus was in league with Satan. They contended these great miracles could only be from the power of the devil. Who else, they asked, would be able to cast out demons?

In his response, Jesus showed that this accusation was both illogical and dangerous: illogical, because Satan would not fight himself and divide his own kingdom. A civil war weakens any nation. If Jesus were working in league with Satan, it would prove only that his Kingdom had been breached and was disintegrating.

This accusation was also dangerous because it indicated that the Pharisees were resisting the Holy Spirit's testimony about Jesus Christ, and dying with that belief would be fatal. Their attributing the Holy Spirit's power to Satan showed the hardness of their hearts. They no longer felt his conviction.

The work of the Holy Spirit is to lead people to Jesus Christ through conviction. When someone is no longer under conviction, the Holy Spirit is no longer striving. As Ephesians 4:18-19 says, "[The unbelieving Gentiles'] minds are full of darkness; they wander far from the life God gives because they have closed their minds and hardened their hearts against him. They have no sense of shame. They live for lustful pleasure and eagerly practice every kind of impurity."

Billy Graham explained today's Bible verse by saying, "The unpardonable sin is rejecting the truth about Christ. It is rejecting, completely and finally, the witness of the Holy Spirit, which declares Jesus Christ is the Son of God who alone can save us from sins."

It is a serious thing to harden our hearts to the Holy Spirit's conviction. Ask God to keep your heart soft and your ears open to the Spirit.

Dark Angels

Jesus demanded, "What is your name?"

And [the spirit] replied, "My name is Legion, because there are many of us inside this man." MARK 5:9

Recently I had an unusual opportunity to visit the Sullivan Correctional Institution in New York and meet with notorious criminal David Berkowitz. He was infamously tagged as the "Son of Sam" mass murderer during the 1970s and is serving a life sentence. He described his days as a killer, saying, "A power overtook me that I knew was demonic." His fascination with *The Satanic Bible* and church cost many innocent people their lives. However, during the last several years, David has turned his life around by making a firm commitment to Jesus Christ.

If you are a Christian, Satan cannot possess you or control you. However, each of us faces a certain level of spiritual warfare. When Satan knocks on your door through opposition or temptation, the best action you can take is to ask Jesus to answer. Pray and ask Jesus to handle the situation. He is far more powerful than Satan. One-third of the angels fell from heaven with Satan and are working against believers, but two-thirds of the angels remain on God's side. You can rest assured that the devil's bunch is outnumbered.

British scholar and preacher Charles Spurgeon (1834–1892) said, "There is something comforting in the thought that the devil is an adversary. I'd sooner have him for an adversary than a friend."

We should be aware that Satan is pursuing us. First Peter 5:8 says, "Watch out for your great enemy, the devil. He prowls around like a roaring lion, looking for someone to devour." How do you have victory over the devil? Is it through chasing him, binding him, or rebuking him? No, James 4:7 says, "Resist the devil, and he will flee from you." That's solid advice whenever Satan pursues you.

Tradition

You ignore God's law and substitute your own tradition. MARK 7:8

Many times I've heard church members say, "We've always done it that way. Why change it now?" Traditions are a part of our lives' fabric. These routines can be helpful when they bring order to our lives, but they can be harmful when they become barriers to God's will. We may need to be especially cautious about religious traditions. Why?

First, religious tradition can emphasize only externals. For example, the religious leaders in Jesus' day practiced specific hand-washing rituals that had nothing to do with hygiene. They were ceremonial rinsings with the purpose of removing ritual defilement when someone touched something unclean. Some of that was required by Mosaic law, but Jesus made clear that God's primary emphasis is not on the external but on the internal, or the heart.

Religious tradition can also add information to God's Word. The Jews often quoted what was known as the *oral law,* a compilation of interpretations and applications of Mosaic law. Unfortunately, this oral law was considered as valid as the Scriptures themselves. Seeing our human traditions as equal with the Bible is dangerous.

Finally, religious traditions can create barriers. Among the Jews, certain people, such as Gentiles and women, were regarded as second class. The Temple was constructed with a series of walled courts to keep each group of people in its proper place. It was a type of caste system. But God is in the business of destroying walls. Christ is the great bulldozer and leveler, and he has no favorites.

Are you holding on to any traditions that make you feel comfortable and secure, yet aren't necessarily part of God's requirements? Sorting that out can take careful soul-searching. Our spirituality is not tied up with what we eat, the words we recite, or our gestures. Rather, it's a relationship to God that's characterized by loving obedience to his will.

A Twist in the Plot

[Jesus] said to them, "The Son of Man is going to be betrayed into the hands of his enemies. He will be killed, but three days later he will rise from the dead." MARK 9:31

The disciples were not expecting Jesus to go to the cross. Like most Jewish people two thousand years ago, the disciples believed the Messiah would be a powerful deliverer. The Bible says that the Messiah will set up his Kingdom and reign from Jerusalem, and the disciples believed they would witness those events.

But the powerful deliverance promised by the Messiah didn't happen right away. First Jesus hung on the cross to pay for the world's sins. Then he rose from the dead and ascended into heaven, where he will remain until his second coming. When Jesus returns again, *then* he will be the deliverer.

The death of Jesus Christ shocked the disciples. Like most people, they were selective listeners and heard from Jesus only what they wanted to hear. Their views of the Messiah didn't allow for death and suffering. The apostle Paul said that the preaching of Christ's crucifixion offended the Jews (see 1 Corinthians 1:23). Yet Jesus' crucifixion was part of God's plan before the foundation of the world (see Revelation 13:8). Jesus often predicted his death, such as in John 10:18: "No one can take my life from me. I sacrifice it voluntarily."

Just as the disciples had expectations about Jesus, many Christians have expectations about how our lives should run. When the Lord doesn't work according to our plans and we experience suffering, we grow confused and disappointed because God didn't follow our scripts.

The Lord has editing rights over the plans for your life. If even Jesus experienced suffering, can we expect a life without it? Trust God to guide your life. Just as his plan for Jesus was right, his plan for your life will be right as well.

God Is Good

"Why do you call me good?" Jesus asked. "Only God is truly good."

MARK 10:18

Many times I've heard people express this sentiment: "He was such a good person. He deserved to go to heaven." These two sentences are used together, yet in reality they are disconnected. Good behavior is not why we go to heaven.

When the first man, Adam, sinned, he generated an innate change in his character, which shifted from innocence to sinfulness. The sin of Adam is passed on to each of us and is a part of our human nature.

Imagine standing at Jackson Lake, located at the base of the Tetons in Wyoming, during the early morning. The lake is perfectly calm and clearly reflects the Tetons. But with one little, flat stone skipped across the surface, the image of the Tetons becomes distorted. In the same way, Adam threw one stone (he sinned), and it marred the human race.

As Paul wrote, "Once you were dead because of your disobedience and your many sins. . . . All of us used to live that way, following the passionate desires and inclinations of our sinful nature" (Ephesians 2:1, 3). Every child has an inborn bent toward selfishness and evil. I've never met parents who will claim their child was such a perfect angel that they had to teach him one or two naughty things to make him normal.

You and I have been polluted from a stream of humanity that flows from Adam, but the great news is that we can be cleansed by the stream that flows from Jesus Christ. He alone is truly good, and he alone can make atonement for our sins. As the song says, "There is a fountain filled with blood drawn from Emmanuel's veins. And sinners plunged beneath that flood lose all their guilty stains." Celebrate the cleansing blood of Jesus Christ in your life.

Church and State

"Well, then," Jesus said, "give to Caesar what belongs to Caesar, and give to God what belongs to God." His reply completely amazed them.

MARK 12:17

Under Roman control during the time of Jesus, the Jews were required to pay tribute money to the emperor. This tax was very unpopular, and some Jews flatly refused to pay it because they believed that payment was an admission that the Romans had a right to rule them. In addition, the Roman emperor was the only person with authority to issue silver or gold coins. Each coin had an engraving of the emperor on one side, and this was offensive to some Jews because the law of Moses forbade anyone to make images.

Yet the taxes served some positive purposes, because they paid for the support of the Roman forces and services. For centuries the Middle East had seen war, and now, under Roman protection, the people enjoyed peace. The Romans also built roads and aqueducts, and many of those ruins still exist today. Without taxes, the government could not function.

When the Pharisees asked their question, they were trying to lay a trap for Jesus. If he answered, "Yes, pay taxes," he would anger the Pharisees and others who hated Rome. If he answered, "No, don't pay the taxes," he might be accused of rebelling against the government. Jesus said neither, and his thoughtful reply amazed his hearers.

Jesus used the Greek word for "render" or "give back," which implied a debt. In other words, he was saying it was right to give taxes to Caesar because those things belonged to Caesar's domain. Romans 13:1-7 and 1 Peter 2:13-15 affirm that it is legitimate to pay taxes. The leaders of government, such as presidents, kings, prime ministers, policemen, and mayors, stand in God's place for the preservation of society.

While Caesar could collect taxes, Jesus told us that we should give to God what belongs to God. What is that? Our worship. Are you giving God the worship that is due him?

Alone

All his disciples deserted him and ran away.   MARK 14:50

Do you know the feeling of being abandoned? Unfortunately, some people experience it when their parents divorce or when a friend or spouse suddenly leaves.

In today's Bible passage, we read that the disciples deserted Jesus and ran away. What was happening to Jesus? He had already experienced a partial separation from the Father because of his human birth. But as he approached the cross, he experienced gradually increasing loneliness. First, all twelve disciples were with him in the upper room, but Judas left. Eleven disciples went with him to the garden of Gethsemane, and then three of them accompanied him a short distance for prayer—yet they fell asleep. After Jesus was arrested, two disciples, Peter and John, went into the nearby courtyard to watch the trial, but Peter denied knowing Jesus three times.

Although Jesus' closest friends had abandoned him, the Father was still with him. In John 16:32, Jesus predicted, "The time is coming—indeed it's here now—when you will be scattered, each one going his own way, leaving me alone. Yet I am not alone because the Father is with me."

Then at the cross, in some way we can't fully understand, the Father forsook the Son, and his wrath at the sins of the world was unleashed. While Jesus was on the cross, God treated him as if by substitution he had lived your sinful life—and mine. Only after that could the Father treat us as if we had lived Jesus' perfect and righteous life.

Jesus Christ took your place so you never have to feel alone. He will never leave you or forsake you. As the song "How Firm a Foundation" says,

> The soul that on Jesus still leans for repose,
> I will not, I will not desert to his foes;
> That soul, though all hell should endeavor to shake,
> I'll never, no, never, no, never forsake!

Please Come In

The curtain in the sanctuary of the Temple was torn in two, from top to bottom.   MARK 15:38

God showed the significance of Jesus' death on the cross in a visible way. From top to bottom, he tore the veil that marked the entrance into the holiest part of the Temple. Now it was possible to enter into the presence of God without barriers, walls, or hierarchy.

This sixty-foot curtain was a cloth divider that separated the Holy Place from the Holy of Holies. Once a year on the Day of Atonement, the high priest carefully entered the Holy of Holies. As Leviticus 16:14 instructed, "He must take some of the blood of the bull, dip his finger in it, and sprinkle it on the east side of the atonement cover. He must sprinkle blood seven times with his finger in front of the atonement cover." This was done to purify the people from their sins, and the task was not taken lightly. The high priest could be struck dead if he entered the Holy of Holies at the wrong time or in the wrong way. The veil was a serious barrier saying, "Keep out." But through the death of the Lamb of God, the sign changed to say, "Come in."

I read one report that, after Jesus' death, the priests sewed up the torn veil and continued with sacrifices until the Temple was destroyed in AD 70. Isn't that typical of people? When God tears the veil of separation, mankind sews it back up. God wants a relationship with us, but we settle for rules and rituals.

Any system that complicates what God made simple is an insult to him. So is any system that puts a person between you and God. Jesus Christ opened the way for you to have a relationship directly with God. Praise the Lord!

Doctor Luke

Having carefully investigated everything from the beginning, I also have decided to write a careful account for you.   LUKE 1:3

The author of the third Gospel was Luke. Although he was not an eyewitness of Jesus Christ's ministry, he culled the best available sources of information to record the story of Jesus in an orderly manner.

Luke was probably a physician in Troas who came to Christ through the ministry of the apostle Paul. We know that he went on the second and possibly the third missionary journey with Paul. Writing for the Hellenic world, Luke's style is more polished and classical than Matthew's, Mark's, or even Paul's.

This Gospel is dedicated to Theophilus, which means "a lover of God." Theophilus was probably a Roman who had become a Christian. Some Bible scholars believe Luke was a slave and Theophilus was his owner, because during this period of history, the wealthy often had their own private physicians.

It's clear that the Gospel writers shared some source material. Of the 1,151 total verses in the Gospel of Luke, it has 389 verses in common with Matthew and Mark; 176 verses in common only with Matthew; 41 verses in common only with Mark; and 544 verses unique to itself.

Luke gives a longer account of Christ's virgin birth than any other Gospel. The doctor records twenty of Jesus' miracles, six of which appear nowhere else in the Bible. He recounts twenty-three of Jesus' parables, and eighteen of these stories are unique to Luke, including the parables of the Prodigal Son and the Good Samaritan. Only Luke includes the story about Jesus walking to Emmaus, which proves the Son of God was still human after his resurrection.

God used many different people to write his words, and they varied from shepherds to kings and from farmers to physicians. The Holy Spirit inspired each author to provide a consistent message of God's love story to redeem mankind.

Christmas in July

Glory to God in highest heaven,
  and peace on earth to those with whom God is pleased.

It may seem disconnected to talk about Christmas in July. But in some ways, the timing is perfect because we need to live out the Christmas message throughout the year.

Many years before Jesus' birth, the prophet Isaiah hinted at the Messiah's mission by calling him the Prince of Peace. On the night Jesus was born, angels announced that peace had arrived on the earth. But according to some calculations, the last four thousand years have included only 286 years of peace. So we wonder, *were those angels mocking the world? Were they ridiculing every generation that has known nothing but war?*

The angels' announcement meant several things. First, they proclaimed that this baby boy would bring ultimate peace through the Kingdom of God. During Jesus' first coming he rode a donkey—a symbol of peace—into Jerusalem (see Luke 19) and came as the King of Peace. Revelation 19 tells us that the second time he returns, he will be on a horse and will return as the Warrior-King and Judge. He will set up his Kingdom and bring eternal peace, putting an end to all war forever.

The angels' announcement also indicated that God's peace is available to all people forever. The Knox translation of Luke 2:14 says, "peace to those men that are God's friends," and all are invited to be his friends.

One day Jesus will reign worldwide—but even now the Prince of Peace reigns in the surrendered heart of anyone who has a personal relationship with him. One day Jesus will come and set up his Kingdom of peace, and he will reign. Until that time, anyone can celebrate Christmas in July. All who yield themselves to the Prince of Peace can have the peace of Christ.

In the comic strip "Dennis the Menace," Dennis asks his father, "Why can't Christmas ever go into overtime?" The message from the angels was that it can. Celebrate the peace of Jesus every day.

Age of Grace

The time of the LORD's favor has come.   LUKE 4:19

Jesus was always accurate in how he used the Hebrew Scriptures. In this passage we see that, by breaking a sentence in just the right place, Jesus revealed an essential understanding of God's plan.

Early in his ministry, Jesus returned to his hometown of Nazareth and visited the synagogue, no doubt seeing many familiar faces. The service likely opened with a prayer for God's blessing, the *Shema* from Deuteronomy 6:4: "Listen, O Israel! The LORD is our God, the LORD alone." Then came readings from the Law.

Jesus then stood in front of the people and read the text of Isaiah 61:1-2. Everyone knew that the rabbis attributed this text to the Messiah, so imagine the shockwaves that rippled through the audience when Jesus declared, "The Scripture you've just heard has been fulfilled this very day!" (Luke 4:21).

It's important to note that Jesus read only part of Isaiah's prophecy. Isaiah predicted the Messiah would not only usher in favor but would also bring judgment. The original prophecy reads, "He has sent me to tell those who mourn that the time of the LORD's favor has come, *and* with it, the day of God's anger against their enemies" (Isaiah 61:2, emphasis added). Why did Jesus stop the prophecy partway? Why was only the portion that he read coming true before the people's very eyes? Because the "time of the Lord's favor" refers to Jesus' first coming, and "the day of God's anger" refers to his second coming and the time of judgment.

The people of Jesus' day were living in the age of God's abundant grace— and so are we. Jesus offers salvation to any who will receive him, and this is still the time of God's favor.

Are you telling as many people as you can about this favor? One day soon, the age of grace will be completed, and the time of judgment will fall. Before that happens, let's tell the Good News to as many people as we can.

A Tale of Two Sinners

[Jesus said,] "I tell you, her sins—and they are many—have been forgiven, so she has shown me much love. But a person who is forgiven little shows only little love." LUKE 7:47

Today's Bible reading tells the story of three people at a dinner—Simon the sinner; a woman who was a notorious sinner; and Jesus, the Savior of sinners. The word *sin* literally means "to miss the mark." Because any sin separates us from God, is one sin greater than another?

Certain greeting rituals were part of Jewish custom, and three things were always done when a guest arrived. First, the host gave the guest a kiss of peace as a mark of respect. Second, because everyone wore sandals and their feet were covered with dust and sweat, the host always provided guests with cool water to clean their feet. Finally, the host gave oils and ointments to help refresh a guest's hot, burned, and cracked feet.

Sometime during the dinner, a woman came into Simon's house and sat down behind Jesus. This woman was known around town; perhaps she was a local prostitute. She let down her hair, which for a Jewish woman was an act of immodesty, and she let her tears fall on Jesus. Then she kissed his feet and put perfume on them—fulfilling the duties of a host that Simon had neglected. Jesus used her as an example of love.

Simon sneered at the woman and at Jesus. He was thinking, *If Jesus were really as holy as I am, he would know her background and wouldn't let her touch him.* He was looking so hard at her sins, he couldn't see his own. God can't stand someone who is so self-righteous that he feels no need for forgiveness.

When you come into contact with sinners, are you filled with pride or compassion? Don't be like Simon. First, acknowledge your own sin. Then learn from Jesus and his tenderness toward sinful people who crossed his path.

Hello, Neighbor

The man wanted to justify his actions, so he asked Jesus, "And who is my neighbor?"   LUKE 10:29

Have you noticed how easy it seems to love people on the other side of the world but how difficult it is to love those who live next door? When Jesus was asked how to obtain eternal life, he answered, "Love God and love your neighbor." But to the person inquiring, a neighbor was someone exactly like him, a fellow Jew.

So Jesus explained that a neighbor is anyone who needs help. Then Jesus told the parable of the Good Samaritan, in which a Samaritan, whom the Jews would have considered an undesirable person, was the unlikely hero of the story. To make his point, Jesus did not have a Samaritan help another Samaritan or a Jew help a Jew. Rather, the parable told of a Samaritan who saw a Jew as his neighbor and rescued him.

Some of the stricter Jews of Jesus' day had become shrewd at complicating God's simplest commandments. They had transformed the Torah (the Old Testament Law) into 613 individual laws, of which 248 were positive commands and 365 were negative.

They never reached a consensus about which of these were binding and which were nonbinding. These religious leaders engaged in endless debates concerning these laws, which resulted in lots of theory but little real practice.

In contrast, the Bible teaches that the measure of our spirituality is seen in the result of our faith: "The Holy Spirit produces this kind of fruit in our lives: love, joy, peace, patience, kindness, goodness, faithfulness, gentleness, and self-control" (Galatians 5:22-23).

Jesus calls us to love our neighbors. As you pray for people and support missions on the other side of the world, don't forget to work on your relationships with your family, your coworkers, and others who cross your path.

Knocking on Heaven's Door

*Keep on asking, and you will receive what you ask for. Keep on seeking,
and you will find. Keep on knocking, and the door will be opened.*

LUKE 11:9

The Jewish liturgy supplied prayers for every occasion. The people prayed before and after meals. They prayed when they saw lightning, a new moon, comets, rain, or tempests. They prayed when they received good news. They prayed when they used new furniture and when they entered or left a city. There were also set times of prayer during the third, sixth, and ninth hours, or at approximately nine in the morning, noon, and three in the afternoon.

Jesus told his disciples to persist in asking, seeking, and knocking, not waiting for midnight emergencies to come to God. Rather, he told them to maintain ongoing communication with him, as we would in any close relationship. When Paul instructed us to "never stop praying" (1 Thessalonians 5:17), he wasn't telling us to spend twenty-four hours a day whispering prayers under our breath. That would be like putting prayer on autopilot. Jesus told us in Matthew 6:7-8, "When you pray, don't babble on and on as people of other religions do. They think their prayers are answered merely by repeating their words again and again. Don't be like them, for your Father knows exactly what you need even before you ask him!" The word Paul used in 1 Thessalonians meant "constantly recurring" or, in other words, returning to prayer on a regular basis. This is distinct from "constantly occurring." We need to make prayer a lifelong priority and not just something we do on Sundays or before meals, as if to say, "Praise the Lord, and pass the potatoes."

Our heavenly Father never tires of hearing from us. Don't be a stranger to the presence of God; come to his throne room often.

Prodigal

We had to celebrate. . . . Your brother was dead and has come back to life! He was lost, but now he is found! LUKE 15:32

Doesn't it feel good to locate something you've lost?

Jesus Christ told three parables about valuable items that were lost and then recovered: first, a wandering sheep; then a lost coin; and finally, a rebellious son.

According to Jewish law, the elder son would receive two-thirds of his father's inheritance, and the younger son would receive one-third. In Jesus' parable, the younger son came to his father with what was certainly a callous attitude and said, essentially, "Give me my share now; I'm going to get it when you die anyway, and I don't want to wait." Then he left home and squandered his money. When he finally wised up and returned home with a properly repentant attitude, his father welcomed him with a great celebration.

When the elder son saw the celebration, he blamed his father for treating his younger son better than he did his first son. He also revealed his discontentment with his place in the family.

The parable of the Prodigal Son reveals two types of sinners: One type is openly rebellious. The other is like the elder brother, whose sin remained hidden in his heart until he opened his mouth.

John Newton was seven when his mother, who had taught him the Scriptures, died. After being reared by a relative, Newton ran away, became an apprentice seaman in the British navy, and planned, in his own words, to "sin my fill." After Newton became involved in the slave trade, his life went from bad to worse. But as the years took their toll, he returned to God, becoming a pillar in the Church of England and writing the hymn "Amazing Grace."

In truth, each of us is a mess, but God can bring the prodigals home. Thank Jesus for saving you, and never give up on your rebellious friend or relative. God is in the business of saving the lost.

Defective Signposts

It would be better to be thrown into the sea with a millstone hung around your neck than to cause one of these little ones to fall into sin. LUKE 17:2

When we drive, we pay attention to road signs because they give direction and tell us the distance to our destinations. But what happens if the signs are inaccurate, unreadable, or simply not there?

One man reminisced, "When I was a lad, I often played on a wide common. Near its center, two roads crossed. Standing at the crossroad was a rickety signpost. One day I twisted it around in its socket and altered the arms so they pointed in the wrong direction. Ever since, I've wondered how many travelers I sent down the wrong road."

It's one thing to send travelers down the wrong path, but consider the eternal consequences of directing someone down the path to hell. There is only one thing worse than going to hell yourself: It's going to hell and knowing that a son, daughter, friend, or neighbor is there because he or she followed you.

Often I've wondered about leaders, musical icons, or even schoolteachers who promote an ungodly agenda. These "role models" can destroy the faith of their audiences.

"Little ones" in today's verse refers to young believers. Luke 15:1 also includes tax collectors and other notorious sinners who are learning to follow Christ.

As Christians, we take care not to cause anyone to sin or stumble on the way to heaven. How can we do this? Ask this question: Will my actions help those watching me or cause them to stumble on their journeys?

Paul expands on this principle when he writes, "You say, 'I am allowed to do anything'—but not everything is good for you. You say, 'I am allowed to do anything'—but not everything is beneficial. Don't be concerned for your own good but for the good of others" (1 Corinthians 10:23-24).

Our lives are signposts to the Savior and heaven. Is your signpost accurate and clearly readable? A lot could be riding on your example.

The Advantages of Being Short

[Zacchaeus] was too short to see over the crowd. So he ran ahead and climbed a sycamore-fig tree beside the road, for Jesus was going to pass that way. LUKE 19:3-4

In 1977, songwriter Randy Newman composed and recorded his highest-charting single ever. The lyrics of this not-so-flattering song about short people were stinging:

> They got little hands, little eyes
> They walk around tellin' great big lies.
> They got little noses and tiny little teeth
> They wear platform shoes on their nasty little feet. . . .
>
> Don't want no short people 'round here.

In today's reading, we learn that shortness has advantages. Zacchaeus climbed a tree to get a glimpse of Jesus. His short stature and curiosity led to his salvation.

Most of the Jewish population would have considered the rich tax collector the scum of the earth. He was barred from both the synagogue and the Temple in Jerusalem. In short (yes, pun intended), he was considered an untouchable, an outcast. But Christ specializes in cultural rejects, untouchables, and "impossible" cases.

Zacchaeus might have been wealthy, maybe even set for life, but that wasn't enough. So when he heard that Jesus was coming to town, he had to see the Messiah and climbed a tree to be able to see. To Zacchaeus's amazement and the amazement of everyone else watching, Jesus stopped at that tree, talked to Zacchaeus, and invited himself to Zacchaeus's home for a meal.

Are there some people you have given up trying to reach for the Lord? They may have questions about the meaning of life tumbling around in their minds. The truth is, from a spiritual perspective, each of us is short: Romans 3:23 says, "Everyone has sinned; we all fall short of God's glorious standard."

At one time, some people thought I was an impossible case, just like Zacchaeus. But when I accepted the invitation of Jesus, the Bread of Life, I discovered that he offers to provide the richest meal anyone can experience.

Heartburn

They said to each other, "Didn't our hearts burn within us as he talked with us on the road and explained the Scriptures to us?" LUKE 24:32

After the Crucifixion, Jesus' disciples were at the lowest point of their lives. Although Jesus had clearly predicted his death, they hadn't expected it. Now, fearing for their lives, the eleven remaining disciples were hiding in a locked room in Jerusalem.

The same day on which the disciples learned of the Resurrection, two of Jesus' followers were walking to Emmaus and discussing what had happened in Jerusalem. While they were talking, Jesus came and started to walk with them. As they talked, Jesus showed them from the Scriptures that the Messiah's death, burial, and resurrection were part of God's redemptive plan.

After Jesus had disappeared, the two people talked about how their hearts had burned as he explained the Scriptures to them. Their hearts apparently did not burn when they talked to him; their hearts did not burn while they talked with each other about him. But when they stopped talking and listened to him, the fire burned inside them.

Notice that their hearts didn't burn because they were hearing a new message. Jesus had reviewed the same Old Testament Scriptures they had heard when they were children, yet this time, the words seemed different, as if someone had opened the curtains and let light pour in.

Sometimes I hear Christians talk about getting a new revelation from God. But the truth is, everything we need can be found in what God has already spoken in the pages of the Bible. We don't need a new revelation. We need a fresh application of the timeless revelation given in the Scriptures.

Maybe Scripture has become familiar to you and dry when you read it. Maybe you still love Christ, but your passion has cooled. Some people say, "God doesn't speak like he once did," but the truth is that people don't listen the way they used to. Consider spending time today just listening for what God's Spirit wants to communicate to you.

August 6   READ JOHN 1:1-18

The First and Last Word

> *In the beginning the Word already existed.*
> *The Word was with God,*
> *and the Word was God.*

JOHN 1:1

Someone once asked why there are four Gospels. Origen, one of the early church fathers, answered, "There are not four gospels but a four-fold gospel." Of the four Gospels, John's is the most unusual. The other three, called the synoptic Gospels, are largely informational, but John's Gospel is both informational and inspirational as he pauses to explain or apply what he has written.

To our Western ears, John opens his Gospel in a strange way by calling Jesus Christ "the Word." But in the first century, this would not have seemed so unusual. The term translated "the Word" came from the Hebrew *memra* as a substitute for the divine name of God. The Greeks used the word *logos* as the self-expression of God. They noticed an ordered universe where the sun rose predictably every day, the stars moved, and the seasons came on a regular schedule. *Why* was there order? Philosophers said it was because there is a *logos*, or word, an ordering principle or reason.

God did much more than speak his words through the prophets or through letters, poems, or stories from inspired writers. God sent his Son as the ultimate "word," or communication, from heaven. As John 1:14 says, "The Word became human and made his home among us."

Imagine John's wonder as he began to understand the origin of Jesus. When John watched Jesus touch a leper, he was seeing God's care for his creatures. When Jesus wept over Jerusalem, it was God weeping over those who rejected him.

Because Jesus came to this world as both God and human, he knows all about you and your needs, fears, and dreams, and he is able to understand everything you feel. What a wonderful Savior!

New Birth

Jesus replied, "I tell you the truth, unless you are born again, you cannot see the Kingdom of God." JOHN 3:3

Until after I was converted, I had never heard the words *born again*. After having watched a Billy Graham crusade and turning to Jesus Christ, I tried to describe my experience. When I heard that Jesus had called it being reborn, I thought, *That's a perfect way to describe what has happened. I feel as if I have a whole new life and I've been born again.*

All forms of life reproduce after their kind, and natural life can't reproduce anything higher than itself. "Humans can reproduce only human life, but the Holy Spirit gives birth to spiritual life," Jesus said in John 3:6.

We can't change our nature. We are born sinners, and we need a new birth if anything about us is going to change. This new birth doesn't come through our bloodlines. We can't say, "My parents were Christians, so I am a Christian." We don't achieve it through our own efforts or through positive thinking. We can't read the right self-help book and apply its principles and hope to get to heaven on the basis of our conformity to those principles. No, the new birth is an act of God's Spirit, and without it, we are lost.

There is a legend about a man who became lost in his travels and wandered into a bog of quicksand. First, Confucius came by and saw him and remarked, "It is evident men should stay out of such places." A few moments later, Buddha saw the struggling man and remarked, "Let this man's plight be a lesson to the rest of the world." Next Muhammad saw the floundering man and said, "Alas, it is the will of God." Finally, Jesus came, reached out his hand, and said, "Take my hand, and I'll save you." It is only when we grab hold of Jesus that we find the true Savior.

Got Water?

Jesus replied, "Anyone who drinks this water will soon become thirsty again."   JOHN 4:13

When Jesus walked the earth, the strict rabbis prohibited other rabbis from speaking to women—even their wives or daughters—in public. One group, called the "Bruised and Bleeding Pharisees," shut their eyes when they saw a woman, even if doing so caused them to walk into walls. If a rabbi was seen speaking to women in public, it meant the end of his reputation.

Jesus didn't cater to the social system of the day, choosing instead to stay focused on people as individuals. He loved people, and the Samaritan woman in today's passage was no exception. Every day she took a forty-five-minute walk to the well to draw water. Jesus used the drinking of physical water to illustrate the spiritual principle of spiritual thirst.

Think about any worldly amusement or life experience that people pursue to satisfy their deep inward thirst. Each time they have to return for more or try something new because they're still thirsty. In their endless quests for satisfaction, they drink from the wrong wells. Perhaps they think, *If I had an affair with that person, I'd be happy* or *If I could attain a level of fame, I'd feel great* or *If I take these drugs, the pain will go away*. If statements like these were accurate, the happiest people on earth would be prostitutes, drug addicts, and people with unlimited financial resources, but that's not true.

People keep returning to the wells of this world because no matter how deeply they have drunk, they are still thirsty. The only way to permanently quench their thirst is to drink of the perpetual well of spiritual life in Christ.

Have you returned to the wells that you left when you came to know Jesus? Do they still hold an appeal for you? If so, be prepared for a long, dry life. But through a vital relationship with Christ, you will see your appetites change to the ones that Jesus alone satisfies.

The Pool

[Jesus] asked him, "Would you like to get well?"

"I can't, sir," the sick man said, "for I have no one to put me into the pool when the water bubbles up. Someone else always gets there ahead of me." JOHN 5:6-7

When I was a kid, I loved to swim, but my swimming pool in California was very different from the pool of Bethesda where the unnamed man in today's reading lived. Originally, this pool was to provide drinking water for the city's inhabitants as well as a place for washing up after the Temple sacrifices. The pool of Bethesda actually consisted of two large pools and was encircled by a colonnaded porch. Below the pool was a subterranean stream that bubbled from time to time. The people believed the bubbles were made by an angel who stirred the water and the first person who entered the pool would be healed. For this reason, it became a gathering place for the hopelessly diseased in Jerusalem.

Jesus came to a man who had been incapacitated for so long that he may have been well known in the community. This man was an ideal person for Jesus' miracle to have its greatest impact.

You've probably heard people say, "God helps those who help themselves." Nothing could be further from the truth. In fact, the opposite is true, because left to his own strength, the man in this account was in a hopeless situation.

Imagine his surprise when Jesus commanded him to get up and carry away his bed. But it was impossible for him to obey such a command. In fact, Jesus' words may have sounded cruel to those who heard them.

How could Jesus say such a thing? Here's how: Whenever God commands something, he also gives the power to obey that command. If God's Spirit has been impressing on you the fact that there is something he wants you to do, do it. God will give you the power you need, and he will be glorified.

Inlet and Outlet

Anyone who believes in me may come and drink! For the Scriptures declare, "Rivers of living water will flow from his heart." JOHN 7:38

Among the various bodies of water in the world, the Dead Sea is unique. It contains no organic life of any kind because it has no outlet. Water pours in from the Jordan, Arnon, and Kidron rivers, yet nothing flows out. Many inlets and no outlets create one Dead Sea. Our lives can be like the Dead Sea if we are always taking in and never giving out.

The account in today's passage took place during the Festival of Shelters, which celebrated Israel's journey in the wilderness and their wandering in tents, or tabernacles. On the last day of the festival, the priests took water from the pool of Siloam and dumped it in the Temple courts to commemorate how God brought water from a rock in the desert.

Today's key verse contains a twofold statement. First, faith in Jesus will quench your own thirst, and second, faith in Jesus will turn you into a conduit through which he will extend satisfaction to others. Many Christians overlook this second part. It's true that when we come to Jesus, we are satisfied, but that is not the point of the promise. The key is that we become vessels or conduits of Christ's refreshment to others.

Much of our modern Christianity is lacking. If you listen to some Christians, you might believe that Christ's purpose was to save them and satisfy them, which makes Christianity nothing more than a bless-me club, and Jesus nothing more than a spiritual Santa whose job is to dispense joy. This kind of thinking produces shallow Christians.

Yes, Jesus gives you joy and meets your deepest needs, but he wants your joy and satisfaction to spill into the lives of others. Is your faith overflowing to others? If so, people will be turning to you to learn the source of your satisfaction.

Storming Death's Castle

Jesus told her, "I am the resurrection and the life. Anyone who believes in me will live, even after dying. Everyone who lives in me and believes in me will never ever die. Do you believe this, Martha?" JOHN 11:25-26

About four hundred years before Jesus came to the earth, Socrates drank poison and lay down to die. "Shall we live again?" his friends asked.

"I hope so, but no man can know," the philosopher replied. If these friends had known Jesus, they might have had a very different perspective.

Experts tell us that it's common for grieving people to experience a progression of emotions that includes denial, anger, bargaining, depression, and finally, acceptance. Periods of withdrawal and outbursts of tears are also typical. In the throes of grief, even rational and spiritual people may say things that they otherwise would not say. When Lazarus died, his sister Martha came to Jesus and forcefully expressed both her disappointment and her faith.

In response, Jesus made his fifth "I am" statement in John: "I am the resurrection and the life." We think of resurrection as an incident, but Jesus emphasizes it as his identity, as if to say, "Wherever I am, I change things. Today I am storming the castle of death. I will show you that I have come to destroy this enemy called death and to bring life."

Jesus asked Martha the question that each of us must answer: Do you believe? If so, it makes all the difference for right now and forever.

Elisabeth Elliot knows firsthand what it is to have her dreams dashed, first when the Waodani of Ecuador killed her husband, Jim, and again when cancer consumed her second husband. In *Facing the Death of Someone You Love*, Elliot wrote, "I cannot thank God for the murder of one and the excruciating disintegration of another, but I can thank God for the promise of His presence. I can thank Him that He is still in charge—in the face of life's worst terrors."

And so Jesus asks each of us, "Do you believe?"

How to Be Happy Every Day

Now that you know these things, God will bless you for doing them.

JOHN 13:17

When feet get dirty and sweaty, they stink. In Jesus' day, when guests had been invited to dinner, they washed and put on sandals. But by the time they arrived at their destinations, their feet were covered with dust. Usually, the host offered water so his guests could wash their feet.

When Jesus washed the feet of his disciples, he was teaching them through his example that they were to humbly serve one another. They knew this truth because Jesus had taught it before, but now he demonstrated it by his actions and told them that they should follow his example.

Our world wants to know, "How many people work for you?" Jesus asks, "How many people are you working for?" The disciples took their cues from worldly structures in which humility was despised and something for only slaves and barbarians, which explains why Jesus' example was so shocking to them.

According to Jesus, happy—or blessed—people are people who serve. In other words, humility leads to happiness. But here's the point: It is not knowledge *about* humility that counts but rather the actions that result from humility. Our reading of this passage can stir us emotionally and challenge us intellectually, but it can't bless us spiritually unless we do what it says.

It's important to note that humility doesn't mean that you think "meanly" of yourself. In fact, truly humble people don't think much about themselves at all. If you want to be a happy person in your everyday life, here's how to do it: Think less about yourself, think more about others, and put into practice what you know to be true about God's will for you.

Jesus Is Praying—for You!

I pray that they will all be one, just as you and I are one—as you are in me, Father, and I am in you. And may they be in us so that the world will believe you sent me. JOHN 17:21

When I was a kid, I used to eavesdrop on my parents and my brothers. I'd walk to the door and listen. If they were on the phone, I'd pick up another one and listen in on their conversations.

Now, eavesdropping isn't a habit we should cultivate, but in today's reading, we get to listen in as Jesus prays his longest recorded prayer. Jesus is praying for his disciples, and we learn what Jesus wants most to express to his Father before he dies on the cross. In a sense, we are able to stand on holy ground and gaze into the heart of God as Jesus prays.

Four times, Jesus prays for the unity of believers. Why is this significant? Today's verse tells us that it is because of the unity of believers that "the world will believe" that God the Father sent Jesus the Son. The unity of Christians proves the authenticity of the Christian message.

Think for a minute about the disagreements churches have about whether to wear robes, the color of pews, styles of music, length of hair, or mode of baptism. The truth is, instead of drawing people toward the church, these issues bring them into an environment characterized by conflict. A bickering and divided church turns people off.

When a recent poll asked people why they don't attend church, it found that 49 percent believed the church was not effective in helping people to find meaning and 56 percent felt the church was more concerned about organizational issues than about spiritual issues.

As Christians, we live before the watchful eyes of the world. What impression of our faith are we giving others?

Finished!

When Jesus had tasted it, he said, "It is finished!" Then he bowed his head and released his spirit. JOHN 19:30

The first words babies speak are pretty much the same. The last words people speak, however, depend on how those people lived.

Today's reading contains the last seven utterances Jesus made during the six hours he hung on the cross. While Jesus Christ was doing his greatest work, he uttered his greatest words: "It is finished."

Make sure you don't misunderstand these last words of Jesus. He did not say, "*I'm* finished," which would have meant, "My life is over." He didn't say, "*We* are finished," which would have referred to the end of everything he had worked for while he was on the earth. If Jesus did not mean those things, what did his words mean? What was finished?

First, Christ had completed his horrendous suffering. Men had done their worst to the Messiah, and never again would the Father turn his face from his Son.

Second, Jesus had completed, or fulfilled, the righteous requirements of the law of God. Humankind was unable to meet God's standard of perfection, but Jesus was. Even today, some people say, "I live by the Ten Commandments, and that's all the religion I need." Yet James 2:10 says, "The person who keeps all of the laws except one is as guilty as a person who has broken all of God's laws."

The third thing that Jesus finished was to break Satan's power to hold humanity captive. In Genesis 3, God had promised that one day Eve's offspring would strike the head of the serpent. Jesus' death and resurrection stripped Satan of his power: "Only as a human being could [the Son] die, and only by dying could he break the power of the devil, who had the power of death" (Hebrews 2:14).

Finally, Jesus' words declared that he had completed our redemption and it would never need to be repeated. The great word of the gospel is not *do* but *done.*

Rejoice that God finishes what he begins.

A Writer's Passion

These are written so that you may continue to believe that Jesus is the Messiah, the Son of God, and that by believing in him you will have life by the power of his name. JOHN 20:31

Writers are often motivated by a passion for their subjects. The verses in today's reading express the passion and purpose driving John as he records the stories and scenes of Jesus' life. Although John's Gospel is clearly evangelistic, its intent is by no means limited to evangelism.

Faith must have content, and the Gospel of John provides marvelous sustenance for faith. John is an inspirational writer, but he also pauses to explain things or to give readers application. The vocabulary is simple—we need to remember that John started as a Galilean fisherman—but the truths are profound.

Two great themes run through the book: faith and unbelief. Frequently John points out either a response of faith or a response of unbelief when people meet Jesus. John included these stories to encourage people to trust in God so they can have life in Christ.

For humanity, life is the highest possible experience, and I'm not referring just to biological life or to existence on an animal level. Real life is broader than a focus on food, drink, or clothing.

Once I saw an old, beat-up Volkswagen bus at a gas station. The vehicle had rust, and the paint was chipped away, but the hippie driver had a huge smile on his bearded face. I understood the reason for the smile when I spotted his bumper sticker, which said, "Without Jesus, you ain't livin'!"

The words from John focus on abundant living. If you want to really live, you need Jesus. Ask the Lord to give you an enthusiasm for life and a sense of expectancy about what awaits you around the corner.

Staying Plugged In

You will receive power when the Holy Spirit comes upon you. And you will be my witnesses, telling people about me everywhere—in Jerusalem, throughout Judea, in Samaria, and to the ends of the earth.   ACTS 1:8

What kind of power does it take to forgive wrongs against us, to have patience in adversity, to love those who treat us unlovingly, or to stand up for what is right when it feels as if the whole world is actively pursuing what is wrong?

Today we began reading the book of Acts, in which Jesus' disciples are clearly different from the fearful men in Luke's Gospel. What happened? How were timid, obscure fishermen transformed into bold figures who carried the message of life? The answer is the Holy Spirit. It is the power of God's Spirit that gives life to those who are lost, directs the selection of missionaries, and provides wisdom for governing the New Testament church.

Before Jesus' followers could "go and make disciples of all the nations" (Matthew 28:19), they had to be equipped for the work. Soldiers don't fight without their weapons, and mechanics don't fix cars without their tools. In the same way, Christians cannot effectively represent Christ unless the Holy Spirit gives them the power to do so. Jesus wanted to make certain his disciples were plugged into the power source of God's Spirit.

From the Greek word *dunamis*, which means "power," we get our word *dynamic*. Jesus wants us to work with a spiritual dynamic. It was only through the empowerment of the Holy Spirit that the disciples spread the gospel in Jerusalem and then moved out in ever-widening circles until they reached the whole world. Their task was enormous, and it required supernatural ability.

If you are feeling burned out spiritually, perhaps you've been attempting God's work in your own power. Get plugged into the power of the Holy Spirit.

Back to Basics

All the believers devoted themselves to the apostles' teaching, and to fellowship, and to sharing in meals (including the Lord's Supper), and to prayer. ACTS 2:42

Sometimes churches can complicate simple things, overshadowing the essentials with the unnecessary, and the truly important with the urgent.

When this began to happen in the counterculture of the 1960s, some reacted with placards that read, "Jesus yes! Christianity no." The protesters felt the church had moved away from the basics and added unnecessary fluff.

Four elements in today's verse characterized a Spirit-directed church in the New Testament, and they can be summed up with four words: *learning* (teaching), *loving*, *worshiping*, and *praying*. This pattern is important for the church as an organization, but it is an equally good model for individual Christians, because these four basics provide a healthy balance for our spiritual lives.

Notice that at the top of this list of basics is the apostles' teaching of the Word of God. Instruction forms the foundation for the other three elements. The Bible teaches us how to love, how to worship, and how to pray. We take our cues from Scripture because it's the Word of God that does the work of God in the lives of the people of God. The believers devoted themselves to this and the other three essentials. How devoted are you to these spiritual priorities in your own life?

Today's church has a need for anointed preaching, but it also needs Christians who listen with their hearts, not just with their heads, and have an openness to receiving God's Word. First Peter 2:2 admonishes, "Crave pure spiritual milk so that you will grow into a full experience of salvation. Cry out for this nourishment." As you approach God's Word today, ask God for the desire and wisdom to apply it to your life.

Perspective

When they heard the report, all the believers lifted their voices together in prayer to God: "O Sovereign Lord, Creator of heaven and earth, the sea, and everything in them." ACTS 4:24

While visiting New York City, my son and I traveled to the top of the Empire State Building and took in the view. From that vantage point, we gained a perspective that showed us the borders of the city, its boroughs and bridges, with a clarity we could not have had on the ground.

Prayer can change our perspective in a similar way. As we go "up" to God in prayer, we can get a different perspective about how we approach life. After the disciples had been arrested and commanded not to talk about Jesus in the city of Jerusalem, they gathered for prayer, and these prayers gave them a clearer perspective, something like looking out from the top of the Empire State Building.

As the disciples began to pray, they realized to whom they were speaking. They were not engaging Herod, the local ruler, or Caesar in Rome. They were talking to the One who held all authority and power. This perspective helped them to get a firm grip on their earthly position and their decisions for the future.

They started with the words, "O Sovereign Lord," literally *despot*, an uncommon title for God in the New Testament. It means an absolute ruler, a dictator, or an autocrat. The disciples took comfort in God's sovereignty.

The best way to begin prayer is with the recognition that you're addressing God, the Autocrat of the universe and the One with absolute authority. The prophet Jeremiah did this when he prayed, "O Sovereign LORD! You made the heavens and earth by your strong hand and powerful arm. Nothing is too hard for you!" (Jeremiah 32:17). If you have a problem, first make a perspective adjustment and boldly address your heavenly Father with a clear sense of who he is.

When God's Kids Fight

As the believers rapidly multiplied, there were rumblings of discontent.
The Greek-speaking believers complained about the Hebrew-speaking
believers, saying that their widows were being discriminated against in
the daily distribution of food.   ACTS 6:1

Satan had failed to destroy the church through persecution, which only made the church grow. Satan also failed to overcome the church through the corruption of Ananias and Sapphira because God swiftly judged their dishonesty, and the message of the gospel spread again.

You've probably heard the old staying, "If you can't beat 'em, join 'em." This tactic of distraction and division is still a problem. Whenever a church is racked with internal conflict, its message is lost in the conflict. When the energy is lost, the church becomes preoccupied with itself and finds it difficult to reach the lost world.

In Acts 6, the church had a people problem that threatened to divide it. The explosive growth in the early church made it difficult for the apostles to minister to everyone. Church growth is a blessing, but it can also have an adverse effect, which is a perceived lack of concern on the part of the leaders. Can't you hear some of the original members of the Jerusalem church lamenting? "We remember what it was like when there were only 120 of us. Oh, for the days of the upper room, when our group was so intimate and loving. It's not the same anymore."

Even if the widows in today's reading were overlooked for a time, murmuring is not the proper response. Proverbs 6:19 reminds us that one of the things God hates is "a person who sows discord in a family." There *was* a problem, and some of the widows *were* neglected, but the murmuring only made the problem worse.

Do you often find yourself complaining about your church? If so, maybe you've made it all about you instead of focusing on Jesus and worshiping him. Instead of complaining, look for ways to encourage your church leaders.

When Hunter Becomes Prey

[Saul] fell to the ground and heard a voice saying to him, "Saul! Saul! Why are you persecuting me?" ACTS 9:4

Many people cross our paths as friends, relatives, or coworkers. You may have prayed for some of them for a long time, even years, and still don't see any change. Do they seem beyond hope?

Saul of Tarsus would have been one of those people. This radical young man never did anything in moderation. In fact, he threw himself headlong into every pursuit. In today's reading, Saul was headed to Damascus, about 160 miles northeast of Jerusalem. The synagogues there already had Christians because many believers had fled to Damascus during the persecution in Acts 8:1. Saul was on a mission to round up the Jewish believers and take them to Jerusalem under arrest. Of course, God had other plans.

As Saul walked along the road, he had an encounter with the living Christ that stopped him dead in his tracks and left him helpless on the ground. Saul, the mighty hunter, had suddenly become the prey of Jesus. Some people just won't listen until they're knocked down.

A humorous story is often told of a stubborn donkey whose owner couldn't get his animal to budge. A neighbor saw his frustration and offered to help. He picked up a two-by-four and knocked the animal squarely between the eyes. Immediately, the donkey cooperated. The surprised owner asked why the donkey complied, to which his neighbor responded, "First I had to get his attention."

David prayed, "I used to wander off until you disciplined me; but now I closely follow your word" (Psalm 119:67). Of course, God doesn't use a two-by-four, but he does discipline us to "get our attention."

The early church thought Saul was beyond reach; in fact, the mention of his name made them fearful. Can you think of someone that you'd consider a lost cause? Don't give up praying. The story of Saul's conversion on the road to Damascus proves that no one is beyond God's reach.

Growing, Growing, Gone!

After more fasting and prayer, the men laid their hands on them and sent them on their way. So Barnabas and Saul were sent out by the Holy Spirit. They went down to the seaport of Seleucia and then sailed for the island of Cyprus. ACTS 13:3-4

How do you know if a church is healthy? What did Jesus have in mind when he said, "You are Peter (which means 'rock'), and upon this rock I will build my church, and all the powers of hell will not conquer it" (Matthew 16:18)? He knew the truth of this saying: When saved people become serving people and serving people become sensitive people, then sensitive people become *sent* people.

In Antioch, prophets and teachers used their spiritual gifts to serve others in the church. Among those believers in Antioch were individuals particularly sensitive to the Holy Spirit's leading as the Spirit identified Christians who should do the specific work of evangelism, and the church sent them out. Today's Bible reading marks the beginning of Paul's missionary journeys.

It is the mark of a healthy church that its members become sent-out Christians. This progression is evident in the book of Acts, where converts become disciples and disciples become apostles, or "sent ones."

Robert Speer (1867–1947), one of the early leaders of the Student Volunteer Movement, said, "If you want to follow Jesus Christ, you must follow him to the ends of the earth, for that is where he is going," and "We cannot think of God . . . without thinking of him as a missionary God."

A sign in front of one church said, "Too many Christians are no longer fishers of men but keepers of the aquarium." With that in mind, let's take our cues from today's Bible reading. Pray for increased sensitivity to God's Spirit.

What steps are you taking today to grow in your faith and to tell the world about Jesus? You can go yourself, or you can send others, but doing nothing is not a viable option.

Fork in the Road

Coming to the borders of Mysia, they headed north for the province of Bithynia, but again the Spirit of Jesus did not allow them to go there.

ACTS 16:7

Guidance is a combination of God's aptitude and our attitudes. The seventeenth-century French writer François Fénelon said, "The wind of God is always blowing, but you must hoist your sail."

Consider for a moment how God directs you and communicates his will. If you are waiting for him to use one particular way, it's time to broaden your expectations, because God has many ways of directing you. As Bible teacher Kent Hughes puts it, "God's guidance is a multifaceted jewel."

When God gave the law to the Jewish people in the desert, he thundered on Mount Sinai. When Jesus was transfigured with Moses and Elijah, the Lord provided another dramatic example of his guiding hand. To Elijah on Mount Horeb, God spoke through "the sound of a gentle whisper" (1 Kings 19:12).

Sometimes God gave guidance through the reading of Scripture; other times God guided his people by stopping them in their tracks. In today's reading, Paul and his missionary team saw God close the door. He told them specifically, "No, you can't go there." God's no is just as important as his "go."

Psalm 37:23 says, "The LORD directs the steps of the godly. He delights in every detail of their lives," but God also directs the "stops" of the godly. And occasionally, God resorts to more severe methods when his people aren't inclined to follow his leading. Do you remember how the Lord handled the stubborn prophet Jonah when he refused to go to Nineveh?

Whichever method God uses to direct your steps, learn to be sensitive to and trust his guidance. Remember the words of Corrie ten Boom, a Dutch survivor of Nazi concentration camps, who said, "When the train goes through the tunnel and it gets dark, you don't throw away your ticket and jump off. You sit still and trust the engineer."

Prepare for Impact

Paul lived and worked with [Aquila and Priscilla], for they were tentmakers just as he was. Each Sabbath found Paul at the synagogue, trying to convince the Jews and Greeks alike.   ACTS 18:3-4

Here's a quick quiz for you:

1. Name five of the wealthiest people in world.
2. Name ten Nobel Prize winners.
3. Name the last six best-actor/actress Oscar winners.

How did you do?

Now, answer these questions:

1. List three teachers who helped you in school.
2. Name three friends who have helped you through a difficult time.
3. Name five people who have taught you something worthwhile.

I suspect that you did much better on the second quiz. The lesson is that the people who have had maximum impact on your life are those who cared about you and showed it, not those with the greatest credentials or the most money or awards.

In today's reading, Paul walked fifty miles south, from Athens to Corinth, where he faced a huge challenge of lust and immorality. Yet during his time there, Paul had maximum impact on the people of that city.

First, Paul had an impact through his relationships. He became friends with Aquila and Priscilla and then lived in their home for a year and a half. Imagine living with the apostle Paul!

Paul also made an impact through his craftsmanship. Paul, a tentmaker, shared this trade with Aquila and Priscilla. As they worked together, the couple could observe Paul's work ethic.

How are you modeling the Christian life for your family and your coworkers?

St. Francis of Assisi said, "Preach the gospel at all times—if necessary, use words." If our lives don't clearly give evidence of the reality of our faith, nothing we say will have any lasting impact.

The Deadly Art of Procrastination

As [Paul] reasoned with them about righteousness and self-control and the coming day of judgment, Felix became frightened. "Go away for now," he replied. "When it is more convenient, I'll call for you again."

ACTS 24:25

It has been said that procrastinators have a creed: "Procrastination is my sin. It brings me naught but sorrow. I know that I should stop it; in fact, I will . . . tomorrow."

In today's reading, Felix, the governor of Judea, was fascinated by Paul's reasoned presentation of the Good News and actually grew terrified as he heard about the coming judgment.

Why did he have such a reaction? Apparently God's truth had produced a level of conviction in Felix. But although Felix heard Paul's testimony several more times, he never budged from his hardened position.

In contrast, when an earthquake awakened the Philippian jailer, he was horrified to find the prison doors wide open. Fearing that the inmates had escaped, he prepared to kill himself. But Paul called out, "'Stop! Don't kill yourself! We are all here!' The jailer called for lights and ran to the dungeon and fell down trembling before Paul and Silas. Then he brought them out and asked, 'Sirs, what must I do to be saved?' They replied, 'Believe in the Lord Jesus and you will be saved'" (Acts 16:28-31).

Here's another question: What must I do to be lost? The answer is absolutely nothing. I personally knew a man who procrastinated about believing in Jesus, and then one day he died in a motorcycle accident. That man was my brother. The road marked "Tomorrow" leads only to a town called "Nowhere."

During the American Revolution, a Hessian commander was playing cards when a courier delivered an urgent message: "General Washington is crossing the Delaware River." The commander put the letter in his pocket and finished the game before reading it. His procrastination was his undoing. Those few minutes of delay cost him his life.

What are you "putting off" until tomorrow? Take action on it today.

Prison Ministry

For the next two years, Paul lived in Rome at his own expense. He
welcomed all who visited him, boldly proclaiming the Kingdom of God
and teaching about the Lord Jesus Christ. And no one tried to stop him.

ACTS 28:30-31

What was Paul's first order of business when he arrived in a city? I've often wondered whether he asked for directions to the city jail so he'd know where he was going to spend the night. Paul spent his share of time in prison throughout his missionary journeys.

How did Paul feel about his confinement? Did he sulk? Did he regret the choices that eventually brought him a prison sentence? Hardly! From his cell in Rome, Paul wrote this to his friends at Philippi: "I want you to know . . . that everything that has happened to me here has helped to spread the Good News. For everyone here, including the whole palace guard, knows that I am in chains because of Christ" (Philippians 1:12-13).

Like a runner who waits expectantly for the shot so the race can begin, Paul anticipated the opportunities that imprisonment brought. For example, he was chained to alternating prison guards who couldn't help but hear the message Paul preached to his many visitors. Paul was the prisoner, but his guards were a captive audience when Paul preached the gospel.

Do you feel chained to something? Maybe you left your career to care for your family, and now you feel confined. I recall a housewife named Susanna Wesley who had nineteen children, including John and Charles Wesley, whose preaching ministry shook the British Isles.

Maybe you feel chained to a bed in a hospital or nursing home. Charlotte Elliott was chained to her room as an invalid, yet she wrote great hymns there, including "Just As I Am." And while confined in Wartburg Castle, Martin Luther translated the New Testament into German.

Perhaps the chains of your circumstances are accomplishing far more than you can imagine. Ask God to give you a new, eternal perspective on your situation today.

Stupid Smart People

Claiming to be wise, they instead became utter fools. ROMANS 1:22

While driving down a highway, a man felt his tire go flat, so he pulled over to the side of the road. He happened to park beside a hospital for the insane, and one of the patients was on the other side of the fence. The patient stood and watched as the man removed the lug nuts, placing them in the hubcap so he wouldn't lose them. But he accidentally tilted the hubcap, and all the nuts spilled into a sewer pipe! Unsure how to repair his tire, the man stood there, scratching his head.

Suddenly, the patient said, "Why don't you take a nut off of each of the other wheels and use them on this wheel? Then you can drive to the filling station and buy replacements." The man looked at the patient in amazement. "Why didn't I think of that? You're in an institution, and I'm not, yet you thought of the solution."

The patient replied, "I may be crazy, but I'm not stupid."

When children peer into a telescope for the first time, they are usually struck with the vastness of the universe, even though they can see only a small part. They may think with wonder, *God must be big and powerful!* Creation is so beautiful and vast that someone must come along and plant lies in children's hearts in order for them *not* to believe in God.

The Bible doesn't say that smart people don't believe; it says the opposite: "Only fools say in their hearts, 'There is no God'" (Psalm 53:1). I believe it takes more faith to believe in evolution than to believe that a loving Creator intelligently designed us. Our universities are filled with "thinkers" who love to put down the idea of God and exalt the philosophies of man. According to God's Word, such "thinkers" are really fools in disguise. Thank God today that you're no fool. Let's celebrate the revealed Creator.

The Word Everyone Hates

Everyone has sinned; we all fall short of God's glorious standard.

ROMANS 3:23

Sin has never been a popular word, the present being no exception; to modern ears it sounds like an outdated and puritanical concept. Most people today believe man is an animal and without moral values unless the outside culture gives them to him.

Today's Bible passage, however, begs to differ. Paul reveals a snapshot of the human heart that portrays its utter sinfulness. In his letter to the Romans, Paul uses the word *sin* some forty-nine times. In the original language, the word for *sin* is an archery term that means "to miss the target." In this game we call life, no person has ever hit the mark with a perfect shot. The Bible declares we are sinners both by nature and by choice, and our good actions won't ever make up for our bad ones. Isaiah 64:6 declares, "When we display our righteous deeds, they are nothing but filthy rags."

I've stood at the base of the Tetons at Jackson Lake in Wyoming. Sometimes, early in the morning, the lake is calm, and a glorious reflection of the Tetons is mirrored on the surface. If you take one little flat stone and skip it across the surface of the water, the image of the Tetons becomes distorted and marred. Adam's sin was like that stone, ruining God's perfect image in mankind. But it doesn't stop there—you and I inherited that broken image, and we further distort God's perfect reflection with our own sinful choices.

It may not be a popular topic, but the Bible makes it painfully clear—sin is real. You're guilty, and so am I. But together let's thank God that we don't have to stay that way: Through Jesus Christ, God can remove our guilt and restore our relationship with him—and the reflection of his beautiful image.

At Peace

Since we have been made right in God's sight by faith, we have peace with God because of what Jesus Christ our Lord has done for us.   ROMANS 5:1

Whenever a judge acquits a criminal, an audible sigh is heard throughout the courtroom. For the accused, peace replaces anxiety with the words *not guilty*.

What if an acquittal from God, the judge of the universe, depended on my works? Some days I might feel peaceful, yet most days I would not. Psalm 130:3 says, "LORD, if you kept a record of our sins, who . . . could ever survive?" Thankfully, God has provided a foolproof plan for his forgiveness—a plan that doesn't depend on good works outweighing the bad ones. Romans 10:9 says, "If you confess with your mouth that Jesus is Lord and believe in your heart that God raised him from the dead, you will be saved."

When we raise the white flag of surrender and call upon Jesus, God makes a conscious declaration of peace between us and himself because of the sacrificial death of Jesus Christ. Sometimes we experience his peace at work within us, but other times we may not. Instead, we must choose to believe by faith that we indeed have peace with God.

Isaiah 48:22 declares, "'There is no peace for the wicked,' says the LORD." This verse doesn't refer to the feeling of peace. Some unbelievers are deceived by their good and peaceful feelings. Their peace is not from God; rather, because of sin, there is enmity between themselves and God. Imagine if a man commits a crime and flees the United States; he may feel great, but if he returns and gets caught, he will be put in jail.

If you've received Jesus Christ as the solution for your sin, you're no longer at war with God. At the cross, Jesus signed the ultimate peace treaty in his blood, bringing peace to our rebel souls and making heaven our home. Pause to thank Jesus for paying the ultimate price for your peace.

The Freedom of Slavery

Now you are free from your slavery to sin, and you have become slaves to righteous living.   ROMANS 6:18

"I am the master of my fate: I am the captain of my soul," wrote British poet William Ernest Henley in his famous poem "Invictus." Unfortunately for the many who subscribe to Henley's philosophy, those words are simply not true. The truth is, we all have a master: We are either a slave to God or a slave to something else. Romans 6:16 puts it this way: "You can be a slave to sin, which leads to death, or you can choose to obey God, which leads to righteous living."

Imagery of a master owning a servant is common in the New Testament. Throughout the Roman Empire, a master totally owned and controlled each slave; there was no such thing as part-time service. The apostle Paul wrote in 1 Corinthians 7:22: "If you were a slave when the Lord called you, you are now free in the Lord. And if you were free when the Lord called you, you are now a slave of Christ."

You may be thinking, *I thought Jesus bought my freedom. What's up with this slavery stuff?* You're right—Galatians 4:5 says that "God sent him to buy freedom for us." But Scripture also teaches that "you must give yourselves to be slaves to righteous living so that you will become holy" (Romans 6:19). You experience true freedom when you are at peace with God, living the rich, full life he desires for you. So today, fix your eyes on your Master and Lord, Jesus, and follow him; you won't regret it because "wherever the Spirit of the Lord is, there is freedom" (2 Corinthians 3:17).

A Soft Pillow for a Tired Heart

We know that God causes everything to work together for the good of those who love God and are called according to his purpose for them.

ROMANS 8:28

Today's verse is a favorite of many Christians who can recount numerous times that its words proved to be true. Evangelist Reuben A. Torrey called this verse "a soft pillow for a tired heart," and I've laid my own head on it during trying times.

It might be easier for you to believe if it read "some things" or even "most things" instead of "everything," but this verse contains no qualifications or limitations. In fact, when we love God, he works in us through our hardest times, no matter what they are.

When Christians fail to understand this, they may become bitter.

During the great San Francisco earthquake in 1906, a woman walked through the debris with a smile on her face.

"How can you smile at a time like this?" someone asked.

"I rejoice because I serve a God who can shake the world," she said.

Think about it. Life is not the result of chance or of impersonal fate. For the Christian, behind everything that happens is a personal God who cares. He approves everything before it comes our way.

Especially in the midst of suffering, it is easy to lose this perspective. But because God has a plan, we can believe Proverbs 3:5: "Trust in the LORD with all your heart; do not depend on your own understanding."

A boy grew frustrated as he tried unsuccessfully to put together a puzzle in which some pieces were bright and others dark, some large and others small. His dad put it together in minutes, saying, "I saw the picture in the puzzle, where you saw only the individual pieces."

We can't see the full picture of our lives because we are living out the pieces. But we can trust our Father, who sees the whole picture.

A Jew for Jesus

My people, my Jewish brothers and sisters. I would be willing to be forever cursed—cut off from Christ!—if that would save them. ROMANS 9:3

I love the nation of Israel. In fact, at one time I lived in an Israeli farming community called a kibbutz.

God has wonderfully provided for this covenant people. Although they make up only one-tenth of 1 percent of the world's population, they have won more than 25 percent of all Nobel Prizes and hold some 30 percent of all awards in music, science, and literature.

Yet as a whole, their nation is blind to the identity of their Messiah, their only hope of salvation. My strong love for Israel and the Jewish people pales when compared to that of Jesus and the apostle Paul.

Jesus wept over Jerusalem and its refusal to acknowledge him as the Messiah: "As he came closer to Jerusalem and saw the city ahead, he began to weep. 'How I wish today that you of all people would understand the way to peace. But now it is too late, and peace is hidden from your eyes'" (Luke 19:41-42).

Imagine someone who has come to know Jesus Christ and yet is willing to be lost forever if it would bring about the salvation of his people. That's the depth of Paul's love and desire that they believe in Christ. In today's verse, Paul declares, "I would be willing to be forever cursed—cut off from Christ!—if that would save them."

Whenever I'm in Israel and visit the Western Wall where Jews still pray, I think of these powerful verses from the New Testament.

As a Pharisee, Paul had been blind to Jesus' identity, too, so he understood how the Jews felt, and his passion was to bring them the hope of salvation. Is your love for the people of your country—or even for your own family—as strong as Paul's? If not, ask God to deepen your concern for the lost world around you.

September 1 READ ROMANS 12:1-21

Squirming off the Altar

Give your bodies to God because of all he has done for you. Let them be a living and holy sacrifice—the kind he will find acceptable. This is truly the way to worship him. ROMANS 12:1

In the Old Testament, sacrifices were part of the worship system. People brought their animals to the altar of the Tabernacle or Temple, where they were killed and then burned. In other words, the sacrifices lost their lives and were consumed in the process. The New Testament listeners understood this imagery when Paul encouraged Christians to become living sacrifices for the glory of God.

As Christians, we may put our lives on the altar and say, "God, I'm yours. I want only to do your will!" Then some time passes, and we reconsider our offers. We try to squirm away and exercise our own wills once again.

Paul encouraged Christians to live a sacrificial life and "walk in the spirit" or act in daily and habitual obedience to the things of the Spirit. If your life is a living sacrifice, you don't follow the crowd (see Romans 12:2).

A biologist performed an experiment with processional caterpillars. He lined them up on the rim of a clay pot so that the head of the leader was next to the tail of the last caterpillar. They circled the rim of the pot for a full week. None of them broke away or went to a plant to eat. Eventually all the caterpillars died from exhaustion and starvation. Following the crowd can be deadly.

Dr. Vance Havner (1901–1986), a preacher and evangelist, said, "We are not going to move this world by criticism of it nor conformity to it but by the combustion within of lives ignited by the Spirit of God."

Every day, place your life on the altar of sacrifice to God, and don't squirm off in the middle of the afternoon. Ask God's Spirit to order your behavior so that it pleases the Lord.

God and the IRS

Pay your taxes, too, for these same reasons. For government workers need to be paid. They are serving God in what they do. ROMANS 13:6

Fortunately, tax season is behind us—for now. But before we know it, we'll be digging through our files for receipts and gearing up for another session with IRS forms.

Today's reading discusses our responsibility to civil authorities and the challenge of fulfilling that responsibility. It is important that we be good citizens without compromising our faith. We can be submissive to Christ without breaking the law. An anonymous letter written to Diognetus sometime in the second century said of believers, "They are passing their days on earth, but are citizens of heaven. They obey the appointed laws, and go beyond the laws in their own lives. . . . Christians are in the world but not of the world."

During the New Testament period, Roman territories extracted exorbitant taxes. They had a poll tax for males between the ages of fourteen and sixty-five and for females from ages twelve to sixty-five. Citizens were charged this tax just for being alive. There was a ground tax, which amounted to one-tenth of all grain and one-fifth of all wine. People living in fishing centers owed a fish tax. And each of these taxes was in addition to an income tax and road, harbor, and import taxes. One Roman writer declared, "I have never seen a monument to an honest tax collector."

We may dispute whether all taxes are just. We know that many tax dollars finance ungodly causes, and yet we pay them because Jesus took a coin with Caesar's face and said, "Give to Caesar what belongs to Caesar, and give to God what belongs to God" (Mark 12:17).

Christians are citizens of heaven, yet Jesus charges us to be faithful and responsible citizens of earth.

September 3

Days of the Week

Some think one day is more holy than another day, while others think every day is alike. You should each be fully convinced that whichever day you choose is acceptable. ROMANS 14:5

Which day is the right one on which to worship God? Is the Saturday Sabbath the true and proper day, as in the Jewish calendar? Or is Sunday, the day that commemorates Christ's resurrection, the suitable day? Does it matter which day Christians worship God, or are the days of the week equal?

Many early assemblies of believers included Judaizers. These individuals who felt compelled to keep the law of Moses were a major influence.

The writings of the early church fathers confirm that the church gathered on Sunday for worship. No portion of Scripture requires us to observe Saturday Sabbath or the sign of the Mosaic covenant rather than the new covenant of the New Testament.

In Acts, the Jerusalem council didn't order Gentile believers to practice the Sabbath. Paul never cautioned Christians against breaking the Sabbath. The seventh day of the week commemorates when God rested after he finished creation. The first day of the week commemorates when Christ finished humankind's redemption through the Resurrection.

In today's Bible reading, Paul wants to prevent any attitude that would diminish the real meaning of Christianity. I love the way Paul handles the issue because he doesn't offer specifics or give the "correct view." Instead, he encourages the believers to make up their own minds and then "be fully convinced" of their choice. There is danger in thinking, "Sunday is God's day, but the rest are all mine." Every day is God's day, and therefore, I believe every day is perfectly suited for worshiping God.

I'm not attempting to persuade you to change your practice or your belief about the proper day to worship. Rather, whatever day you choose, be sure you are worshiping God with your whole heart.

A Little Help from My Friends

Gaius says hello to you. He is my host and also serves as host to the whole church. Erastus, the city treasurer, sends you his greetings, and so does our brother Quartus. ROMANS 16:23

When you got to Romans 16, was it tempting to skim it and think, *This is just a list of names. They're not important*? Would it have made a difference if your name were on the list?

In today's reading, Paul greets twenty-six individuals, including Jews and Gentiles, men and women, and slaves and nobility. Thirteen of the names appear in documents related to the emperor's palace in Rome, implying that those people are of noble birth. Nine of the twenty-six are women. Paul wasn't a lone-ranger missionary. He was a part of a team and had key relationships in the Roman church.

The New Testament uses the phrase *one another* or *each other* more than seventy times, and more than thirty occurrences appear in the writings of Paul. These verses point out a vital truth: We were created to be interdependent, and we need each other.

The Scriptures include many examples of people who took initiative in their relationships. Consider Ruth and her relationship with her mother-in-law, Naomi. Or consider Jonathan, the son of Saul, and his relationship with David. Because Jonathan took the initiative, they became close friends.

During World War II, our enemies conducted experiments to discover the most effective way to get information from prisoners. They found that solitary confinement was their most effective tool. After just a few days completely alone, most prisoners would reveal anything. We need others, because without them we become easy prey for temptation and for abandoning our values.

No one should be able to provide fellowship better than Christians. Do you tend to be solitary? It's okay to be a private person and be alone for a time to recharge, but you also need relationships with others. God wired you that way.

How is your vertical relationship with God? How are your horizontal relationships with others?

Polarized and Paralyzed

Some of you are saying, "I am a follower of Paul." Others are saying,
"I follow Apollos," or "I follow Peter," or "I follow only Christ."

1 CORINTHIANS 1:12

Some historians estimate that if the American colonies had been more unified at the time of the American Revolution, we could have won our independence in a single year. But because of division within our own ranks, the war went on for eight years.

Believers can learn a lesson from this. Sometime after Paul left Corinth, the household of Chloe brought the news that there were divisions among the believers there. So Paul was trying to teach the Corinthian church that when the church becomes polarized, especially around strong personalities, it also becomes paralyzed.

The need for unity was on Paul's heart as he wrote, "Has Christ been divided into factions? Was I, Paul, crucified for you? Were any of you baptized in the name of Paul?" (1 Corinthians 1:13). The people had taken their eyes off the One who had atoned for their sins, and they had gravitated to their leaders of choice.

Notice that Paul takes these Christians back to the Cross, the common denominator of our faith. When Christians reach heaven, they will not find their local leaders on the throne; they will see them bowed down before it.

For humans, division comes naturally. Abraham's and Lot's herdsmen argued about their territorial allotments. James and John tried to grab the spotlight when they asked Jesus if they could have the most prominent positions in the Kingdom. Paul and Barnabas split over a disagreement about John Mark. And the Jerusalem church experienced conflict over food distribution to the widows.

According to Paul, the church is like a body, and like a body, it is intended to operate smoothly with the parts working in unity. Jesus is the head of his body, the church, and we should look to him first for direction. Are you rallying around Jesus or around some other leader?

God's Toolbox

God chose things the world considers foolish in order to shame those who think they are wise. And he chose things that are powerless to shame those who are powerful. 1 CORINTHIANS 1:27

Imagine you are a member of God's selection committee. Would you choose smart people, because God knows everything? attractive people, because God is resplendent in his glory? powerful people who know how to get things done? members of the nobility? (After all, you don't want to surround God with riffraff.) You submit your list, and your document comes back in shreds.

In today's reading, Paul was saying, "Take a look around, Corinthians, at those God called. They are God's tools." The reality is, God's Kingdom is backward and upside down: The weak are strong. The humble are exalted. The last are first. The poor are rich, and fools become wise.

Chuck Colson, the founder of Prison Fellowship, said, "The Kingdom of God is a Kingdom of paradox, where through the ugly defeat of a cross, a holy God is utterly glorified. Victory comes through defeat; healing through brokenness; finding self through losing self."

Jesus' own disciples reflected this paradox. The majority of them were fishermen; one was a despised tax collector, and all of them were from Galilee, which was not considered a place of culture. Not one would have appeared in a "Who's Who" in ancient Israel.

Why does God choose this way? He does it so he gets all the glory. As you get close to any of the heroes in the Bible, you can quickly see they are flawed. Check out Abraham or Moses or David. Their imperfections make their selection all the more wonderful. It adds to the mystery and glory of God.

Any surgeon can operate in a modern hospital, but in a hut in the jungle, with only a knife and some disinfectant, a surgeon's skill really shines. God's work in our world is more dramatic because he has chosen inferior "tools." Take a few moments to reflect on how God is "operating" through your life.

Are You Crazy?

Those who are spiritual can evaluate all things, but they themselves cannot be evaluated by others. 1 CORINTHIANS 2:15

My first day of integrated zoology class in college, the professor asked, "How many here are dumb enough to believe in God?" I felt awkward as I raised my lonely hand. Let's face it: This world doesn't get us. Unbelievers typically view Christians as ignorant or naive.

I once heard a humorous story about an atheist and a Quaker. The Quaker was talking about his belief in God when the atheist interrupted, "Have you ever seen God?"

"Nay," replied the Quaker.

"Have you ever touched God?" the atheist continued.

"Nay."

"Well then, have you ever smelled God?"

"Nay."

"Then how do you know that there even is a God?"

The Quaker began to question the smug unbeliever: "Hast thou ever seen thy brain?" he asked.

Impatiently, the atheist responded, "No, of course not!"

"And hast thou ever touched or smelled thy brain?"

"No!"

The Quaker asked with a smile, "Then how dost thou know that thou even *hast* a brain?"

Most people don't understand faith in Jesus Christ. Stories about our conversions earn either a blank stare or a condescending smirk. Paul tells us that without the Spirit's enlightenment, it's impossible to grasp spiritual things. Unbelievers don't have the capacity to get it.

Even Albert Einstein said, "Certainly there is a God. Any man who doesn't believe in a cosmic force is a fool, but we could never know Him."

But we *can* know God if the Spirit has awakened our senses. As you tell others what Jesus has done for you, ask God's Spirit to shine the light of his truth into the hearts of the spiritually blind so that they want what you have.

Gray Areas

You say, "I am allowed to do anything"—but not everything is good for you. And even though "I am allowed to do anything," I must not become a slave to anything. 1 CORINTHIANS 6:12

Some scriptural principles are black and white. We know certain things, such as sexual sin, murder, and stealing, are wrong. We know worshiping God and loving people are right. But we also deal with gray areas, such as music, clothing styles, and alcohol. The three questions that follow will help to determine your perspective on those and other issues.

1. *Is it helpful to you?* In 1 Corinthians 6, Paul says that although you have freedom, "not everything is good for you" (v. 12). Will what you're considering help you or hinder you? Some music may plant the kinds of thoughts in your mind that will tear you down.

2. *Will it control you?* Again, the apostle counsels that, although you may have freedom to engage in certain activities, you "must not become a slave to anything" (v. 12). Will one glass of wine lead to a second and then a third? If so, perhaps it controls you.

3. *Is it beneficial to others?* When you consider the gray areas of life, you can't stop with evaluating what an activity will do to *you*; you must also consider what effect it will have on *others*. This consideration is part of loving your neighbor as yourself. Will what you want to do set the right kind of example or the wrong kind? A younger Christian from a family where alcoholism is a problem may get the wrong signal, even if you're having a soft drink. God wants you to be sensitive to others' weaknesses.

Learn to filter your choices through the little grid above. When you include these three considerations, decisions concerning the gray areas come more easily.

To Marry or Not to Marry

I wish everyone were single, just as I am. Yet each person has a special gift from God, of one kind or another. 1 CORINTHIANS 7:7

Years ago George Gilder wrote a book titled *Men and Marriage,* in which he described the single man as "disposed to criminality, drugs and violence. . . . He is irresponsible about his debts, he is alcoholic, he is accident prone and susceptible to disease." That's quite a description.

Some ancient Jews might have agreed. They believed it was a sin not to be married, and it is said that they actually had a list of the kinds of people who couldn't go to heaven. The top two groups on that list were Jewish men without wives and wives who had no children.

Prominent newspaper man and political commentator H. L. Mencken said, "It is impossible to believe that the same God who permitted his own Son to die a bachelor regards celibacy as an actual sin." That's an interesting point, of course, but far more important than what H. L. Mencken believed is what the Bible itself teaches.

The Bible never said that singleness is wrong. Unfortunately, when some people read Genesis 2:18, in which God declared, "It is not good for the man to be alone," they inferred from those words that if it was not good to be alone, then it was wrong to be unmarried. But, in fact, Scripture sees both marriage and singleness as gifts.

Whatever your status is today—whether single or married—determine to serve God to the best of your abilities and giftedness. Thank the Lord for his plan for you, and ask him to help you to be content where you are right now. It may not always feel like it, but it is his gift to you at this time.

The Amazing Race

Don't you realize that in a race everyone runs, but only one person gets the prize? So run to win! 1 CORINTHIANS 9:24

One of Paul's favorite analogies for the Christian life is a race. It seems apparent that he loved sports and was knowledgeable about them, because he uses the race metaphor so frequently. In Philippians 3:14, he wrote, "I press on to reach the end of the race and receive the heavenly prize." In his second letter to Timothy, Paul wrote, "I have fought the good fight, I have finished the race" (2 Timothy 4:7).

True athletes must be disciplined if they are to stay the course. If someone offers them a hefty slice of chocolate cake, they will likely refuse it because they want to stay in top condition. As Christians, we need to be in top condition spiritually in order to stay usable and faithful in serving God and his Kingdom.

Unfortunately, it's hard to describe many Christians as running. Some may be "strolling" or "meandering." Others may *look* like athletes, but all they really do is wear the uniform, wait until another runner comes along, and then *act* as if they've been running. Still others collapse on the side of the track and gasp, "I'll never make it." They may be close to quitting.

Still others have left the track to sit in the bleachers and watch other Christians run. They may never spend any time running, yet they are often the first ones to offer advice to those still in the race. One sports fan remarked, "Sports like baseball, football, basketball, and hockey develop muscles. That's why Americans have the strongest eyes in the world."

Ask God to give you the strength to finish your race well. The Christian life isn't a fifty-yard dash; it's a marathon. So don't quit. Don't just go through the motions. When you come to the end of your life, you want to be able to celebrate your successful finish and your victory in Jesus.

Wanted: Role Models

You should imitate me, just as I imitate Christ. 1 CORINTHIANS 11:1

Edgar A. Guest, an American poet, wrote, "I'd rather see a sermon than hear one any day; I'd rather one should walk with me than merely tell the way!"

The apostle Paul is a good model. He taught others using two methods: precept and example. He drew principles about life from the Old Testament Scriptures and the words of Jesus Christ. Throughout his eighteen months in Corinth, he lived out his beliefs openly for people to see and emulate. If a picture is worth a thousand words, a real-life example is worth a thousand wise statements.

We can use those same methods, whether we are teaching our own children or a Sunday school class or preaching in the pulpit. It has been estimated that children spend about one percent of their time in Sunday school, 7 percent of their time in school (whether public or private), and 92 percent of their time at home. Children hear what their parents say and watch what their parents do, and that's a critical part of their overall learning.

Charles Spurgeon said, "Before a child reaches seven, teach him all the way to heaven. Better still the work will thrive, if he learns before he's five!" Little children learn first by example and then through instruction.

We need good role models. Young boys and girls need the examples of strong yet sensitive godly men and women. Christians need biblically sound and morally pure teachers and leaders.

Have you considered becoming a mentor to someone who is spiritually younger in the faith? Take a moment and see whom the Lord brings to your mind. Was it someone specific? If so, take the initiative and plan a regular time to meet and build godly experience into that person's life. As you follow Jesus Christ, you, like Paul, can teach and live in a way that has an impact on another person for eternity.

Spiritual Gifts

A spiritual gift is given to each of us so we can help each other.

1 CORINTHIANS 12:7

Have you ever thought about your spiritual gift? There are several keys to consider.

First, *spiritual gifts are given, not earned.* When people hear of a ministry that sounds exciting, they say, "That's what I want to do." In their own strength, they plunge into work God never intended for them; then they grow frustrated and want to quit. They don't understand that they have tried to create their own places in the body of Christ rather than work within the gift Jesus has given them.

Second, *spiritual gifts are given to help the church, not build up ourselves.* Whenever Paul speaks of the church and gifts, he uses the analogy of a body in which all the parts must cooperate if the body is to function properly. It's important to understand that your spiritual gift is not a goal in itself but a gateway to ministry within the church. Peter wrote, "God has given each of you a gift from his great variety of spiritual gifts. Use them well to serve one another" (1 Peter 4:10).

One morning in 1854, Luigi Tarisio was found dead, with little of value in his home except a collection of more than a hundred violins. These masterpieces, several of them made by Antonio Stradivari, were crammed into an attic, and the best one was found in a rickety bureau. Through his devotion to violins, he had robbed the world of the music they could have produced. When the greatest of his collection, now known as the Messiah Stradivarius, was first played, it had been silent for more than a hundred years.

Don't keep your spiritual gift stored away. Like those fine violins, it was meant to be used. Use the gift God has given to you for his glory and the benefit of all his children.

All You Need Is Love

Three things will last forever—faith, hope, and love—and the greatest of these is love. 1 CORINTHIANS 13:13

In 1875, Marcel de LeClure sent the longest love letter on record to Magdalene de Villalore. It read, "I love you" 1,875,000 times, or 1,000 times the calendar year of 1875. If that sounds romantic, don't get too excited, because LeClure hired someone else to do the actual writing.

We all want unconditional love and acceptance. When we are young, we dream about the person we will marry and about what our lives will be like. Of course, in our dreams we live happily ever after. As we grow up, we try to find the kind of love we've dreamed about and spend time planning whom we will date. We want to make our dreams come true.

As Christians, we should be highly skilled at love. God has poured such amazing love into us that it should be overflowing to others. The love of the early Christians was so evident that it had a huge impact on unbelievers. In AD 200 an unbelieving Greek writer who observed the loving fellowship of the Christians said, "It is incredible to see the fervor with which the people of that religion help each other in their wants [needs]. They spare nothing. Jesus has put it into their hearts that they are brethren."

First Corinthians 13 is commonly called the love chapter or the Beatitudes set to music. Paul takes the Christian life and summarizes it in an irreducible minimum of three elements—faith, hope, and love. And of those three attributes of faith, hope, and love, love is the greatest. Love has the greatest influence, longevity, and power.

Our world is desperate to see real love in action. I'm talking about unconditional love that forgives, heals, helps, and even confronts when necessary. Do others see this type of love when they look at you?

Not Afraid to Die

O death, where is your victory?
O death, where is your sting?

1 CORINTHIANS 15:55

From almost any list of the ten greatest chapters in the Bible, 1 Corinthians 15, which talks about the resurrection of Jesus Christ and believers, is likely to be on it.

When Jesus rose from the dead, he took the souls of those who had died in faith with him into paradise. Since then, when a believer dies, the soul goes immediately into the presence of God. Paul taught this clearly: "We would rather be away from these earthly bodies, for then we will be at home with the Lord" (2 Corinthians 5:8).

The Bible compares death to falling asleep because when Christ returns, those who have died will awaken. We may fear the *process* of dying, but if we love Jesus, we need not fear our death itself any more than we fear going to sleep.

As a young man, Benjamin Franklin had composed his own mock epitaph: "The Body of B. Franklin Printer; Like the Cover of an old Book, Its Contents torn out, and stript of its Lettering and Gilding, Lies here, Food for Worms. But the Work shall not be [wholly] lost: For it will, as he believ'd, appear once more, In a new & more perfect Edition, Corrected and Amended By the Author." Franklin's words reflect the hope we have as Christians.

Death isn't the end of our journey. Though we die, we move on to be with Christ forever.

A Christian man was once asked, "What is your age?"

He said, "I'm on the right side of seventy."

When the inquirer learned the man was seventy-five years old, he was puzzled and asked further, "You said you were on the right side of seventy?"

"I am—on the side nearest heaven."

Whether you are young or old, celebrate your assurance of living eternally with Jesus.

September 15

Why We Suffer

He comforts us in all our troubles so that we can comfort others. When they are troubled, we will be able to give them the same comfort God has given us. 2 CORINTHIANS 1:4

Discouragement is no respecter of persons. It affects even someone as close to God as the apostle Paul. Charles Spurgeon once wrote, "I am the subject of depressions of spirit so fearful that I hope none of you ever get to such extremes of wretchedness as I go to."

So why do Christians suffer so much? If we are God's own children, why do we sometimes experience suffering even greater than that of unbelievers (see, for example, Psalm 73)? There are many reasons, but let's examine three of them.

First, *we suffer so we can change.* It is through the "tumbling" of trouble that God smooths our rough edges. The smoothest and most polished stones are not found in quiet coves. They are found on the shore, where the pounding waves smooth and shape them. In the same way, God uses the buffeting of life's storms to smooth and polish his people.

Second, *we suffer so that we can be consoled.* When we suffer, we draw closer to God and experience his comfort and presence in deep ways. Those who walk with Christ during periods of suffering have a depth of relationship with God that is noticeable.

Finally, *we suffer so that we can give comfort.* The Lord uses us as his instruments of comfort to others. As I have read about how other Christians faced their struggles, I have been comforted. When I listen to the hymn "Just as I Am," I remember that Charlotte Elliott was an invalid when she wrote it. As I read *The Pilgrim's Progress*, I find encouragement in the knowledge that Bunyan wrote it while imprisoned in England's Bedford Gaol.

What steps are you taking to ensure that your share of suffering is used to help others? Keep a journal and record what God teaches you from times of suffering.

The Sweet Smell of Salvation

[God] has made us his captives and continues to lead us along in Christ's triumphal procession. Now he uses us to spread the knowledge of Christ everywhere, like a sweet perfume. 2 CORINTHIANS 2:14

I once heard a great saying: "Blessed are the flexible, for they shall not be broken!"

In today's short section, Paul addresses the reason his plans to visit the Corinthian Christians had changed. He went from Troas to Macedonia because God had spoken to him in a vision. Neither Paul's plans to go to Corinth nor his plans to rendezvous with Titus in Troas worked out. But that didn't distract him from his larger focus. Wherever God took Paul, the apostle was victorious through Christ.

Today's verse recalls the imagery of a Roman triumphal procession. If a commander won a complete victory on foreign soil and killed at least five thousand enemy soldiers, he was entitled to a procession through the streets of Rome when he returned from the conquest. The victorious legions paraded through Rome, and the commander rode in a golden chariot. This procession included the captives or trophies of war and ended at the Circus Maximus. The parade route was adorned with garlands of fresh flowers, and burning incense perfumed the air.

Paul compared his mission to a triumphant procession. Jesus, the commanding officer, came to foreign soil, defeated Satan, the enemy of our souls, and took captive those who were slaves of sin. How did he work such a feat? He gave his own life for their salvation. With Christ's victory over Satan, it's no wonder he cried out from the cross, "It is finished." Those words were his victory shout.

What Paul was saying to the Corinthians was, "Whether we march in Troas or in Corinth, the spiritual army of Jesus Christ disseminates the gospel, and our actions smell good to God."

How flexible are your plans for today? If God changes them, will you still faithfully spread the pleasant aroma of the gospel?

Visit to the Spa

That is why we never give up. Though our bodies are dying, our spirits are being renewed every day. 2 CORINTHIANS 4:16

I never used to be a "spa goer." I always held the notion that such pampering used too much time and cost too much money—until I tried it. For our anniversary, friends treated my wife and me to a day at a spa. Neither of us had ever felt as relaxed and renewed as we did after that visit. But as renewed and refreshed as we felt, the truth is that whether our bodies are pampered or not, one day we will die. Our aches and pains remind us of our physical limitations and tell us that our outer person is gradually wearing out.

Paul suffered not only the wear and tear of his itinerant lifestyle, but also a body that had been weakened from the many punishments he endured for preaching the gospel. At the same time, however, he experienced an inward rejuvenation, a type of spiritual spa treatment that renewed him inwardly. He saw his present earthly troubles as "small" and not of very long duration in the light of eternity (see 2 Corinthians 4:17).

What is your attitude about your earthly afflictions? Do you make a mountain out of a molehill? Is your focus on all the bad stuff in your life? Paul handled it in the reverse fashion and turned a mountain into a molehill by weighing the struggles of the moment, as difficult as they were, on the scales of eternity, and that gained him a new perspective.

From a human standpoint, Paul carried an unbearably heavy weight. Yet when he compared those difficulties to the glory of eternity, his troubles appeared to be light.

You need frequent treatment in the Lord's spiritual spa. Get your daily massage in the Word of God, soak your days in prayer, and engage in regular worship washes. The spiritual spa experience will make a dramatic difference in your attitude and in how you view what's ahead for you this day.

The Great Exchange

God made Christ, who never sinned, to be the offering for our sin, so that we could be made right with God through Christ. 2 CORINTHIANS 5:21

When I first heard the gospel on television and heard that Christ became our substitute and took on our sins in order to free us from guilt, I thought, *God is getting a bad deal.* Yet this substitution was the only way to make us right with God.

I once read about a new product in the marketplace. Each package of disposable "guilt bags" contained ten brown paper bags and these instructions: "Place the bag securely over your mouth, take a deep breath, and blow out all your guilt. Dispose of the bag immediately." The Associated Press reported that twenty-five hundred kits quickly sold at $2.50 per kit.

Unfortunately this gimmick doesn't work. The only way for our guilt to be removed is through Jesus Christ. His death and resurrection allow our restoration to fellowship with the Lord of the universe. God treated Jesus Christ as if his perfect Son were guilty of all our sins. Jesus took the treatment we deserved for our sins. And because he did, God can treat us the way Jesus Christ in all his perfection deserves to be treated by his Father. In other words, because Jesus bore our sins, we can bear his righteousness.

Isaiah 53:4-5 says, "It was our weaknesses he carried; it was our sorrows that weighed him down. And we thought his troubles were a punishment from God, a punishment for his own sins! But he was pierced for our rebellion, crushed for our sins. He was beaten so we could be whole. He was whipped so we could be healed."

Only in the eyes of an infinite God could that substitution ever make sense, but we can accept it with faith and gratitude. Talk about the price for forgiveness!

Mismatch

Don't team up with those who are unbelievers. How can righteousness be a partner with wickedness? How can light live with darkness?

2 CORINTHIANS 6:14

A certain kind of alligator has a reputation for being lazy. Instead of hunting for its dinner, it lies near the water's edge with its mouth open and acts as if it were dead. Flies begin to buzz around its moist tongue, and other insects gather. These insects attract bigger game. Before long, a lizard approaches to feed on the bugs, and a frog joins the gathering. In a short time, a whole menagerie has gathered in the alligator's mouth. There is a sudden "earthquake" and a loud noise, and without warning, the giant jaws snap shut. The party is over because the insects and larger animals were hanging out in the wrong company.

In today's reading, Paul warns the Corinthian Christians not to be in partnership with unbelievers. The passage's primary focus is the need for Christians to separate from the false teachers who were troubling the church at Corinth, but the principles of the passage can also apply to other alliances of Christians and non-Christians, such as marriage and business.

Because marriage is the emotional and spiritual yoking of two people, a believer and an unbeliever should not marry. Picture two animals harnessed side by side to pull a plow. A wise farmer selects two animals that have similar size, strength, and temperament so that they will work well together. Otherwise, the animals may try to pull in two different directions.

God knows that a marriage between a Christian and a non-Christian won't be happy because each person will be drawn in a different direction. When there is a mismatch, life becomes one big tug-of-war. Believers need not end all associations with unbelievers. That would undermine the purpose for which God saved us and left us on the earth—to draw others to him. But God does want us to make wise spiritual choices as we form partnerships, whether in marriage or in business.

Giving Joyfully

You must each decide in your heart how much to give. And don't give reluctantly or in response to pressure. "For God loves a person who gives cheerfully." 2 CORINTHIANS 9:7

A farmer's motivation for planting seeds doesn't matter. Whether the seeds were planted for money or for pride, what matters is that they have the right conditions for growth. Soil and water, not the farmer's motivation, are key.

But when Christians give, motivation *is* the issue: "People judge by outward appearance, but the LORD looks at the heart," says 1 Samuel 16:7.

You can be a sad giver who gives grudgingly, a mad giver who gives out of necessity, or a glad giver who gives with joy. I've heard some people say that we need to give "until it hurts." Others give with an attitude that says, "The church is ripping me off again this week." If that's your attitude, then you need to keep your money, because God doesn't need it. Maybe you are giving out of necessity because you feel compelled to follow a particular rule or feel pressure from the church to give a certain amount. Has the leadership contended that the church will go under without your gift? This sort of pressure works because guilt is one of the strongest forms of motivation. Of course, you don't want to be insensitive to the needs of a church or ministry, but you also don't want to fall into the temptation of giving out of a sense of guilt.

The right way to give is with a willing heart, or as today's verse says, "Decide in your heart how much to give." I love the fact that this passage does not mention a percentage. The amount you give is between you and God. The J. B. Phillips translation says, "Let everyone give as his heart tells him." Giving begins in your heart, because "God loves a person who gives cheerfully."

The Gift of a Thorn

To keep me from becoming proud, I was given a thorn in my flesh, a messenger from Satan to torment me and keep me from becoming proud.

2 CORINTHIANS 12:7

As Christians, we know that God gives blessings but also permits burdens. These burdens have a good purpose and are not meant to break our backs or bend our knees—except in prayer.

In today's verse, Paul says God gave him "a thorn in my flesh." We know this thorn wasn't the little sliver you get when you garden or cut wood. The word used refers to a sharp stake of the type used to torture or impale and implies that Paul had a type of severe or nagging physical affliction.

Some commentators speculate that Paul had epilepsy, migraines, or malaria. Most scholars believe this thorn was eye disease and that Paul suffered from partial blindness. Perhaps after his encounter with Jesus on the road to Damascus, his eyes were never the same. Maybe the stoning he suffered at Lystra caused lasting damage.

Let's examine the wording for this verse carefully where it says, "a thorn in my flesh, a messenger from Satan." The tense in the original language indicates that although it was a "messenger from Satan," it actually came from the Lord. Just as he did in Job's life, God permitted one of Satan's messengers to "torment" Paul in some way. Both God and Satan were at work with different purposes. Satan wanted to destroy Paul's faith, and God wanted to use this difficulty to build Paul's faith and keep him humble.

We may not understand God's purposes, but we do know the Lord is in control and permits some things for his glory and our good. The mixture can be compared to chemistry, in which the right combination of harmful chemicals produces beneficial results. If you combine two poisons, sodium and chlorine, in the right amounts, they produce table salt.

Rejoice in the beneficial mixture of God's blessings and burdens in your life.

Forever Cursed

Let God's curse fall on anyone, including us or even an angel from heaven, who preaches a different kind of Good News than the one we preached to you. GALATIANS 1:8

Paul's letter to the Galatians was Martin Luther's favorite book of the Bible. "It is my letter; I am wedded to it," Luther wrote. In his day, the religious establishment considered Luther a radical, just as Paul was in his day. The apostle gave up everything to travel the world with the message of the gospel, and he never compromised on that. Anything less than the message of the grace of God was to be rejected.

Some of the young churches Paul had founded were already being infiltrated with legalism and attempts to get the Gentile followers of Jesus to observe the law of Moses. These false teachers were saying that faith in Jesus Christ was not enough.

Why did Paul use such strong language in today's verse? Because he knew that God was perfect and holy and that humanity was sinful and unholy. No one can earn right standing before God. The prophet Isaiah declared, "We are all infected and impure with sin. When we display our righteous deeds, they are nothing but filthy rags" (Isaiah 64:6). Law and grace are mutually exclusive.

Anytime I point to *my* righteousness, *my* faithfulness, or *my* good deeds as a basis for salvation, I am denying that only Jesus saves. The only type of righteousness God accepts is the righteousness of Jesus Christ.

In 1829, George Wilson robbed the U.S. mail, and in the process, he killed someone. Wilson was arrested, brought to trial, found guilty, and sentenced to be hanged. Wilson's friends secured a pardon from President Andrew Jackson, but Wilson refused to accept it. Although he had an official pardon, his own pride kept him bound.

As you tell people how to get to heaven, make sure you are teaching a pure message of God's grace that is freely given to helpless sinners. We have a responsibility not to compromise the message.

How Amazing Is Grace?

No one will ever be made right with God by obeying the law.

GALATIANS 2:16

The gospel transformed the life of John Newton, a former slave trader. He wrote one of the most famous hymns of all time: "Amazing Grace." He said, "I remember two things: that I am a great sinner and that Christ is a great Savior!"

One of the challenges the early church faced was the idea, held by a group called Judaizers, that belief in Jesus the Messiah was not enough. People still needed to keep the requirements of Moses. This belief exalted human efforts and denied the utter sinfulness of humanity and, in addition, denied that Christ's death on the cross was sufficient for salvation. In contrast, Paul wrote, "Everyone who believes in [Christ] is declared right with God—something the law of Moses could never do" (Acts 13:39).

Although God gave the law through Moses, over time, religious leaders made it increasingly complex. In fact, the first section of the Talmud, a compilation of Jewish tradition, has twenty-four chapters devoted to Sabbath laws alone. One law specified that the legal limit for a Jew to walk from home on the Sabbath was thirty-one hundred feet. Yet if food had been placed six thousand feet from home, a Jew could walk that distance to eat. Because food was considered an extension of the home, a Jew could go an additional three thousand feet. If a rope was placed across a street or alley or group of buildings, the entire area was considered part of a person's "greater home." Can you imagine how burdensome it became to try to keep track of all the rules when the Sabbath was intended to be a day of rest?

If you believe in Jesus, learn to rest in his acceptance of you. Of course, you have room to grow and become more like Christ. But God will never accept you or love you more than he does right now. Now that's amazing!

Project Perfection

How foolish can you be? After starting your Christian lives in the Spirit, why are you now trying to become perfect by your own human effort?

GALATIANS 3:3

When I was a boy, my brother Bob kept a journal and often wrote about what he called "Project Perfection." Bob struggled to master some old habits, and when he had a good day, he wrote, "Project Perfection was successful today." When he gave in to those old habits, Bob wrote, "Failed today on Project Perfection." My brother's approach was doomed from the start.

Jesus told us that although our spirit may be willing, our flesh, or natural state, is weak. Only by the power of the Holy Spirit can we accomplish our spiritual goals. We can't engineer such success on our own.

Someone asked a multimillionaire about the reason for his wealth. He said, "When I was first married, I was poor. I took my last nickel and bought an apple. I polished that apple until it was shiny and sold it for ten cents. I took the dime and bought two apples and polished them. The next day, I sold them for twenty cents. With that money, I bought four apples and sold them for forty cents. I did that until I reached $1.60. I worked hard and sweated. Then my wife's dad died and left us a million dollars."

Our spiritual strength is not the result of fasting longer or praying harder than others any more than that man's wealth was the result of his efforts. Instead, our spiritual strength is rooted in the power of Christ's Spirit, who is in the process of changing us day by day.

If a bridge to heaven were built and it came from 99 percent Christ's work and one percent my effort, it would still break. Our lives have to be built 100 percent on Jesus. Our own efforts contribute nothing to our standing. Have you learned to rest completely in what Christ has done for you?

Is God Ever Late?

When the right time came, God sent his Son, born of a woman, subject to the law. GALATIANS 4:4

Why was Jesus born when he was—at a point in history more than two thousand years ago? Wouldn't three thousand years ago or even a century ago have been just as timely? Actually, no. God's timing in sending his Son was perfect—not a moment too soon or too late.

Jesus arrived at the right spiritual time. Around this period of history, there was a noticeable religious yearning. As Gentiles grew increasingly unfulfilled, they questioned the polytheism, or worship of multiple gods, of the Greeks and Romans.

Even Jews were experiencing some of this emptiness. Since their captivity in Babylon, they had met in synagogues for the study of the Scripture, and their yearnings grew as they read about the Messiah's coming.

Jesus arrived at the right cultural time. The world had become more unified than ever before. Greek was the common language, and this brought cohesion to worldwide communication and enabled the Good News about Jesus to be written with incredible linguistic precision.

Jesus arrived at the right political time. The Roman Empire was at its pinnacle, and although many saw the government as rigid and oppressive, it brought economic and political stability. Roman roads connected the parts of the world and allowed those who carried the gospel message to travel extensively.

Jesus arrived at the right prophetic time. The Jews had always believed in the Messiah. A common prayer was, "I believe in the coming of Messiah, and even though he tarry, yet I will wait for him every coming day."

In every way, Jesus was born at exactly the right time. The eternal God is never early, and he is never late. In every season of life, we can trust his perfect timing.

Emancipated

Christ has truly set us free. Now make sure that you stay free, and don't get tied up again in slavery to the law. GALATIANS 5:1

As a part of America's fabric, the word *freedom* holds different meanings for different people. Artists celebrate freedom of expression; politicians are conscious of freedom of speech and the democratic system. Young idealists see freedom as permitting nonconformity and allowing them to forge their own paths for the sake of a cause.

As Christians, we have the ultimate freedom to resist sin through the power of the Holy Spirit who lives in us, and we have been released from trying to get right with God through our own performance.

One freedom we don't have, however, is the freedom to indulge. Paul wrote to the Galatians, "You have been called to live in freedom, my brothers and sisters. But don't use your freedom to satisfy your sinful nature" (Galatians 5:13). We can never say that because we're Christians, we have the freedom to live as we please. This attitude only makes us slaves to the appetites of the flesh, and that is not freedom.

Instead, Paul told the Galatians that they now have "freedom to serve one another in love" (Galatians 5:13). In effect, they were free to choose to become willing servants.

Later in the New Testament, the apostle John wrote, "If we love our Christian brothers and sisters, it proves that we have passed from death to life" (1 John 3:14). Ours is a freedom *from* sin, not freedom *to* sin. And this kind of freedom leads to the joy and fulfillment we were created for.

As you explore your freedom in Christ, learn to say no to the cravings of your old nature. Instead, use your energy to please Christ. Look for people who need your assistance. When they ask why you're being so helpful, you can tell them about the freedom Jesus has given you to love and serve others.

The Battle Within

The sinful nature wants to do evil, which is just the opposite of what the Spirit wants. And the Spirit gives us desires that are the opposite of what the sinful nature desires. These two forces are constantly fighting each other. GALATIANS 5:17

Do you ever feel as if you're in a constant state of war? When you accepted Jesus, you received a new nature that battles with your old, sinful nature, which you inherited from Adam. Your new nature is the product of your new birth (see John 3), and the battle between the old nature and the new one is a uniquely Christian conflict.

Your new nature wants to serve the Lord, but your old nature responds, *You need a break. Be good to yourself!* Your new nature wants to start the day with prayer and Bible reading, but the old nature says, *Stay in bed a few more minutes. You have a hard day ahead of you.* Your new nature wants to go to church, but your old nature says, *You're not in a crisis right now; you can go next Sunday.* These types of battles rage continually.

Even the great apostle Paul—Mr. Spiritual himself—experienced it: "I don't really understand myself, for I want to do what is right, but I don't do it. Instead, I do what I hate" (Romans 7:15). The only solution is to live each day guided by God's Spirit. That doesn't mean you live in perfection, but it does mean you live with purpose and in obedience to Christ.

Cultivating your new spiritual nature is like cultivating a garden of fine flowers. You can't just throw seeds on the ground and expect them to grow. You must water and fertilize the seeds. In the same way, it's important to nurture your spiritual dimension.

Remember, it doesn't take any effort on your part for weeds to grow. They'll sprout anywhere without fertilizer or assistance. What we grow spiritually depends on what we are fed. Nourish your spiritual nature with frequent feedings from God's Word.

When Christians Sin

If another believer is overcome by some sin, you who are godly should gently and humbly help that person back onto the right path. And be careful not to fall into the same temptation yourself. GALATIANS 6:1

Can any other institution be likened to the local church? In *The Edge of Adventure*, Bruce Larson and Keith Miller compared a neighborhood bar to the church, noting that "it's an imitation, dispensing liquor instead of grace, escape rather than reality, but it is a permissive, accepting, and inclusive fellowship. It is unshockable. The bar is an unshockable place. . . . With all my heart, I believe Christ wants his church to be unshockable."

Unfortunately, the church has its share of legalistic people who make great finger-pointers, always telling others what's wrong with them. Instead of having hearts interested in restoration, these rule minders have a bent toward condemnation. In my years as a pastor, I've found the church is just as likely to shoot those who are wounded as it is to salvage them.

Ministering healing to fallen brothers and sisters takes the skill and care of mature believers, godly Christians who possess three qualities:

First, *they want to help others rather than hurt them.* Their actions are marked by open arms rather than pointing fingers.

Second, *they have great sensitivity.* They restore others gently and help them get back on their feet. When they see dirt on others, they help to remove it with tenderness, not with scalding words of criticism, not with an icy, formal approach, and not without water, by harshly scraping off the dirt and taking the skin with it. Think of how gently Jesus must have washed his disciples' feet.

Finally, *they are humble and keep themselves pure.* They are mindful of their own susceptibility to sin and therefore don't think of themselves as morally superior to others.

Do you demonstrate these qualities when brothers or sisters sin? If so, you can reach out to them with the healing touch of Jesus Christ.

You're Always on His Mind

Even before he made the world, God loved us and chose us in Christ to be holy and without fault in his eyes. EPHESIANS 1:4

When did God start thinking about you? Were you an afterthought? Did the Lord let you into his Kingdom arbitrarily or haphazardly? No, long before the events of Genesis 1, you were on his mind, and his plan was firmly established. This idea bothers some people. They resist the thought that God has a right to make choices about people before they even exist.

But Charles Spurgeon said, "I am quite certain that, if God had not chosen me, I should never have chosen Him; and I am sure He chose me before I was born, or else He never would have chosen me afterwards."

Think about this: Jesus knew all about his disciples' future failures, but he still chose them. Jesus knew Peter would deny him, Judas would betray him, and Thomas would doubt him. He even told them, "You didn't choose me. I chose you" (John 15:16).

God also knew everything about you, and yet he chose you, long before you could have any desire at all for him.

Centuries ago, a huge block of marble from the Carrara quarries arrived in Florence. As the story goes, one of the artisans planned to sculpt a statue from it, despite its many visible imperfections. It lay in the cathedral yard while many came to see if it would suffice for their next projects, but no one who saw it selected it.

Then one day, after examining the stone, an artist declared excitedly, "There's an angel inside, and I must set it free." For two years he worked, chipping and chiseling, until at last, in 1504, he unveiled his masterpiece—*David*, Michelangelo's most famous sculpture.

Jesus sees us like a block of marble. Though we are flawed in so many ways, he can make something beautiful of our lives. So he works in us to reveal the ultimate masterpiece—his own image.

What's in Your Bankbook?

I pray that your hearts will be flooded with light so that you can understand the confident hope he has given to those he called—his holy people who are his rich and glorious inheritance. EPHESIANS 1:18

William Randolph Hearst (1863–1951) invested a fortune in priceless art from all over the world. One day, Hearst came across a description of a priceless treasure and decided he had to have it. After a frantic search, Hearst discovered he already owned it. Does this story sound familiar to you?

Many Christians search for an extraordinary spiritual experience in contrast to their "ordinary" Christian lives. If only they knew the richness of all they already possess!

In today's reading, Paul emphasizes the wealth of what we have and who we are in Christ. Is it possible to understand how rich we are?

Many times before Billy Graham spoke at a crusade, George Beverly Shea sang, "Oh the wonder of it all, just to think that God loves me." When some Christians consider the wonder of God's love, they say, "I'm not good for anything." Be careful. You're talking about God's property. Just look at the Cross to see the value of your salvation. God sacrificed his Son to redeem you. Later in Ephesians, Paul says his desire is that God's people will understand "how wide, how long, how high, and how deep [God's] love is" (Ephesians 3:18).

Author and composer Frederick M. Lehman wrote, "Could we with ink the oceans fill, / And were the skies of parchment made, / Were every stalk on earth a quill, / And every man a scribe by trade, / To write the love of God above, / Would drain the ocean dry. / Nor could the scroll contain the whole, / Though stretched from sky to sky."

When one theologian was asked to give the most profound truth he knew, he responded, "Jesus loves me." Rejoice today in God's immeasurable love for you.

But God

God is so rich in mercy, and he loved us so much, that even though we were dead because of our sins, he gave us life when he raised Christ from the dead. (It is only by God's grace that you have been saved!)

EPHESIANS 2:4-5

As Christians, we've gone from the graveyard to glory. In Ephesians 2, Paul describes the journey from the graveyard of sin to the throne of glory, and today's reading starts in "Death Valley" and ends in "Graceland" (I'm talking about God's home, not Elvis's). From birth, we are spiritually dead on arrival, separated from God by our sin. The Bible doesn't say that people are sick—without Jesus, they are spiritually dead. Non-Christians can go to the best schools, and they'll come out educated sinners. They can go to psychotherapists, and they'll end up better-adjusted sinners. To experience true and lasting change, unbelievers need Christ.

Paul wrote to the church at Rome, "Most people would not be willing to die for an upright person, though someone might perhaps be willing to die for a person who is especially good. *But God* showed his great love for us by sending Christ to die for us while we were still sinners" (Romans 5:7-8, emphasis added).

Joseph's brothers abused him and sold him into slavery, but Joseph's perspective in retrospect was this: "You intended to harm me, *but God* intended it all for good. He brought me to this position so I could save the lives of many people" (Genesis 50:20, emphasis added).

The two little words *but God* provide some of the most significant transitions in the literature of the Bible. They capture the essence of the gospel and change our perspective on any situation.

In some way, every Christian's testimony is similar to Joseph's statement: *I was going my way on the path of life, but God changed everything when I met Jesus.* Spend a few moments in praise for the times the words *but God* invade your life each day.

Do You Want to Know a Secret?

Both Gentiles and Jews who believe the Good News share equally in the riches inherited by God's children. Both are part of the same body, and both enjoy the promise of blessings because they belong to Christ Jesus.

EPHESIANS 3:6

In today's reading, Paul speaks a message of belonging to the church: God loves you! The great mystery of the church is that God's love is inclusive. God took Jews and non-Jews and brought them together in fellowship.

The apostle Paul's instruction about an inclusive church especially surprised the Jews, who thought they were better than the Gentiles because they were God's chosen people. Verses like Deuteronomy 7:6 do describe God's unique love for them: "You are a holy people, who belong to the LORD your God. Of all the people on earth, the LORD your God has chosen you to be his own special treasure." But the Jews mistakenly assumed God loved only them. Their separatist attitude kept them from seeing God's love as inclusive.

No wonder Jewish leaders opposed the different message of the church. John 3:16 says, "God loved the world so much . . . everyone who believes." Jesus meant salvation was for anyone in the world who would believe.

Jesus, the Good Shepherd, mentioned this to his disciples in John 10:16: "I have other sheep, too, that are not in this sheepfold. I must bring them also. They will listen to my voice, and there will be one flock with one shepherd."

But it took time even for the disciples to understand that Jesus meant for the church to include non-Jews. Eventually God gave Peter a vision in which God instructed him to eat both clean and unclean animals, which represented his inclusion of both Jews and Gentiles.

The church was a mystery. Gentiles were brought to God through a Jew, and soon both Jews and Gentiles ate together. Now all believers regularly celebrate the mystery of the Lord's Supper.

The disciples uncovered the secret that God loves all people and anyone can be part of his church.

October 3 READ EPHESIANS 4:1-32

How Much Do You Weigh?

I, a prisoner for serving the Lord, beg you to lead a life worthy of your calling, for you have been called by God. EPHESIANS 4:1

The Greek word for *worthy* includes the idea of balance or equality. To say a person was worthy of his pay meant his day's work corresponded to his day's wages (see Luke 10:7). When people were worthy of honor, their accomplishments corresponded to their accolades. If Christians' lives were worthy, their actions corresponded to their calling or their position as children of God.

John the Baptist told the crowd, "Bear fruits worthy of repentance" (Matthew 3:8, NKJV) or, as the New English Bible puts it, "As God has called you, live up to your calling" (Ephesians 4:1). In today's Bible reading, Paul calls Christians to consistency and to live up to the name of Jesus Christ. Paul calls himself the "Lord's prisoner," meaning that his life revolves around the Lord's will.

Soon after Jesse James killed a man in a bank robbery, he was baptized in a church in Kearney, Missouri. The outlaw went on to kill another man—and then joined the church choir and taught hymn singing. He couldn't always show up for church on Sundays; twice he was busy robbing trains. The English statesman and philosopher Francis Bacon (1561–1626) said, "A bad man is worse when he pretends to be a saint." He might as well have been describing Jesse James!

Christians are called to walk worthy and to be genuine, which is the opposite of being phony. Paul is urging the Ephesians to replace any hypocrisy with integrity.

While four in five Americans say they're "Christians," only a third, or 35 percent, claim to be born again. In the midst of such inconsistency, we are called to be consistent.

Newspaper columnist Erma Bombeck pointed to inconsistency by writing, "Never go to a doctor whose office plants have died." In the same way, people don't look for guidance from a Christian who can't seem to direct his own life. Is it evident that you are living a consistent, godly life?

Check Your Oil!

Submit to one another out of reverence for Christ.   EPHESIANS 5:21

A friend neglected to check the oil in his Blazer. Over time, the oil reached a critically low level. Then, one day, the engine seized on the freeway and dropped out.

Engines have finely machined parts with the potential to stick, crack, or wiggle. Without the viscosity of the oil permeating all the parts, an engine can't operate smoothly or efficiently.

Relationships are like engines. The more people you have in your family or your church family, the more lubrication is needed. In today's Bible reading in Ephesians 5, Paul covers the various parts of the family machine. He lifts the hood and looks at each component. He singles out the role of each and how it fits with other parts and then puts them back together. Paul calls for submission as the lubricant to make the home run smoothly.

Some men who study this chapter focus only on the instruction to wives to submit to their husbands—without noticing Paul's instructions to husbands in verse 25: "Love your wives, just as Christ loved the church. He gave up his life for her."

Submission is for the whole family. To submit means to line up, get in order, or arrange. In a military sense, to submit means to rank beneath someone. Paul means for us to "get under one another." Submission is mutual—not for just one but for all.

This overarching command in verse 21 is followed by four paragraphs giving examples of submission in the microcosm of the family. Submission isn't just for wives. It is also for husbands (see verse 25), children (see verse 6:1), and parents (see verse 6:4).

As part of our submission to God, we accept this call even when doing so isn't easy.

How to Fight

Put on all of God's armor so that you will be able to stand firm against all strategies of the devil. EPHESIANS 6:11

Do you think of Christians as fighters or as peacemakers who act with love and gentleness? Paul reminds you that you entered a spiritual battle zone when you came to Christ. When you became a friend of God, you inherited the Lord's enemies.

With the vivid images in this third section of Ephesians, the apostle Paul transports us to a battlefield to see the smoke of war. The Christian life is not a playground.

The first essential in military intelligence is to know information about your enemy. Our Commanding Officer, God, plainly points to the enemy as the devil and his buddies (see verse 12). Though some people think the devil is simply a symbol of evil, we know that Jesus Christ dealt with a literal Satan. In Luke 10:18, he said, "I saw Satan fall from heaven like lightning." Then in Luke 22:31, Jesus spoke about the devil like any other person, saying, "Simon, Simon, Satan has asked to sift each of you like wheat."

Evangelist Dwight L. Moody knew Satan was real. He said, "I believe Satan exists for two reasons: first because the Bible says so and second because I've done business with him!"

When the people of ancient China wanted security, they built the Great Wall, which was too high to climb over, too thick to break, and too long to go around. Yet in the first hundred years after it was built, China was invaded three times by enemies who simply bribed the gatekeeper and marched through a gate. The Chinese had relied too much on their walls when they should have built character into the gatekeepers.

God has provided the perfect spiritual armor for Christians, but it is useless unless you wear it. Daily put on the protection of God to face the enemy. Consciously ask God to help you wear your weapons and fight courageously.

The Unfinished *Work of Christ*

I am certain that God, who began the good work within you, will continue his work until it is finally finished on the day when Christ Jesus returns.

PHILIPPIANS 1:6

From across the room in a furniture store, I noticed a beautiful antique piano. On closer inspection, I realized the piano had no insides—no strings or hammers or keys. Only the outer walnut case had been refinished. God works the opposite way. God's work in us is an inside job. Although we spend too much of each day concentrating on outward appearances, God's primary concern is the internal people we are. Today you may be discouraged because so many aspects of your life seem like unfinished projects. Take heart! You are seeing only part of the whole picture. Your life is a work in progress.

God has a specific plan for you. He is preparing you for a meeting with Jesus Christ. As the "author and finisher of our faith" (Hebrews 12:2, NKJV), God won't stop working until you are finally glorified like Jesus Christ. God will never say, "I quit because you're a hopeless job." God created a whole complex universe in only six days, not resting until he could declare the work finished. The Lord is not going to rest in working with you because you are still under construction. Today's key verse promises that he who began his work will continue until it is finally finished. What God starts, he finishes.

Evangelist Charles Spurgeon said, "There is not a spider hanging on the king's wall but has its errand; there is not a nettle that grows in the corner of the churchyard but has its purpose. . . . And I will never have it that God created any man, especially any Christian man, to be a blank, and to be a nothing. He made you for an end. Find out what that end is; find out your niche and fill it."

Rejoice that the Creator of the universe has a specially designed purpose for your life.

The God of the Backstage

I want you to know, my dear brothers and sisters, that everything that has happened to me here has helped to spread the Good News.

PHILIPPIANS 1:12

The believers in Philippi were watching Paul's life as if it were a play unfolding on a stage. As the scene darkened and Paul was imprisoned, they were shaken. So Paul, in his letter, took them "backstage" to reassure them about God's work even in such apparently ominous circumstances.

While Paul the evangelist was chained in a prison cell, he was afforded numerous opportunities to advance the gospel. The palace soldiers who guarded Paul day and night were a captive audience. Because Paul had to be chained to a Roman guard around the clock, each guard took a six-hour shift. By sheer proximity, these guards were forced to listen to Paul's message of salvation in Christ. If you've ever tried to share the gospel with someone who ignored you or simply walked away, imagine the experience of having that listener chained up to the Good News!

The longest period of Paul's confinement amounted to his greatest period of ministry—at the expense of the Roman government! Besides his continual preaching to his captors and fellow prisoners, during this time, Paul wrote the New Testament books Philippians, Philemon, Ephesians, and Colossians.

Paul could see what God was doing "backstage." In effect, Paul was backstage himself. These days, most people are dissatisfied with a backstage role. Some people aspire to be center stage. They long for the limelight and the resulting accolades from being "seen." Even in the Christian world, visibility is too often equated with God's "anointing" or with spiritual effectiveness. But consider Paul's *backstage* experience. Instead of seeing his guards as a nuisance, Paul saw them as his own mission field. What appeared to be a disappointment was God's appointment.

Whenever the scene of your life story turns dark, dare to peek backstage and look for God's providential hand at work. From God's perspective, your dark situation could become the greatest scene of your life.

The Way Up Is Down

When [Christ Jesus] appeared in human form,
he humbled himself in obedience to God
and died a criminal's death on a cross.
Therefore, God elevated him to the place of highest honor
and gave him the name above all other names.

PHILIPPIANS 2:7-9

The soul has a cancer that, if left undiagnosed and untreated, will destroy your spiritual life. This cancer is pride. Pride took Lucifer out of heaven, Adam out of Paradise, Saul from his throne, Nebuchadnezzar out of Babylonian society, and Haman out of the Persian court.

Jesus' life exemplified humility from the very start. Jesus, who is God, arrived in humility and not in a way that anyone expected. The Messiah wasn't born in luxury at Rome General Hospital; he was born in an animal stall. His birth wasn't announced to the world with a public address system hung from the moon; angels appeared to lowly shepherds in a lonely field. God could have threatened people with cosmic annihilation if they didn't respond to his message; instead, Jesus died on a cross to pay for the sins of humanity, and his first prayer while hanging on the cross was, "Father, forgive them." Jesus Christ came to earth as a servant, not to be served.

Because of Jesus' humility, the Father exalted and glorified him. After Jesus was resurrected, he ascended into heaven. Now he dominates heaven and sits at the right hand of the Father's throne. Eventually, Jesus will rule and reign over everything.

Jesus Christ is Lord, and yet he humbled himself. And guess what? We need to follow his example and similarly humble ourselves for God's purposes and for his service. Jesus compared the prayers of a Pharisee and a dishonest tax collector. In humility, the tax collector begged God for mercy. Jesus concluded his story, saying, "Those who exalt themselves will be humbled, and those who humble themselves will be exalted" (Luke 18:14).

As believers, we find that the way up is the way down, and the way down is always the way up.

How to Glow in the Dark

Live clean, innocent lives as children of God, shining like bright lights in a world full of crooked and perverse people.   PHILIPPIANS 2:15

Fireworks are awesome—while they last. Next time you see a fireworks display, linger after the skyrockets fizzle out and the Roman candles are dark. Eventually, you will see stars that won't sputter out or sparkle only momentarily. The darker it is, the better the stars glow.

Some believers are like candles whose warm glow draws people to Jesus. Others are "flashlight believers" who shine the light and lead others out of darkness. Daniel 12:3 says, "Those who are wise will shine as bright as the sky, and those who lead many to righteousness will shine like the stars forever."

According to Paul, Christians need to glow in the dark, living in purity before a worldly audience that watches their every move. If we're ever going to glow with impact, we need to live the Christian life around and among an unbelieving world. Staying around other Christians all the time would be like shining a three-hundred-watt bulb outdoors on a sunny day. Useless!

In Matthew 5:15-16, Jesus says, "No one lights a lamp and then puts it under a basket. Instead, a lamp is placed on a stand, where it gives light to everyone in the house. In the same way, let your good deeds shine out for all to see, so that everyone will praise your heavenly Father."

In 1963, it took about two hours for the world to learn about the death of John F. Kennedy. In 1999, it took minutes to hear about his son's death in a private aircraft over the Atlantic. More than two thousand years ago Jesus Christ, God's Son, died on a cross, yet half the world still doesn't know about it.

You can't reach the whole world by yourself. But if we all glow a bit more where we live, work, and play, then the dark world will notice. Maybe a few people will step out of their darkness to live in the light.

Has Your Joy Sprung a Leak?

Whatever happens, my dear brothers and sisters, rejoice in the Lord.
I never get tired of telling you these things, and I do it to safeguard
your faith.   PHILIPPIANS 3:1

The little book of Philippians originated in a Roman jail. I've visited people in jail, and I've heard words of remorse or anger—not joy. Yet twelve times in Paul's letter to the church at Philippi, he wrote, "Rejoice."

Was Paul lying through his teeth or trying to sound spiritual? Neither. The apostle had discovered that real joy isn't tied to circumstances.

Maybe the Philippian readers got tired of hearing about joy so often, but Paul wasn't tired of reminding them. Paul wanted to warn them to beware of the joy stealers and grace killers that try to rob Christians of their joy.

The Philippian church faced the dangers of Judaizers, who taught that observance of the law was a prerequisite for salvation. They opposed Paul and his message about grace-based Christianity, clinging instead to a bootstrap religion that glorified their works instead of the finished work of Jesus Christ on the cross. No wonder Paul urged the Philippians to safeguard their faith and joy!

Dr. Eugene Peterson, author of *The Message*, wrote, "There are people who do not want us to be free: they don't want us to be free before God, accepted just as we are by his grace. They don't want us to be free to express our faith originally and creatively. . . . Without being aware of it we become anxious about what others will say about us. We are obsessively concerned about what others think we should do." Dr. Peterson is describing the joy stealers!

Under difficult circumstances or around difficult people, joy can spring a leak. When we focus on the trouble instead of on God's power and character, we can lose our joy altogether. The first way to guard our joy is to remember that it's easily lost.

Protect your pure joy, which is yours in Jesus Christ.

How to Run a Marathon

I press on to reach the end of the race and receive the heavenly prize for which God, through Christ Jesus, is calling us.   PHILIPPIANS 3:14

The Christian life is like a long-distance marathon. For a lifetime of following Jesus, you need passion to live day in and day out through varying conditions, moods, circumstances, and changes.

The Olympic runner shows such strong desire. The athlete pours every ounce of energy, mind, and body into the race. Every part of him contributes to help him win. His sweat glands release a liquid to cool his overheated body. As his muscles require more fuel, his pancreas releases a hormone that tells his liver to release stored sugar into his bloodstream. As his legs and heart demand more oxygen, his brain signals the heart to beat faster. Blood flow shuts down in 80 percent of his upper body, and blood vessels dilate 400 percent to ensure maximum blood flow to his legs and heart. His lungs take in more air. Psychologically, the athlete is prepared. His face reveals intense determination: *I want to win this race more than anything else in the world.* His drive, determination, and attitude will not allow him to quit.

In the movie *Chariots of Fire*, world-class runner Harold Abrahams suffers his first defeat. After the race, he pouts and angrily declares, "If I can't win, I won't run." He thinks his defeat might be a good excuse to quit. His wise girlfriend retorts, "If you don't run, you can't win." Abrahams goes on to win the 1924 Olympic gold medal in the one-hundred-meter race.

Are you straining to win? Exerting any spiritual energy? Are you following Jesus Christ with passionate pursuit? Are you involving your whole self—heart, soul, mind, body, strength—with an eye on the prize?

Paul never gave up or quit running his race. Whatever your own age or condition, don't quit. God has a purpose for the race of your life.

Don't Worry

Don't worry about anything; instead, pray about everything. Tell God what you need, and thank him for all he has done. PHILIPPIANS 4:6

According to the National Institute of Mental Health, thirteen million Americans feel anxious every day. Worry is a big problem—with negative results.

A British clinic found that one-third of five hundred patients had visual problems because of stress. Dr. Leonard Fosdick noted that tooth decay is accelerated because worry restricts the flow of saliva, which neutralizes mouth acids. A survey of five thousand students in twenty-one colleges proved that worriers get the lowest grades. Medical research repeatedly demonstrates that worry breaks down resistance to disease.

So go ahead and worry—if you want to be a blind, diseased flunky with no teeth!

Jesus provides his followers a better way. The cure for anxiety is prayer. Rather than directing your energy inward with mental perturbation or outward with frenzied activity, you are encouraged to "give all your worries and cares to God, for he cares about you" (1 Peter 5:7). Giving worries to God includes thanking him for his sovereign control even if you can't understand his plan at the time. We need to be anxious for nothing, prayerful in everything, and thankful for all things.

One dark night a man walked down an unfamiliar road with a deep ravine on either side. Suddenly he stepped into space and began to fall. As the man flailed his arms, he found a bush on the side and held on for his life. Every minute he hung was sheer agony, and his body grew numb. Finally in weakness and despair, the man let go and dropped. It was only six inches to the bottom of the ditch. His anxiety had been needless.

The great hymn "What a Friend We Have in Jesus" says,

> O what peace we often forfeit,
> O what needless pain we bear,
> All because we do not carry
> Everything to God in prayer!

If you are holding on to some worry, through prayer trade it for God's peace.

What Holds It All Together?

He existed before anything else, and he holds all creation together.

COLOSSIANS 1:17

Jesus Christ is the only person who ever lived before he was born. During his ministry, Jesus told the religious leaders, "I tell you the truth, before Abraham was even born, I Am!" (John 8:58). Because Jesus is one with God, he created the well-ordered universe out of chaos. And, as today's key Bible verse tells us, Jesus remains responsible for holding creation together.

Matter is composed of rapidly moving particles with opposite charges, yet they retain cohesion and balance.

The earth's distance from the sun is perfect for sustaining our world. The sun's temperature measures twelve thousand degrees Fahrenheit, and it is located ninety-three million miles from the earth. If it came even as close as Venus, our world would burn. If the sun were as far away as Mars, we'd freeze.

The earth rotates 365 times a year, at one thousand miles per hour, sustaining our days and nights as it travels around the sun. If it rotated at one hundred miles per hour, our days and nights would be ten times longer, and the alternating heat and cold would burn and freeze all life from our planet.

Because the earth is tilted 23$^1/_3$ degrees on its axis, we have the four seasons, and our atmosphere is a perfect balance of oxygen and other gases. Imagine if our atmosphere were 50 percent oxygen and 50 percent nitrogen; then the first person to light a match would end everything.

Even the depth and dimensions of our oceans matter. At half their present dimensions, we'd receive only a quarter of our rainfall. And if the oceans were an eighth larger, the earth's annual rainfall would swamp the planet.

Aren't you glad someone monitors these details? We can trust Jesus Christ to hold the universe—and our lives—together continually and consistently. As you have emotional and spiritual needs, turn to the Creator with fresh confidence because of the evidence in nature of his wonderful design and sustaining control.

When God Clears the Path

Through him God reconciled
everything to himself.
He made peace with everything in heaven and on earth
by means of Christ's blood on the cross.

This includes you who were once far away from God.

COLOSSIANS 1:20-21

Once a hurricane pushed through a densely grown, forested area of North Carolina where I was visiting. I tried to reach the cabin where I was staying, but the road was clogged with trees, stones, and debris. Until a path was cleared, access was impossible.

This concept of clearing a path aptly represents one of the Bible's most important ideas: reconciliation. Reconciliation means to "alter or change completely, to turn hostility into friendship." *The Living Bible* paraphrases the idea of *reconcile* as "to clear a path for everything to come to him."

Sin creates an impenetrable barrier to any relationship and destroys its harmony. I may want to reach God, but I can't accomplish this with my own sinful effort. My efforts to break through this barrier would be like trying to break through a concrete slab with a plastic hammer.

Jesus Christ was sent on a mission to remove this barrier—and Jesus used the dynamite of his own death and resurrection to blow it away.

Reconciliation changes your relationship with God. Before reconciliation, he was God, and you were a fallen human creature. As you put your personal faith in Jesus Christ, God becomes your heavenly Father, and you become his child. What a change! Second Corinthians 5:17 tells us that "anyone who belongs to Christ has become a new person."

Because we are reconciled to God, we can clear the broken pathways between ourselves and others. Scottish theologian John Eadie (1810–1876) said, "The cross which slew Jesus also slew ... hostility! ... The cross is God's answer to Judaizing, racial discrimination, segregation, apartheid, anti-Semitism, bigotry, war and every other cause and result of human strife." Recall a lost friendship and be willing to begin the process of reconciliation. Take steps today to be reconciled to one another.

The Danger of Philosophy

Don't let anyone capture you with empty philosophies and high-sounding nonsense that come from human thinking and from the spiritual powers of this world, rather than from Christ. COLOSSIANS 2:8

Ancient peoples revered their philosophers, but they were not always all they were cracked up to be. During the early church age, the prevalent false teachers elevated philosophy over scriptural revelation. These Gnostics built a system of religious philosophy combining Eastern mysticism and Jewish legalism. On the surface, it sounded intelligent, yet it was deadly. And believers who were young in the faith and ignorant of Scripture were most susceptible to these traps.

Philosophy means "the love of wisdom," yet the Bible is clear: "Fear of the LORD is the foundation of true knowledge" (Proverbs 1:7). Through the years, many Christian fads and trends, involving a range of philosophies, have come and gone. For example, a yearning for the "deeper life" sounds wonderful, but if the teaching isn't anchored in the Bible, people can get distracted from the central truth about Christ.

At the age of eighty-three, the preacher E. Stanley Jones affirmed, "Christ has been, and is, to me *the Event*." Jones had learned the danger of becoming sidetracked. He wrote, "I once traveled during my formative evangelistic years with a very great man. I learned much from him. But when his emphasis shifted from Christ to varying other areas of human interest—antiwar programs, social justice, birth control, spiritualism—he was less than effective; he was a blur. He would exhaust these topics in a year or two and have to shift to a new one. But you do not exhaust Christ—He is the inexhaustible. Events come and go; but *the Event* remains unchanged amid the changeable."

It's good to love wisdom, but only the wisdom built on a foundation of true knowledge: the fear of the Lord. Spiritual growth comes through consistent nutrition from the Word of God. Draw the nourishment for your spiritual life from Jesus Christ.

Ripping Up Tickets

He canceled the record of the charges against us and took it away by nailing it to the cross. COLOSSIANS 2:14

I have a confession to make. One night a policeman gave me a ticket for speeding. I hate the shame, the threat of higher insurance, and having to pay a fine. But the passenger in the backseat of my car called her cousin at the central police station, who was a friend of this officer. My ticket was ripped up and my debt canceled. I should feel terrible, but I don't. I love forgiveness!

The Greek word for "charges against us" in today's verse refers to the handwritten certificate on which a debtor acknowledged his debt to be paid. Can you imagine the gratitude of the debtor if the person holding this record destroyed it?

Every person owes God an unpayable debt for violating his law. But Paul says that God took our debts and canceled the record of our sins.

The crimes of a crucified criminal were written up and nailed to a cross as a public declaration of his guilt and violation. When Jesus, who was sinless, was on the cross, his sign said, "This is Jesus of Nazareth—King of the Jews." There were no crimes to list. Instead, our sins were put against Jesus Christ's account, and he paid the price for them.

Can you imagine a court trial where you are the accused, Satan is the prosecuting attorney, and Christ is your defense attorney? The newspaper coverage of the trial would read, "Sinner pardoned and gone to live with Judge."

The Cross canceled the debt of the sins for humankind from the past, present, and future. We failed to keep all God's requirements, and yet the long record of charges against us was wiped clean by the blood of Jesus. A favorite hymn declares, "Jesus paid it all, / All to Him I owe; / Sin had left a crimson stain, / He washed it white as snow."

Heavenly Minded and *Earthly Good*

Think about the things of heaven, not the things of earth.

COLOSSIANS 3:2

You've heard it said that people can be "so heavenly minded they're no earthly good." The reverse is also true. People can get so bogged down with earthly concerns that they forget their ultimate destination. The Bible tells us that when we keep heaven in mind, we think clearly and live purely. "We are already God's children, but he has not yet shown us what we will be like when Christ appears. But we do know that we will be like him, for we will see him as he really is. And all who have this eager expectation will keep themselves pure, just as he is pure" (1 John 3:2-3). Keeping our minds focused on heaven teaches us how to live responsibly and well here on the earth.

Paul doesn't advocate disengaging from life and culture. He is not stipulating that Christians are not to be involved in business, sports, or civil events. He isn't telling Christians to withdraw from normal duties and responsibilities. This passage doesn't prohibit Christians from becoming lawyers or doctors or entrepreneurs. Bible heroes such as Joseph and Daniel were highly involved and visible in society.

The key is to understand your priorities. Earthly concerns should not dominate our thoughts. Why? Because wherever you focus your mind, it will govern your priorities. Jesus said it best, "Wherever your treasure is, there the desires of your heart will also be" (Luke 12:34). When I travel overseas, I miss my family. I enjoy the different food, the winsome fellowship of believers in other places, and the exotic sights of being in a foreign country, but my mind remains set on home. I'm engaged in what I'm doing, but my priority is my family at home.

As you walk through this world, remember that you're just passing through. Run your thoughts through an eternal grid that considers everything in light of eternity. That kind of heavenly mindedness will help you accomplish a world of earthly good.

Marketplace Christians

*Work willingly at whatever you do, as though you were working for the
Lord rather than for people.* COLOSSIANS 3:23

The workplace is one platform, or stage, where others can closely observe
your Christian faith. You may be the only evidence of Christ that your
unchurched coworkers will see. From looking at you, they find the answers
to their questions: How do Christians act when they come to work on a
Monday? How do Christians react to work pressures? How do Christians
make ethical decisions on the job? How do Christians treat other employ-
ees and their employer? The marketplace provides a great opportunity
for Christians. They work hard and display a good attitude in order to
help unbelievers with their questions. But they also work wholeheartedly
because they know that they aren't the only ones watching. God watches
as well.

God gave us work as part of his good creation—and not after the Fall, as
part of man's curse. Genesis 2:15 says, "The LORD God placed the man in
the Garden of Eden to tend and watch over it." God's first task for Adam was
to employ him as a gardener. Then in God's top-ten list of commandments,
the Lord further exonerated work, saying, "You have six days each week for
your ordinary work" (Exodus 20:9).

American workers admit they spend more than 20 percent of their work
time goofing off. That figure amounts to one full day each week. A joke goes
that an employee died, went to heaven, and complained to Peter, "I'm only
thirty-five. I'm too young to die." Peter checked the records and said, "Well,
according to the hourly work reports you've been turning in, you should be
ninety-seven."

Christians have a God-directed motivation for working conscientiously
and truthfully on the job. They know their ultimate authority is God. How
well does your service to your employer reflect your commitment to Christ?
Seize this incredible opportunity to witness to others through excellence
in your work.

Put Your Mouth to Good Use

Let your conversation be gracious and attractive so that you will have the right response for everyone. COLOSSIANS 4:6

When your doctor says, "Stick out your tongue," he knows your throat reveals something about what is going on inside you.

About the tongue, Jesus said the same thing: "Whatever is in your heart determines what you say" (Matthew 12:34). Whatever people are on the inside, their mouths will give evidence of on the outside. If angry people harbor grudges, eventually they will express those bitter feelings. Those filled with lustful thoughts will eventually express those feelings with crude remarks. People who are genuinely loving and kind will express those qualities through their words.

You may wonder about the importance of your actual words. Does it really matter what you say? The apostle James said it best: "We all make many mistakes. For if we could control our tongues, we would be perfect and could also control ourselves in every other way" (James 3:2).

Jesus set an example of gracious speech: "Everyone spoke well of him and was amazed by the gracious words that came from his lips" (Luke 4:22). It is unfortunate, but some Christians speak in a manner that would be labeled anything but gracious. The Scottish Bible scholar Henry Drummond (1851–1897) said, "How many prodigals are kept out of the Kingdom of God by the unlovely characters of those who profess to be inside?"

Beyond avoiding obscenity or gossip or belittling words, our speech should never be dull and lifeless. Our words represent the Lord Jesus Christ. We must strike a balance between an attractive message and speech so pointed and clear that there is no misunderstanding.

Throw out any religious mumbo jumbo you've accumulated over the years. As you get rid of the pat answers and sanctuary tone in your voice, speak to others with clarity and respect about your beliefs.

What Kind of Church to Choose

As we pray to our God and Father about you, we think of your faithful work, your loving deeds, and the enduring hope you have because of our Lord Jesus Christ. 1 THESSALONIANS 1:3

The churches available to you might be as varied as the types of restaurants in your neighborhood. Some emphasize liturgy, others stress music, and others are centered on Bible teaching. Finding the right church is not simple, but Paul's words about the church at Thessalonica provide a starting point. Paul noted this church's three noteworthy virtues, and John Calvin called this description a "brief definition of true Christianity."

Paul's three virtues are not abstract qualities or lofty doctrinal statements. They are productive virtues of real people—not a place or a building—that will produce concrete and practical results.

First, this church had an *active faith*. This church put its faith to work. These believers translated what they believed into their everyday lives. James the brother of Jesus affirmed in James 2:20, "How foolish! Can't you see that faith without good deeds is useless?"

Second, Paul praised this church's *active love*. Even when faced with difficulties or struggles, they behaved in a way that was sustained with love. You might say, "When the going got tough, the tough kept loving." Love is a principle earmark for Christians. John 13:35 says, "Your love for one another will prove to the world that you are my disciples."

The third and final productive virtue was *active waiting*. As the members of the church in Thessalonica lived with the hope of heaven, it changed the way they lived. For Christians, the anticipation of Jesus' return is one of the most powerful forces for purity.

No matter where you choose to go to church, remember that you *are* the church, or at least a part of it. Locate a group of believers that reflect these three priorities, and then practice these principles in your own life.

Balanced Leadership

As apostles of Christ we certainly had a right to make some demands of you, but instead we were like children among you. Or we were like a mother feeding and caring for her own children. . . . And you know that we treated each of you as a father treats his own children.

1 THESSALONIANS 2:7, 11

I imagine the great apostle Paul as a strong, masculine leader. Paul knew how to lead from the front, take the hits, and keep going. In 1877, in the Yale Lectures, Phillips Brooks (1835–1893) said, "Courage is the indispensable requisite of any true ministry. . . . If you are afraid of men and a slave to their opinions, go, and do something else. Go and make shoes to fit them. Go even and paint pictures you know are bad but which suit their bad taste. But do not keep on all your life preaching sermons which shall say not what God sent you to declare, but what they hire you to say. Be courageous. Be independent." Paul fits that description.

Yet Paul also had a nurturing side. The apostle didn't want to abuse his authority. He wanted to love these young believers selflessly. In his instruction, Paul mixed the encouraging tenderness of a mother with the value-laden discipline of a father. Paul wrote, "Even if you had ten thousand others to teach you about Christ, you have only one spiritual father. For I became your father in Christ Jesus when I preached the Good News to you" (1 Corinthians 4:15). Paul nurtured believers.

Good leadership is balanced leadership. A leader needs to be strong and to be soft, to lead and to love, to be courageous and to be consoling. If a leader is always cuddly and sentimental, the kids could become unruly. But if a leader is always stern and unmovable, people will miss the personal touch and become hard to reach. Ask God to make you a balanced blend of truth and tenderness.

The Power Eaters!

We never stop thanking God that when you received his message from us, you didn't think of our words as mere human ideas. You accepted what we said as the very word of God—which, of course, it is. And this word continues to work in you who believe. 1 THESSALONIANS 2:13

In Coney Island, New York, one man consumed fifty-nine and a half hot dogs in twelve minutes to take the power-eaters' championship at the annual hot dog–eating contest. That's a dubious honor at best. I'd rather excel in another area of consumption: spiritual appetite.

The Bible, the best-selling book of all time, has more copies in more languages than any other book in history. The Scriptures are available to 97 percent of the world's population, and yet the Bible is one of the least-read books. Job said, "I have treasured the words of His mouth more than my necessary food" (Job 23:12, NKJV). What about you? Do you feed on this spiritual food?

The apostle Paul commended the Thessalonians for treating the Bible with great respect and with hunger for its truth. When he wrote that they accepted what was said, the words conveyed the meaning of welcome. They welcomed the Scriptures into their ears, their brains, their hearts, and their lives. These believers were spiritual power eaters.

One research group says, "Only 25 percent of born-again Christians read their Bibles every day." This means that 75 percent of Christians who read their Bibles only do it once a week; presumably at church.

The real power of the Bible comes when a strong spiritual appetite is combined with subsequent life application. Besides reading God's Word, you should learn to feed on it, taking nutrition that sustains and enables all activity. It takes about seventy-one hours to read from Genesis to Revelation; over a year you could do it in twelve minutes a day. Read God's Word as your daily meal, and make it a regular and vigorous habit. The experience will give you a spiritual appetite for life-changing transformation.

Sexual Purity

God's will is for you to be holy, so stay away from all sexual sin. Then each of you will control his own body and live in holiness and honor.

1 THESSALONIANS 4:3-4

Sex was God's idea. The Lord's design included the pleasure of those who are married and also the propagation of the human race. Yet because sex is God given, it must also be God governed, set apart, holy.

Primarily, we stay holy sexually by practicing abstinence and keeping clear of any activity that might tempt us. God doesn't command sexual purity because he wants to cramp your style. He's trying to save you years of potential heartache, legal proceedings, emotional suffering, and sexually transmitted diseases. God wants you to be fulfilled. As your creator, he knows what you need to be fulfilled. God gives rules for our protection and satisfaction. God gave the commandment "You must not commit adultery" (Exodus 20:14) to put a protective wall around marriage.

Sex can be compared to a fire. In the fireplace, the fire is beautiful and great with heat that feels wonderful and satisfying. Yet when the fire burns outside of the hearth where it belongs, it quickly becomes destructive.

So be careful what you allow yourself to watch, read, and hear. The battle regarding sex begins in the mind. Remember King David, who saw another man's wife while he was enjoying the view one night. He could have looked away. But he fell into sin with Bathsheba. There is an old saying, "You can't stop a bird from flying over your head, but you can stop it from building a nest in your hair." Don't let sexual temptation come to stay.

Leonard Ravenhill said, "The greatest miracle that God can do is to take an unholy man out of an unholy world and make that unholy man holy and put him back in an unholy world and keep him holy." God can make you that holy person, even in this unholy world.

Raptured!

Together with [the Christians who have died], we who are still alive and remain on the earth will be caught up in the clouds to meet the Lord in the air. Then we will be with the Lord forever.   1 THESSALONIANS 4:17

An old farmer brought his family to the city for the first time to see skyscrapers and all the sights. The farmer dropped off his wife at a department store and took his son to the tallest building. In the lobby, they saw something they'd never seen before. Two steel doors opened, a rather large and elderly woman walked in, and then the big doors closed behind her. The father and the son watched as the dial over the door swept to the right and then back to the left. Suddenly the doors opened, and a beautiful young lady walked out. The old farmer, amazed, said to his son, "Wait right here. I'm going to get your mother and run her through that thing."

Christians look forward to an instant moment of transformation (see 2 Corinthians 5:2). When Christ returns, the Christians who are alive will be taken up to heaven, instantly and totally transformed into resurrected bodies.

New Testament Greek scholar Kenneth Wuest translated 1 Thessalonians 4:17 this way: "As for us who are living and are left behind, together with them we shall be snatched away forcibly in [masses of saints having the appearance of] clouds for a welcome-meeting with the Lord in the lower atmosphere." *Rapture* is a good word to describe this grandest of events. Our change will be complete. As Christians we are constantly changing and growing in our faith; this process is called *sanctification*. When Jesus returns for his church, our transformation will become an instant accomplishment, or glorification.

This event will signal the end of walking by faith and the beginning of being in the presence of Jesus forever. No matter what has happened to you in the past, remember that your best days are yet to come! Keep your eyes forward and upward.

Tribulation

*You know quite well that the day of the Lord's return will come
unexpectedly, like a thief in the night. When people are saying,
"Everything is peaceful and secure," then disaster will fall on them as
suddenly as a pregnant woman's labor pains begin. And there will be
no escape.*   1 THESSALONIANS 5:2-3

Of all the prophecies in the Bible, few include more detail than the "Day of
the Lord." This Old Testament term refers to the full and final judgment of
God, and it does not mean a literal twenty-four-hour day but rather a season
or a whole series of events. The emphasis is on the Lord because when the
Day of the Lord arrives, humankind's day is over.

The Day of the Lord will mark the end of the "day of grace," that long
period of time between the first coming of Christ and the second coming
of Christ. The Day of the Lord will not be a peaceful time but a time of great
wrath, a time when judgment will fall on this earth.

Often the Bible talks about this coming period of tribulation as a birth.
Birth is a wonderful yet painful process. The birth of the Kingdom of God
here on the earth will be a great yet painful process as well.

Paul described the glorious deliverance of Christians, when the saints
are caught up in the air when the Lord returns "like a thief in the night."

Jesus told us to "keep alert at all times. And pray that you might be strong
enough to escape these coming horrors and stand before the Son of Man"
(Luke 21:36). Let's get busy telling those around us about Jesus the Great
Deliverer.

Learn to Say Thank You

Be thankful in all circumstances, for this is God's will for you who belong to Christ Jesus.   1 THESSALONIANS 5:18

One of the most important pursuits for a Christian is to pursue God's will. Ultimately, of course, God's eternal will is for us to be in heaven. As for knowing God's will for us now, we have some direct guidelines in God's Word.

Today's Bible reading provides several directives about God's general will for our attitudes, and the first on the list is thankfulness. God begins here because he works on the heart attitudes that will later produce outward actions.

God doesn't expect you to say, "Thank you, Lord, for the Holocaust" or "Thank you that people are dying in wars" or "Thank you for all the sinful things around me." Yet God does want you to be thankful in spite of a particular situation—thankful that God is still in control, that he is with you, and that he'll never forsake you. You can maintain a grateful spirit as you acknowledge that God is in charge. Psalm 103:2 says, "Let all that I am praise the Lord; may I never forget the good things he does for me."

In the book *The Hiding Place*, Corrie ten Boom told about how she and her sister, Betsie, were transferred to the German prison camp Ravensbruck, where the barracks were overcrowded and infested with fleas. That day the sisters read 1 Thessalonians 5:16-18, and Betsie told Corrie to stop and thank the Lord. At first, Corrie flatly refused to thank God for fleas, but Betsie insisted. During their months at the camp, they were surprised to find how openly they could hold Bible study and prayer meetings without any guard interference. Months later, they learned the guards would not enter the barracks because of the fleas.

Spend time thanking God for what he is bringing and will bring into your life. Maintain this attitude of gratitude in spite of your circumstances.

October 27

I've Got Good News and Bad News

[Those who refuse to obey the Good News of our Lord Jesus] will be punished with eternal destruction, forever separated from the Lord and from his glorious power. 2 THESSALONIANS 1:9

The car in front of me had a bumper sticker that read, "Jesus is coming soon . . . and boy is he mad!" That sticker wasn't telling the whole story, but the end of the world will reveal both good and bad news.

When the Lord returns, he will come back as King, saying in effect, to every politician and voter, "Move over! Let me show you how it's to be done!" That's good news.

The bad news is that Jesus' return will also mark "eternal destruction." The word *eternal* means exactly what it says. It will be unending. For the majority of people on the earth, this experience will not be a warm feeling as they pass through a tunnel and are embraced by the light. Instead, they will have the woeful experience of darkness and judgment.

The classic preacher Charles H. Spurgeon described the bad news, saying, "Your heart will be beating with a high fever; your pulse rattling at an enormous rate in agony . . . every nerve a string on which the devil shall ever play his diabolical tune of Hell's Unutterable Lament; your soul forever and ever aching, and your body palpitating in unison with your soul. Fictions, sir? They are no fictions, but as God lives, solid, stern truth."

This topic isn't a pleasant subject, and almost everyone disdains it. But if you love people, then you'll tell them the truth, the whole truth, and nothing but the truth. Ask God to help you live expectantly as you wait for Jesus to return. And also ask God for the strength to tell people about how they can avoid the bad news.

How to Send "Knee-Mail"

We keep on praying for you, asking our God to enable you to live a life worthy of his call. May he give you the power to accomplish all the good things your faith prompts you to do. 2 THESSALONIANS 1:11

In 1973, when researchers asked people what they considered essential, computers were not on the list. Ten years later, only 4 percent thought computers were a necessity. Today, many of us say we couldn't live without them.

You can receive e-mail on your laptop or a PDA from anywhere. Prayer is somewhat like e-mail. Prayers can be sent instantly from anywhere. And if our prayers aren't perfect, the Holy Spirit will convey our thoughts to the Father perfectly (see Romans 8:26). Sending e-mail requires an open connection. Sending "knee-mail" requires an open life, free from unconfessed sin.

To send e-mail, you must have the right address, or it will be returned to your computer. To pray effectively, you must send it to God through his Son, Jesus Christ. Once you have the right connection and the right address, your prayers should also have the right intentions. Paul's prayers were always God centered. They had the aim of God's glory being demonstrated through his people on the earth.

Some view prayer as room service or a way to order God around as if he were a "divine bellhop." These people believe God is like a personal heavenly genie where all you have to do is rub the prayer lamp. But these concepts are not taught in the Bible.

Jesus Christ taught us to pray, "Our Father," not "Our Butler." We're to say, "Your will be done," not "God, please make sure my will gets done."

Maybe you'll relate to a little girl saying prayers. She always asked God for something. One night, as a sweet afterthought, she said, "And now, Lord, what can I do for you?" As you pray today, ask God to accomplish his will in your life and to enable you to fulfill his good intentions.

The Ultimate Lie

[The man of lawlessness] will exalt himself and defy everything that people call god and every object of worship. He will even sit in the temple of God, claiming that he himself is God. 2 THESSALONIANS 2:4

After British statesman Lloyd George met with Hitler for an hour, he called Hitler "the greatest living German." A year later, he wrote, "I only wish we had a man of his supreme quality at the head of affairs in our country today" and applauded Hitler for "the moral and ethical side of the National Social program, its clear stand for religion and Christianity, and its ethical principles." What a misperception!

The Bible predicts another leader who will come on the world scene. Charismatic and awe inspiring, he will have answers for many of the maladies of our time. People will be drawn to his unusual appeal and his promise of peace.

Someone predicted that he will have the oratorical skill of John Kennedy, the inspirational power of Sir Winston Churchill, the respectability of Mohandas Gandhi, the charm of Will Rogers, and the genius of King Solomon.

Of course, this leader will be a counterfeit. Paul believed that this was the ultimate lie (see 2 Thessalonians 2:9-11). From the beginning, Satan has been a liar. Lucifer tried to convince heaven that he was as good as God (see Isaiah 14:13-14). Then in the Garden of Eden, the devil told Eve that she could be like God if she followed his dishonest plan (see Genesis 3:5).

From the beginning of time, the devil has wanted people to believe the key lie that humans are divine. This man of lawlessness will convince many that he is to be worshiped as God. Is that unthinkable? For many Europeans, Hitler's twisted plan was unthinkable, yet for a period of history, it thrived. Practice humility as you bow before the Lord God today, and thank him that you know the true Lord of the universe and the Hope of the world.

Stand Your Ground

With all these things in mind, dear brothers and sisters, stand firm and keep a strong grip on the teaching we passed on to you both in person and by letter. 2 THESSALONIANS 2:15

One day, two cowboys went out to capture a wild steer and took along a little gray burro. They tied the burro to the steer, neck and neck, and then let them go. At first, the steer threw the small animal all over the place, banged him against trees, threw him on top of rocks and down into the bushes. Time after time, both went down. Then the burro had an idea. No matter how often the steer threw him, every time, the burro got to his feet and took a step in the direction of the corral. The animals continued in this pattern for days. After a week, the burro showed up at the corral with the tamest and sorriest-looking steer you've ever seen. How'd the burro do it? He stood his ground, one step at a time.

As Christians, we have certain principles on which we must stand our ground. The basics are Bible study, prayer, fellowship, and telling others about Jesus. We should never lose ground and give up on these practices.

In our Bible reading today, Paul expresses the idea that we need to maintain our course. I've always found it amusing that people will speak to or make funny faces at or chide the guards at Buckingham Palace, but no matter what they do, the guards stand their ground.

As followers of Jesus Christ, we must stay at our posts and not retreat just because some situations are difficult. We can be reassured that God has a plan. As we've read through the Bible over the past months, we've watched Samuel stand his ground. Joseph remained steady like Ruth, Esther, Daniel, and a host of others.

Are you wavering or floundering spiritually? Maybe you need to hear the Holy Spirit saying, "Steady." Stand your ground.

October 31 READ 2 THESSALONIANS 3:1-5

Nine-Tenths

Dear brothers and sisters, we ask you to pray for us. Pray that the Lord's message will spread rapidly and be honored wherever it goes, just as when it came to you. 2 THESSALONIANS 3:1

Nine-tenths of an iceberg lies below the waterline and out of sight. Above the surface, only one-tenth is visible. The bulk of the mass, which lends stability and enormity to the floating island of ice, is the lowest and hidden part. Prayer and effective service are like an iceberg. Nine-tenths of the effectiveness for any ministry occurs from prayer.

In today's verse, we learn that Paul wasn't some independent loner who carved his own way and needed no one. In fact, Paul knew his greatness came from a powerful God combined with a solid network of prayer partners. Those prayers from so many people were the underpinnings of Paul's powerful ministry.

I keep old calendars. Each week has a different name printed on it. This individual or family made a covenant to pray for me during that week of the year, and their efforts bathe my entire year in prayer. These brothers and sisters in Christ have been my nine-tenths and provided stability and effectiveness for my own ministry.

Bible teacher A. W. Tozer said, "If the Holy Spirit was withdrawn from the church today, 95 percent of what we do would go on and no one would know the difference. If the Holy Spirit had been withdrawn from the New Testament church, 95 percent of what they did would stop, and everybody would know the difference." We need to consider our activities and make sure the Holy Spirit is directing them.

Every iceberg needs a base to support its blue and white beauty, and your life needs spiritual stability. Plan today to form a network of friends who can pray for one another about weekly schedules, challenges, and ideas. You need the nine-tenths to be effective, and so do your friends.

Arm's Length

Dear brothers and sisters, we give you this command in the name of our Lord Jesus Christ: Stay away from all believers who live idle lives . . . refusing to work and meddling in other people's business.

2 THESSALONIANS 3:6, 11

When I was a young boy, my father regularly spoke with me about the necessity of selecting the right types of people as friends so I wouldn't be harmed by the influence of bad company.

In the early church, some lazy people in Thessalonica were free to meddle in other people's affairs. Paul tells these meddlers to "get a life"—and he tells the rest of the church to steer clear. There's a big difference between putting your nose in other people's business and putting your heart in other people's problems. But is this "arm's length" approach still loving? Is this the same guy who wrote the great love chapter of 1 Corinthians 13?

Yes. In fact, the Scriptures tell us to deal firmly and swiftly with such people, or they will poison others in the church. Like a healthy body, a strong church can purge itself of disease. Whenever your skin is cut, the leukocytes rush to the area in order to clean up the infection and accelerate the healing. This is similar to what Jesus commanded of the spiritual body. He instructed his followers to lovingly approach a sinning brother, first one-on-one and then in increasing numbers. If this brother refused to hear repeated correction and wouldn't even listen to the whole church, he was to be treated like a pagan (see Matthew 18; see also November 17).

Today, take a moment and evaluate your circle of friends. Are there any professing Christians you need to lovingly but firmly approach about an issue in their lives? According to Scripture, a reproof could be the very best thing for this person. And if there is anyone who is dragging you down, whether a believer or not, think hard about whether you might, as Paul says, need to just stay away.

Peace on Earth

May the Lord of peace himself give you his peace at all times and in every situation. The Lord be with you all.   2 THESSALONIANS 3:16

The threat of a nuclear war inspired one retired couple to move to the country least likely to be affected by a nuclear war. After careful research, they moved to the Falkland Islands and breathed a sigh of relief. Months later, their haven turned into a war zone when Great Britain and Argentina clashed in a major battle for occupation. You just can't find peace on the earth.

Some scholars estimate that in more than thirty-one hundred years of recorded history, the world has been at peace only 8 percent of the time—a total of 286 years. During this period, eight thousand treaties have been made and broken.

As Paul closes this letter to a young, afflicted church, he reminds them that God's people are to be different from the rest of this turbulent world. They are to receive the soundness of soul that Jesus Christ referred to when he said, "I am leaving you with a gift—peace of mind and heart. And the peace I give is a gift the world cannot give" (John 14:27).

Despite his Pax Romana, Caesar Augustus was no stranger to war and other stresses of his extensive rule. When he heard about a certain man of Rome who slept quietly and at peace even though he had great debts, the emperor bought the man's bed, thinking there must be some secret in its comfortable design. Of course, he learned it was a useless purchase.

Peace is laying your head on your pillow at night in right relationship to God. According to J. Oswald Sanders (1902–1992), peace is not the absence of trouble; it's the presence of God. And the apostle Paul says the same thing in today's verse: Essentially, "The Lord's peace is wherever the Lord himself is!" No matter what external or internal struggles you face, you can experience God's presence, and that's peace you can count on.

Raising Spiritual Kids

I am writing to Timothy, my true son in the faith. May God the Father and Christ Jesus our Lord give you grace, mercy, and peace.   1 TIMOTHY 1:2

Paul's young protégé named Timothy was converted during Paul's first missionary journey. He was the son of a religiously mixed marriage; his mother was a Jew, and his father was an unbeliever. During Paul's second missionary journey, Timothy joined him.

Over time, Timothy matured spiritually, and Paul increasingly involved him in ministry opportunities. Timothy was a breath of fresh air to Paul; the apostle saw in him a fellow spiritual soldier who shared his values. In fact, he noticed that Timothy's love for people was equal to his own: "I have no one else like Timothy, who genuinely cares about your welfare" (Philippians 2:20).

Timothy loved people because Paul mentored him to do so. For the apostle Paul, Timothy was not only his spiritual son and servant; he was also his substitute. Faithfulness and excellence of character open the door to fruitfulness.

Are you a mature Christian? Perhaps you've personally known the Lord for some time, and now you are looking for ways to be used in God's work. Let me suggest that you consider having a spiritual "kid." If you have led someone to Christ, or if you have a new believer in your sphere of influence, God may have a mentoring relationship in store for you. Or, if you are young in the faith and having a hard time with certain spiritual "basics," take the bold step of asking someone who is older in the faith than you to help you grow spiritually.

The Worst Sinner Ever

This is a trustworthy saying, and everyone should accept it: "Christ Jesus came into the world to save sinners"—and I am the worst of them all.

1 TIMOTHY 1:15

Looking at his later life, you might never imagine that Paul would call himself the worst of all sinners. But because of his early life, that is exactly how he felt. As a Christian, Paul was sensitive to his past, when he had been determined to stop the early Christian movement.

As a young rabbi, Paul was filled with fierce religious zeal that fueled his hatred of Christians. There's nothing wrong with zeal in itself—depending, of course, on the object of your passion and the character of your pursuit of it. Paul (going by Saul then) had been sincere in his zeal, but he was sincerely wrong. Any good thing can become a bad thing if it keeps you from achieving the best thing.

Paul's words call to mind some of Jesus' own. Jesus said a person enters the Kingdom of God through being poor in spirit and repenting of past sins that offended God (see Matthew 5:1-34). This poorness of spirit would be interpreted by some Christians today as an injured self-esteem. But there is a difference. Paul is not prevented from living a healthy life because he reflects on his wrongs. Recognizing who you are in the light of who God is always produces a humble reaction.

You would never impress the Boeing Corporation with a paper airplane. You would never impress a great conductor with "My Dog Has Fleas" on your ukulele. And God isn't impressed with your background, your education, or even your religious zeal. We have all fallen short of the glory of God. Like Paul, we should recognize where we have done so and rejoice in God's mercy that is evident in our lives.

Pause for a moment today and thank God for saving you from your sins. Then ask the Lord to show you how he might want to use your past for his glory.

Building Bridges

There is only one God and one Mediator who can reconcile God and humanity—the man Christ Jesus. 1 TIMOTHY 2:5

When I was growing up, an old steel bridge spanned a river about five miles from our home in California. The bridge connected the dusty town of Apple Valley and the growing metropolis of Victorville. Our family of four boys loved to cross the bridge into the land of shopping and fun.

A gulf separates God and man for some pretty obvious reasons. God is perfect, and we are imperfect. God is totally unique, holy, and pure, while we are all alike in being naturally sinful. Apart from God's grace, the concept of God and man ever getting together is as far-fetched as moving the sun next door to a skating rink to obtain additional light inside. The light is everywhere; what's needed is a way for the light to get in. What's needed for us to be connected to God is a mediator, or bridge. That's where Jesus comes in.

The word *mediator* means a "go-between," someone who intervenes to make peace between two parties. As the God-man, Jesus Christ was the perfect—and only possible—Mediator between a holy God and sinful mankind. In Jesus, God actually became a man. There is only one God and only one possible mediator, Jesus. Because he was both God and man, and because he was sinless and yet he took our sins on himself to the cross, Jesus was uniquely qualified for this role. His substitutionary death was sufficient to bring the two parties together.

As Christians, we should follow Jesus' example of being a bridge builder. Some people act like spiritual terrorists, blowing up bridges. Instead, we ought to be peacemakers and reconcilers. Guard your heart; don't be a fault-finder or a sin sniffer. Today, follow Jesus' example and look for ways you can, in his strength, build a relational bridge to him.

Applying for Ministry

This is a trustworthy saying: "If someone aspires to be an elder, he desires an honorable position." 1 TIMOTHY 3:1

Today's reading lists qualifications of a spiritual leader. Are you sensing a tug to enter leadership ministry? True leadership, particularly that of a church or mission field, is a great responsibility. How do you know if you're called into such an esteemed service?

First, learn whether you're already a leader or if some other form of ministry is more suitable to you. One way to determine if you are a leader is to turn around and look behind you. Is anyone following your lead? Natural leaders are apparent and easy to locate because their actions inspire the people around them.

Second, leaders, as all ministers, should possess a holy joy for their work. This underpinning of joy drives their motivation and fosters the qualities of hard work and responsibility. As the great Victorian preacher Charles Spurgeon wrote in *An All-Round Ministry*, "If you plan to be lazy, there are plenty of avocations in which you will not be wanted; but, above all, you are not wanted in the Christian ministry." Look over the other characteristics of a leader in today's Scripture text and see whether exhibiting them would be a joy or a hardship to you.

Third, if you are to be in full-time leadership ministry, your spiritual gifts will match your desire. Other people will notice that God enables your ability to complete the work of the ministry. If you're called to be an evangelist, people around you will be coming to know Christ. If you're called to be a pastor, people where you minister will grow spiritually.

Your first step to enter this ministry is to apply in person: Ask God directly. As you seek God's will for your life, he will reveal whether he has a leadership position in store for you or if he wants to use you somewhere else. The key is to always be open to God's direction in your life.

Youth Movements

Don't let anyone think less of you because you are young. Be an example to all believers in what you say, in the way you live, in your love, your faith, and your purity. 1 TIMOTHY 4:12

Statistics have shown that at least 75 percent of those who ever come to Christ make their decisions before the age of eighteen. In the past century, some of the most powerful spiritual movements have been initiated and led by youth. During the 1940s, Youth for Christ began to hold rallies that attracted the young and energetic; Billy Graham was among those young preachers who reached out to the youth. During the 1960s, the Jesus Movement saw the gathering, and return, of thousands of young people who had previously been turned off by the organized church. I was one of these young people who made a serious decision for Christ and later went into full-time ministry. It's been said that this century, even more than the last, wears the face of the young.

But the ancient world of the New Testament respected age, and they were suspicious of young leaders. With this background, we can understand Timothy's problem and why Paul felt a need to address it in the verse above. Timothy didn't bear the etchings of experience on his face or the color of it in his hair.

But even if we do have one or two such merit badges of the aged, we all can hear Paul in this passage essentially saying, "No matter what you think your disadvantages are, don't quit reaching out with the gospel." Do listen to wise counsel, but guard your heart against false expectations and restrictions, whether from your own fears or from those around you—even those in the church. Always be sure to take your cues from Scripture first.

We should never forget the words from the Lord Jesus to his band of disciples, who were predominately young and unmarried when he called them. Jesus told these disciples to go everywhere and preach the gospel. "Change the world. Do it in my name." These words from Jesus Christ are a challenge, and God calls us to take them up at any age. Make a commitment today to accept the challenge, and God will take your life and use it for his glory.

Pay the Preacher

*Elders who do their work well should be respected and paid well,
especially those who work hard at both preaching and teaching.*

1 TIMOTHY 5:17

During the days of the early church and Timothy's ministry, leaders were devoting increasing amounts of time both to preparing messages and to ministering to the people's needs. These ministers needed some financial help since they were not able to carry on other employment. As the verse above clearly states, the church is to financially support the individuals who work in the teaching ministry.

Although Paul himself chose to support his missionary endeavors through tent making, he defended those who received financial support (see 1 Corinthians 9:1-14). God's plan was for the local church to meet the needs of his servants. If the church is not faithful in meeting the needs of its minister, then it is a poor testimony to the unbelievers in the community. The relationship of honor between the pastor and his congregation is the underlying idea of today's Bible reading.

But money is not all that is due to the pastor. Here are a few disturbing numbers about this relationship at present.

First, every month sixteen hundred ministers leave the ministry for many different reasons. Second, 50 percent of the pastors who presently serve in churches say they feel so discouraged that they'd leave the ministry if they had any other way to make a living. Finally, 85 percent of those head pastors who have left the ministry pinpointed their greatest problem, and it was the same: They were sick and tired of dealing with the people problems that included disgruntled elders, deacons, worship leaders, board members, and assistant pastors.

Today make plans to show your pastor your support, whether by a note of encouragement or some other gesture you're sure would be welcome. Express your appreciation for his hard work, and see how you can minister to his needs. God can use your efforts in ways that are exceedingly abundantly above all you can ask or think.

A Suitcase in the Casket

We brought nothing with us when we came into the world, and we can't take anything with us when we leave it.   1 TIMOTHY 6:7

The ancient Egyptians believed that treasures stored in one's tomb could be enjoyed in the afterlife—which explains their elaborate embalming methods and ornate tombs. Abundant treasures found in their burial chambers show that these people believed you really can take it with you. Even in our culture, people are buried with a portion of their valuables; some eccentrics are even buried in their favorite cars or in caskets wired for sound so they might enjoy communication from their graveside visitors.

Such beliefs are contrary to the instruction in the Bible. The Scriptures are clear: We arrive here empty-handed, and we leave that way. That means what material possessions we acquire should be used. They should be regarded as tools to be invested, not goods to be carried over to eternity in a suitcase.

Have you ever heard that money is like manure? As the saying goes, stack it up, and it stinks; spread it around, and it makes things grow. If you hoard your money, you'll smell up your life. Instead, invest your money and other possessions in spiritual endeavors.

Consider the difference between the Middle Eastern tombs of King Tut and Jesus Christ. Tut believed in the afterlife and wanted to take his possessions with him. The walls of his tomb were covered with precious materials, and he was buried in a golden, inscribed sarcophagus. In stark contrast, Jesus Christ believed the truth about the afterlife. He was buried in a simple, rock-hewn cave containing no treasure—and finally, no body. Jesus had no reason to store up possessions. His goal was to fulfill the will of his heavenly Father, and he eventually returned to his presence—the greatest treasure one can gain.

Ask God to reveal how you can use what you have, however little or great the amount, for his glory. If you don't use it, you will eventually lose it.

Trickle-Down Spirituality

I remember your genuine faith, for you share the faith that first filled your grandmother Lois and your mother, Eunice. 2 TIMOTHY 1:5

The old hymn "Faith of Our Fathers" celebrates the rich heritage of faith behind us. If someone were to write a hymn about the faith of our mothers, in particular, such a song would tie directly to today's key Bible verse.

Once four scholars argued about which translation of the Bible was the best one. One contended it was the King James Version because of its majesty. Another argued for the *New American Standard Bible* because of its accuracy. The third stood by the New Living Translation because of its clarity. Finally, the fourth scholar said, "I like my mom's translation best." They laughed, but he explained, "She translated each page of the Bible into life with the most convincing translation I've ever seen."

Paul's letter to Timothy made no mention of the faith of Timothy's father. We only learn about the faith of Timothy's mother and grandmother. From generation to generation, faith characterized the lives of Lois, Eunice, and finally, Timothy. Many scholars believe Timothy's father died when he was young, so his mother and grandmother principally raised him.

English preacher G. Campbell Morgan (1863–1945) had four sons, and all of them became preachers. During a family reunion, a friend asked one of the sons, "Who's the greatest preacher in your home?" He expected to hear a response like "My brother" or "My father." Instead, the son answered, "My mother."

And Morgan himself said, "My dedication to preaching the Word was maternal. The first Bible stories I heard came from my mother. I lined up my sister's dolls and preached to them."

Are you practicing "trickle-down spirituality" in your family? If not, take some proactive steps in that direction today.

A Friend's Refreshment

May the Lord show special kindness to Onesiphorus and all his family because he often visited and encouraged me. He was never ashamed of me because I was in chains. 2 TIMOTHY 1:16

Dawson Trotman, founder of The Navigators, died an unusual death. He was an excellent swimmer, yet he drowned during a boating accident. Because he knew his fellow passenger couldn't swim, he held her up until she was rescued, but he drowned in the process. As a caption in the posthumous *Time* magazine article featuring him put it, Dawson Trotman was "always holding someone up."

A newspaper in England once sponsored a contest to search for the best definition of the word *friend*. The winning definition read, "Someone who comes in when the rest of the world has gone out." By that definition, Dawson Trotman was a friend indeed.

True friendship will not always require such a price. But it should always inspire us to make daily choices that strengthen our love for others. Hebrews 3:13 says we should "encourage one another daily" (NIV).

Consider the importance of your encouragement to any fellow servant of Jesus Christ. It doesn't take much for you to engage in this endeavor. We see in 2 Corinthians 7:6 that sometimes all it requires is showing up: "God, who encourages those who are discouraged, encouraged us by the arrival of Titus." But like the rescue of a strong swimmer when we're in deep waters, the encouragement of a friend at the right time can be vital. Last year, a couple flew out from California and then drove with us the entire length of a joint trip we had planned. This encouragement through the simple gift of their presence greased the gears of our ministry.

Each of us has opportunities to reach out and encourage others; we just need to be proactive in looking for the opportunity and seizing it. Who needs encouragement in your life? What are your opportunities for meeting that need?

Reproducers

You have heard me teach things that have been confirmed by many reliable witnesses. Now teach these truths to other trustworthy people who will be able to pass them on to others.   2 TIMOTHY 2:2

An older, wiser leader gave me one of the best pieces of advice. He said, "Meet regularly with a few men and give them yourself. The big meetings are fine, and you're a fine preacher, but to take just a few men and share your life with them will impact them forever." His words were in the style of Jesus, who did more than speak to the crowds. The Lord spent his time training twelve disciples, who carried his message to the ends of the earth.

Every Christian needs to strike a balance between the activities of input and output. You need to be fed, nourished, and trained in God's Word; there's no substitute for Bible study and solid biblical preaching. Yet that's only half of the equation. If you receive all input with no output, then you will become spiritually obese, a fat and sassy Christian. Everyone needs a place to upload into the life of another person, to give out what's been gained through instruction and experience.

This type of "spiritual reproduction" is often called discipleship. It's when a mentor transfers personally what he or she knows into another person. And it's one of the key ways to weave the fabric of God's Kingdom.

Remember, Jesus said, "Anyone who believes in me may come and drink! For the Scriptures declare, 'Rivers of living water will flow from his heart'" (John 7:38). The image is of water flowing in to refresh you, and water going out from you to refresh others. If you're only giving out without taking in, you'll soon dry up. Each of us needs to drink in spiritual nourishment. Yet if you only take in and never give out, the life-transforming truth gets bottle-necked.

Take a moment to evaluate your own spiritual reproduction. Are you taking in enough nourishment and giving out to others?

Who Really Wrote the Bible?

All Scripture is inspired by God and is useful to teach us what is true and to make us realize what is wrong in our lives. It corrects us when we are wrong and teaches us to do what is right.   2 TIMOTHY 3:16

The Bible is often referred to as special revelation. Though God has revealed himself *generally* through his creation, without the Lord's *special* revelation, we would never know about his love, forgiveness, plan for the future, or judgment. Through the Scriptures, God reveals himself to us more fully. In today's key Bible verse, Paul calls the Word of God *inspired*. The most literal translation of this word is "God breathed." The words of Scripture are the direct result of God's "breathing" through men. While many different people penned the words, God superintended the process, so he guided the exact outcome or result.

When we talk about God's Word, we are not referring to natural inspiration—an activity with a high level of human achievement. For instance, after attending a play we might hear someone say, "They gave an inspiring performance." But the Bible isn't on the same level as a play, a Picasso, or a concerto in D major. Some people try to relegate the inspiration of the Bible to that of merely creative and smart men. Yet I wonder, would smart men write a book that condemns them all and offers salvation through belief in only one person—and not one of them?

No, God is the real Author behind the Bible. Through its historical accuracy, we can test it. Through its transmission over time, there is manuscript evidence as well as archaeological evidence and predictive prophecy. We can read our Bibles with a clear conscience as well as an open heart.

But the main thing is that we do read it. Charles Haddon Spurgeon was fond of saying, "A Bible that is falling apart usually belongs to someone who isn't." Does your Bible show signs of frequent use?

Last Words of a Legendary Saint

I have fought the good fight, I have finished the race, and I have remained faithful.   2 TIMOTHY 4:7

Paul was under guard on his journey to Rome and was imprisoned for the two years he lived there (see Acts 28). During this time, the apostle wrote four letters: Ephesians, Philippians, Colossians, and Philemon. After two years, Paul was released to enjoy freedom for about a year. Then he was rearrested and imprisoned—probably in the underground Roman holding place that was later known as the Mamertine prison—and was eventually executed. It was in this dark place that he penned these final words to his apprentice and friend, Timothy.

Paul knew he was about to leave this earth. Just before today's verse he says, "The time of my death is near" (v. 6). I have heard people who are close to death say that they have an incredible sense of clarity. Some have regrets, and many wish they could do things differently. With this end-of-life clarity, Paul saw his life as complete, fulfilled, and without regret. He had accomplished all that God had for him to do. As God's soldier, he didn't go AWOL but remained faithful. As God's athlete, Paul stayed in the race and was about to cross the finish line in victory. As the guardian of God's message, Paul kept the truth intact and shared it at every possible opportunity.

The second letter to Timothy was Paul's swan song. He was ready to die and depart the earth to heaven. The Greek word for death draws on several images, including the pulling up of an anchor to set sail, the folding up of a tent, or the removal of the yoke from an ox. Paul was ready to sail to heaven, move into his permanent home, and lay aside his earthly service to Christ.

What about you? Are you living today so you won't die with any regrets?

Is Doctrine Important?

As for you, Titus, promote the kind of living that reflects wholesome teaching. TITUS 2:1

Doctrine is an unnerving word to many people. Many associate it with old churchmen who have nothing better to do than dwell on lofty, ethereal subjects and use a bunch of big theological words. What does doctrine have to do with real life? The answer is that it undergirds everything. The word *doctrine* means "right teaching." And the Bible, of course, is our primary source of right teaching about God, mankind, our origin, and eternity.

Every so often the church has historically needed to reassess the basic tenets of its belief system. Through these self-evaluations over time, the church has reaffirmed its doctrine, contributing to a new era the right teaching of Scripture regarding the person and work of Jesus Christ, the nature of God, and the Trinity. Though it can have a low profile within certain churches, doctrine has always been extremely important to the church at large.

Consider what radio teacher and pastor James Montgomery Boice (1938–2000) wrote in his *Foundations of the Christian Faith*: "We do not have a strong church today, nor do we have many strong Christians. We can trace the cause to an acute lack of sound spiritual knowledge. . . . Ask an average Christian to talk about God. After getting past the expected answers you will find that his god is a little god of vacillating sentiments."

Ignorance is anything but bliss when it comes to understanding doctrine. Spiritual illiteracy compromises the effectiveness of the average believer. When you are driving a car, you need the right directions in order to stay on the course to your destination. In the same way, you need the right teaching to stay on the right spiritual path. Learn to discern between what is right teaching and wrong teaching, and also between truth and error.

Another way to look at doctrine is as your foundation: With doctrine firmly in place, you can build a solid life to withstand any storm of doubt, fear, or hardship.

Radical Surgery

If people are causing divisions among you, give a first and second warning. After that, have nothing more to do with them. TITUS 3:10

Scorpions live on insects, but they also kill and devour their own species. One man's experimentation with them revealed their killer instincts. First, he placed a hundred scorpions in a large glass vessel; after a few days only fourteen remained, having eaten the others. Then, he put a pregnant female in a glass vessel; she devoured her young as soon as they were born. One scorpion escaped and took refuge on its mother's back—but then this little one exacted revenge, killing its mother. Finally, the experimenter discovered that, if cornered with no possible escape, a scorpion will actually sting itself to death.

Have you ever met a scorpion-like Christian? These believers are ready to attack anyone who gets in the way. Given an opportunity, these Christians choose a course of action that divides instead of unites.

What are we supposed to do with divisive people within a church? According to Scripture, we are to approach them and warn them twice. After two warnings, it's three strikes, and they're out of the church.

It sounds harsh, but the warning intended by this passage is a gentle but firm confrontation based on Jesus' teaching. He said, "If another believer sins against you, go privately and point out the offense. If the other person listens and confesses it, you have won that person back. But if you are unsuccessful, take one or two others with you and go back again, so that everything you say may be confirmed by two or three witnesses. If the person still refuses to listen, take your case to the church. Then if he or she won't accept the church's decision, treat that person as a pagan or a corrupt tax collector" (Matthew 18:15-17).

Carrying out such a teaching is hard, and some Christians would say it's not true to a loving God. But actually, confrontation as Jesus and Paul describe is one of the most loving things you could ever do for the church. Just as our physical bodies must be protected against attack, so the body of Christ—the church—must be protected from those who would willfully release the poison of sin and resentment into the congregation. And if loving confrontation doesn't work, it's time to protect the body from the scorpions.

A Friend Indeed

If he has wronged you in any way or owes you anything, charge it to me.

PHILEMON 1:18

While Paul was imprisoned in Rome, he led a runaway slave from Colossae to faith in Christ. This slave, Onesimus, had fled his master, Philemon, possibly after robbing him. After running away, Onesimus met Paul and received God's forgiveness and was set free from his sin. Now, after his conversion, Paul wanted him to go back to his master and make things right. Evidently, Philemon was a believer in Colossae—which would make Onesimus his new Christian brother.

Notice how Paul offers to be a part of the solution and the restoration process. He sends Onesimus back to Philemon, encouraging their reconciliation. Furthermore, he is willing to be personally responsible for any loss that Philemon might have incurred. When Onesimus came to Christ, it did not cancel his debts to his master. But this letter tells Philemon to charge Paul. Why?

Paul knew that's what God had done for him. He had benefited from the principle of imputation, whereby God placed all our debts from our own sins onto his Son, Jesus. Anything we owed God was charged to Jesus' account; as our substitute, he paid the debt in full. Now, Paul was placing the debts of his spiritual son on himself. And even though he was in great need himself in prison, Paul let his new friend Onesimus go so that reconciliation could take place between him and Philemon.

Proverbs 17:17 says, "A friend is always loyal, and a brother is born to help in time of need." Paul demonstrated this kind of friendship while he was in prison. What about you? Take a moment and think about your friends. Is there anyone whom you could contact today and offer a word of encouragement? Someone who is in a different sort of time of need? Consider how you might be a true friend to that person.

God's Final Message

Long ago God spoke many times and in many ways to our ancestors through the prophets. And now in these final days, he has spoken to us through his Son.   HEBREWS 1:1-2

A little boy wrote this short letter to God: "Dear God, Grandpa says you were around when he was a little boy. Just how far back do you go?" That sweetly innocent letter expresses two powerful concepts: first, that God has been around for a long time, and second, that communication with God is possible.

Throughout time, God has spoken to people on earth through special messengers called prophets. God spoke from outside our time-and-space continuum to those within it. Finally, he spoke to mankind by the most direct means possible. He entered our world as a man so people could see and understand what God was like. Jesus Christ, his Son, was God's ultimate Communicator to the world. As he said, "Anyone who has seen me has seen the Father!" (John 14:9).

Others have acknowledged great things about Jesus. The ancient historian Josephus called him "a wise man, if it be lawful to call him a man . . . a doer of wonderful works." The French ruler Napoleon said that he knew men—and that Jesus was more than a man; French philosopher and atheist Ernest Renan acknowledged him as the greatest among the sons of men. German philosopher Leo Strauss called Jesus "the highest model of religion." Yet each of these descriptions fell short of the full truth.

Jesus was God's final message. Through Christ, God said everything he had to say to humankind. That's why your relationship to Jesus is central to your salvation. It's why you should believe the right things about Jesus and then place your full trust in him. When was the last time you shared with someone else God's great message to us through Jesus?

Entropy

We must listen very carefully to the truth we have heard, or we may drift away from it.   HEBREWS 2:1

Entropy is the scientific term for the phenomenon by which, in any closed system such as our material universe, the amount of heat energy will diminish—in other words, energy will be lost over time. We can see entropy at work everywhere. A natural deterioration or breakdown is always taking place; things tend toward decay rather than order. I believe this principle is also true in the spiritual world.

Many who came to Christ with great enthusiasm and excitement tend to lose energy over time. Unless they are tended, the fires of devotion die down and can even flicker out.

Perhaps you've heard about the newly retired couple who bought an RV and hit the open road. When the husband needed a rest, the wife took over and enjoyed the use of cruise control until they crashed—while she had stepped away on a bathroom break. Cruise control is no substitute for engaged driving, either on the highway or on the spiritual journey.

What about you? Can you look back to a time when you walked closer to Jesus Christ than you do right now? Possibly you grew up in church, and as a child you felt more tender toward God.

Could it be that you have drifted from what you knew to be true? Possibly you are experiencing spiritual entropy. If so, you can reverse the trend. Determine to respond to God's truth the moment you hear it. Decide to practice the biblical principles you read about or hear from a pulpit or radio program. You may want to carry a small notepad to write down certain things the Holy Spirit is telling you through his word.

When asked how to start a revival, evangelist Rodney "Gypsy" Smith (1860–1947) said you should lock yourself in a room, draw a chalk line around yourself, and pray for God to start a revival within that line. Ask God today to begin a revival with your life.

Commoners in the Palace

So let us come boldly to the throne of our gracious God. There we will
receive his mercy, and we will find grace to help us when we need it most.

HEBREWS 4:16

In almost every ancient religion, priests represented the common people. Ancient Jews had priests who stood in the gap between themselves and God. The book of Hebrews was written to young Jewish converts to the Christian faith, who were familiar with the priesthood. Many of these Hebrew Christians were returning to their old religious practices because of pressure or because they felt more comfortable in their traditions. To encourage them to remain in their new faith, the writer of Hebrews emphasized Jesus Christ as our High Priest, whose ministry is from heaven.

Jesus is the *Theanthropos,* or the God-man. Fully God, Jesus was sinless, the perfect substitute for sinners. At the same time fully human, he experienced emotions, hunger, and pain. He wept at the tomb of Lazarus, and he sweat blood in the garden of Gethsemane. Then he passed through the heavens and was seated at the right hand of God, where he is right now—and not as a figurehead, but as a man who represents all humankind.

Because of Jesus Christ we can always come boldly into God's presence. You might say that although we're mere commoners in the Kingdom, because of Jesus we have been made children of the King. When my son, Nate, was a small child, I taught him that he could always have access to me. Although I pastored a large church and had many serious conversations with adults, I wanted my own son to know I always had time for him.

In the same way, God is letting us know that at any time, without fear and with confidence, we can boldly approach our Father. Remember that when Jesus, our great High Priest, offered himself as a living sacrifice, the veil to the Holy of Holies ripped apart, symbolizing total access for all people. Freely go into the Father's presence today.

Stunted Growth

You have been believers so long now that you ought to be teaching others.
Instead, you need someone to teach you again the basic things about
God's word. You are like babies who need milk and cannot eat solid food.

HEBREWS 5:12

Years ago, I worked in the medical field. Every now and then, we'd see someone whose development had been limited by linear growth retardation. This ailment is typically caused by malnutrition, infection, or a compromised mother-infant interaction. All three causes are critical, but the first is a major international problem. Though in our own country we do not see the same figures, malnutrition affects more than one-third of the world's children and nearly 30 percent of people of all ages in the developing world, making it the most damaging physical condition worldwide.

There is a parallel problem in the spiritual world. Spiritual malnutrition can be just as devastating as its physical counterpart. When we don't eat well, we don't grow well, and our whole lives can be affected. Similarly, when we don't take in proper spiritual nutrition, we will be spiritually stunted.

Why were some of the Hebrew Christians mentioned in today's verse not maturing? Why were they experiencing a "second childhood"? Their hearing wasn't right, and hearing is the spiritual equivalent of eating. These Christians' problem wasn't poor teaching but poor listening.

In the physical realm, a child who doesn't advance from milk to solids will have stunted growth. In the spiritual realm, when we don't advance to the point that we can teach someone else what God has shown us, our growth is also impaired. Sharing spiritual truth is a mark of Christian maturity. That doesn't mean you need to be a pastor or a Sunday school teacher. But each of us can give what we have to others. And we must share with others the spiritual food that God is giving us—not just for the sake of our own development but also for that of others. Think today about someone you could and should share your spiritual insights with.

Why Religion Doesn't Work

With his own blood—not the blood of goats and calves—he entered the Most Holy Place once for all time and secured our redemption forever.

HEBREWS 9:12

When an ancient Hebrew went to the Temple for worship, he brought an animal to offer as a sacrifice on the altar. The priest carefully examined this sacrifice to be sure it had no spot or blemish. But the priest never inspected the person. Why? It was the blood of the animal, not a man's own condition, that covered his sin.

A key emphasis of the book of Hebrews is the sacrificial work of Christ. It will never need to be repeated, unlike the priestly sacrifices of the Old Testament. Nothing was permanent about the Jewish sacrificial system. For their entire lives, Hebrew worshipers had to bring these animals for sacrifice because the animals' blood never removed sin; it only covered it. Now, because of Jesus, the blood of Christ contains infinite value and all-sufficient power to actually cleanse all sin. Seeing Jesus, John the Baptist cried, "Look! The Lamb of God who takes away the sin of the world!" (John 1:29).

Of course, the devil would love for you to lose your confidence and focus on your spots and blemishes. Satan will suggest, "You've failed over and over. You're blemished. You can't come to God right now; you can't worship him because you're soiled." When you hear these whispers from Satan, remember that it's the lamb that is inspected, not the one who brings the lamb.

Jesus lived the perfect, spotless life we never could have lived, and then he shed his own blood in atonement to cleanse us from our sins. In an instant, Jesus did what religion could never do in a lifetime. As hymn writer Robert Lowry (1826–1899) put it, "What can wash away my sin? / Nothing but the blood of Jesus. / What can make me whole again? / Nothing but the blood of Jesus."

Your salvation is secure. Pause for a few moments and thank the Lord for his sacrifice.

Anatomy of Faith

Faith is the confidence that what we hope for will actually happen; it gives us assurance about things we cannot see. HEBREWS 11:1

Often those people who highly value empirical truth will ridicule people of faith. Prominent newspaperman H. L. Mencken (1880–1956) mockingly said, "Faith may be defined briefly as an illogical belief in the occurrence of the improbable." For some, faith requires the leap famously suggested by Danish philosopher Søren Kierkegaard (1813–1855). Yet it shouldn't be presumption or blind optimism—after all, biblical faith is based on the objective truths of the historical life of Christ and a proven track record of the prophetic Scriptures. But what *is* it?

First, faith is confident assurance. According to Bible commentator William Barclay (1907–1978), "So often we have a kind of vague, wistful longing that the promises of Jesus should be true. The only way to enter into them is to believe in them with the clutching intensity of a drowning man."

When you discover a promise from God in the Bible, what do you do? If your answer is, "I underline it," you're missing the point. Have you held onto God's promises with a drowning man's grip? Biblical faith is basically betting your eternal life on Jesus—because he's good for the bet.

When my son was small, I'd pick him up and toss him in the air. He'd laugh and enjoy the experience because he trusted me. Although he was floating in the air in an unusual situation as high as ten feet off the ground, Nate had reason to trust because I never dropped him. While you will certainly be in situations you don't understand, you can trust the outcome to the Lord because you know the trustworthiness of God.

But, second, faith is the evidence of what we can't see. A man of faith acts on what he believes, even when his senses can't grasp it—otherwise, what good is it?

For faith to be worthwhile, it must be both sure and unwavering. What state is yours in?

On the Track

Since we are surrounded by such a huge crowd of witnesses to the life of faith, let us strip off every weight that slows us down, especially the sin that so easily trips us up. And let us run with endurance the race God has set before us.   HEBREWS 12:1

Have you heard about the marathon runner who had fallen so far behind that the guy just ahead actually started to mock him? He snickered, "Hey, buddy, how does it feel to be last?" Retorting, "Do you really want to know?" the slower man dropped out of the race.

We've already seen that one of the Bible's favorite analogies of Christianity is *the race*. Paul mentioned it often in his books, and some scholars believe he also wrote the book of Hebrews, which features the athletic illustration above. Paul loved the comparison between running a race and living the Christian life. We each run our own race of personal obedience to Christ.

And we're in good company. Others before us have run the race of faith. Some of them are listed in the Hebrews 11 "Faith Hall of Fame." One interpretation of this passage is that these heroes are now in a heavenly arena cheering us on. Through their own faithful examples, they have demonstrated that we, too, can endure this marathon of faith.

They also show that the race doesn't require elite spiritual status. Those listed in today's Scripture reading were ordinary folks with challenges of their own—but they trusted God to pull them through. Now it's our turn to run the race of faith. If we are on course, we can run it just as well as they did. Why? Because we trust in the same Lord they did. Our God is their God, and the same promises sustain us.

If you feel as if you've dropped out of the race or wandered off course, ask God to help you get back on track. And let the example of those who have gone before spur you on.

How Temptation Works

*Temptation comes from our own desires, which entice us and drag us
away. These desires give birth to sinful actions. And when sin is allowed to
grow, it gives birth to death.*   JAMES 1:14-15

Today's reading, from the book of James, describes the path of temptation
leading to sin. Understanding these principles helps us determine where
we are and stop sin in progress.

The first stage of temptation is desire. All of us have natural desires that
we want satisfied, and nothing is inherently wrong with that. In fact, we
couldn't function without desire. If we didn't become hungry, we would
never eat; unless we grew thirsty, we would never drink; if we had no
sexual drive, there would be no human race. Yet these desires can lead to
sin. How?

The second stage of temptation is the lure. In this stage, we are drawn
away from safety like an animal led to a trap. Hunters and fishermen use
bait to attract their prey from a place of safety: The basic idea is to exploit
a desire. Bait is attractive and in itself isn't harmful if it's managed—but it
can lead to a trap.

The third stage of temptation, the trap, is sin. The choice is made, and
the bait is taken. A person who is constantly yielding to temptation lives
enslaved to sin like an animal.

The final stage is death. The end result does not satisfy or produce more
pleasure. After momentary delight comes spiritual corruption.

Learn to resist the devil by fleeing temptation. Seem cowardly? Tell that
to Joseph, who ran from temptation and saved his integrity (see Genesis 39).
Avoiding danger is three-fourths of the battle. Are you steering clear of the
danger zones in your own life?

Like Joseph, some need to run from ungodly gratification of natural
desires for things like sex or food. The temptation for each of us will be
different, but the need to run is universal. Understanding how temptation
works will help arm you for the battle against it.

Are Your Feet Attached to Your Ears?

Don't just listen to God's word. You must do what it says. Otherwise, you are only fooling yourselves. JAMES 1:22

It's one thing when the devil deceives us. It's quite another when we fool ourselves. During the times of the New Testament, the Pharisees made this mistake. Condemning their self-deceit, Jesus said, "On judgment day many will say to me, 'Lord! Lord! We prophesied in your name and cast out demons in your name and performed many miracles in your name.' But I will reply, 'I never knew you'" (Matthew 7:22-23).

Believers, too, can be self-deceived. Some of the believers in Corinth thought they were spiritual because they identified with leaders like Paul, Peter, or Apollos. But their true spiritual condition was the exact opposite of what they had thought (see 1 Corinthians 3:3-4). Perhaps the most common occurrence of self-deception is when we listen to the Word of God, nod in agreement, and never put the principles into practice. J. Vernon McGee (1904–1988) used to say that every Bible should be bound in shoe leather: in other words, that believers should walk out the truth they hear.

I ask you, are your feet connected to your ears? Do you put into practice what you read in the Bible or hear at your church? Many Christians have the mistaken idea that if they regularly attend a Bible-teaching church and hear good sermons, they will automatically grow spiritually. But spiritual growth doesn't occur at the turn of a switch; it takes intentional action over time. The Bible is like a map. Reading a road map will never take you to your destination, but it will direct you to the destination as you get on the road.

One day, Dwight L. Moody and a friend saw another man whom Moody guessed to have been in the army. His friend, who knew the man, wondered how Moody had known. "By the way he walked," said Moody. How are you walking? Make sure your walk is marked with the evidence of the truth you hear.

Faith without Batteries

How foolish! Can't you see that faith without good deeds is useless?

JAMES 2:20

An angry customer once stormed into his auto mechanic's shop. "Six months ago, when I bought this premium battery, you said it would be the last battery my car would ever need. It has already died after just six months!" Stunned, the mechanic apologized, "I'm very sorry. I didn't think your car would last longer than that."

Like a car with a dead battery, faith that doesn't work is useless. In today's reading, James argues that real faith takes action and produces results. For a few reasons, Martin Luther took such issue with the book of James that he famously called it a straw epistle. Among the issues was his opinion that James and Paul were in disagreement about salvation and that James was insisting salvation came through works and not by faith.

James never claims that works can save. But he does contend that real faith must run powered by the battery of action. He makes a clear contrast between two kinds of faith: living and dead. Living faith saves and is dynamic. Dead faith cannot save because it is lifeless itself, stagnant. Living faith is not mere intellectual contemplation, nor is it an emotional sensation bringing a temporary feeling of well-being. Living faith is that which leads to willful obedience as a lifestyle rather than an isolated event.

Eventually, Martin Luther agreed with the apostle James, writing about faith's being such a living thing that it cannot help but be at work. If your faith is real, it will show itself. How does that happen? Through obedience. Every believer must obey God even when the path ahead is uncertain. Today, ask God what practical ways he might have for you to put your faith into action.

Only You Can Prevent Forest Fires!

The tongue is a small thing that makes grand speeches. But a tiny spark can set a great forest on fire. JAMES 3:5

A snail is an interesting creature because it is both slow and tough. The snail actually has teeth on its tongue—thirty thousand of them, according to one scientist. It keeps this secret weapon rolled up like a ribbon. Though small, the snail can saw through tough leaves and stems, destroying the entire plant.

The Scriptures tell about another small thing that can inflict great damage—the human tongue. Some of us are like human flamethrowers with our mouths, wounding others and their ministries with loose lips. What kind of fires can the tongue spread?

First, there's the fire of profanity. It is in every form of the entertainment industry and in every workplace across America. Profanity degrades our speech and thoughts.

The second fire from the tongue is deceit. Proverbs 6:16-19 lists seven things God hates, one of which is "a lying tongue." The ninth commandment is about testifying falsely against your neighbor—a breach of integrity (see Exodus 20:16). Deception may start small, but as C. S. Lewis said, "A little lie is like a little pregnancy; it doesn't take long before everyone knows."

The third fire from the tongue is destructive or abusive language, usually due to anger. Some people make excuses, saying, "I'm temperamental." Sure—that's 90 percent temper and 10 percent mental. We need to think before we speak in anger; a lot of damage can be prevented that way.

A final fire from the tongue is gossip, which includes repeating something without confirmation. This time, the problem is with not only the one speaking but also the person listening to it. There wouldn't be so many open mouths for gossip if there weren't so many open ears.

The tongue has power to do evil—but you can exert willpower over it. By controlling your speech, instead of starting fires, you can prevent them.

How to Start a War

What is causing the quarrels and fights among you? Don't they come from the evil desires at war within you?   JAMES 4:1

Years of controversy tore apart the congregation of an old Scottish church. One morning after the worship service, this note was found in one of the pews: "To dwell above with those we love will certainly be glory; to dwell below with those we know, well that's a different story!"

How do you start a war? Gather enough people bent on having their own ways, add some selfishness and other vices, and before long a battle will begin. War is basically the extension of people not getting what they want. When that condition escalates, it can spread from a family feud to a church fracture or an international conflict.

Think back to the last war you were in—a fight you had with someone. It probably stemmed from an unmet expectation, with one party failing to please the other. Perhaps one person's selfishness was prominent, but soon you both dug in your heels. This is war on a personal level. Of course, it can also break out on other levels.

Consider ecclesiastical war: conflict within the church. Churches split because some faction doesn't like the pastor or the policies or the other people. We need only look to the early church heresies, the Spanish Inquisition, or the issues dividing mainline denominations today to remember that the church itself has never been exempt from war.

Don't be like Alexander the Great, whose driving ambition to rule the world caused him to fall down and weep once there were no other worlds to conquer. As President Herbert Hoover said, "Peace is not made at the council tables, nor by treaties, but in the hearts of men and women." As followers of Christ, we should be driven to spread peace throughout the world in the hearts of our neighbors.

War, especially on the personal level, is easy to start. Work instead at being a promoter of the peace of Christ—the peace that surpasses all understanding.

Blessed Are the Flexible

Look here, you who say, "Today or tomorrow we are going to a certain town and will stay there a year. We will do business there and make a profit."

JAMES 4:13

In the pattern of the Beatitudes from the Sermon on the Mount, someone once said, "Blessed are the flexible, for they shall not be broken." There is a great deal of wisdom in daily seeking God's plan for your life.

Throughout the ancient Mediterranean world, businessmen made their plans apart from God. Being entrepreneurial in the trade markets, James the brother of Jesus watched them plot their travel schedules with confidence and boldness. He noticed their attitudes of self-sufficiency and self-centeredness.

James doesn't condemn planning or strategizing. There's nothing wrong with preparation. However he *does* condemn those who plan without considering the fact that God has "editing rights" over our lives. Here are two facts we should never ignore: First, we are finite and have limited knowledge about our futures. We can't predict exactly what will happen. The fact that life flows in a certain rhythm is no reason to believe it will never change. Second, life itself is uncertain. Like a vapor of smoke, life appears and then vanishes. Since life is so short, we shouldn't merely *spend* our lives. We should invest them in God's plans for today and for what he has planned for us in eternity.

The prophet Jeremiah wrote, "'I know the plans I have for you,' says the LORD. 'They are plans for good and not for disaster, to give you a future and a hope'" (Jeremiah 29:11).

Evaluate your level of flexibility. Are you open to seeing God change your schedule? As you commit each day to the Lord, your life will take on new meaning. When God superintends your schedule, interruptions and diversions can become exciting adventures rather than annoying distractions.

Does Prayer Really Work?

The earnest prayer of a righteous person has great power and produces wonderful results. JAMES 5:16

Maybe you've heard about the man who rarely prayed until one Sunday, while hunting, he climbed over a ridge and met a bear nose to nose. When the bear roared fiercely, the man fell down the hill, lost his gun, and broke his leg. As the drooling bear came bounding up to him, the man prayed, "Lord, make this bear a Christian!" Immediately, the bear fell to his knees, folded his paws, bowed his head, and prayed aloud, "Lord, bless this food to the nourishment of my body."

What's your view on prayer? Does it work? Does God always answer? Jesus Christ said, "Keep on asking, and you will receive what you ask for. Keep on seeking, and you will find. Keep on knocking, and the door will be opened to you" (Matthew 7:7).

That fiery Old Testament prophet Elijah performed eight major miracles during his lifetime. James tells us that Elijah's prayers had powerful results not because he was great, but because he trusted in a great God. When Elijah prayed, God suspended the rain for three and a half years; during Elijah's confrontation on Mount Carmel, God answered his bold prayers to defeat the 450 priests of Baal.

Every child of God has access to our heavenly Father to ask for help, encouragement, and resources. Every prayer of a child of God—and I mean *every prayer*—is answered. I've heard some say that God didn't answer their prayers. I believe God did answer—just not with the expected answer. Sometimes God says yes, sometimes no; and sometimes he says wait. Each answer flows from his heart of love. Remember, Jesus said that God knows exactly what we need (see Matthew 6:8).

Ruth Graham, the late wife of Dr. Billy Graham, used to say, "If God had answered all my prayers, I would've married the wrong man—several times!" Spend time rejoicing that God hears and answers every prayer in the way that's best for you.

Loving without Seeing

You love [Christ] even though you have never seen him. Though you do not see him now, you trust him; and you rejoice with a glorious, inexpressible joy.   1 PETER 1:8

The prophet Isaiah wrote, "Truly, O God of Israel, our Savior, you work in mysterious ways" (Isaiah 45:15). The God of the universe seemed hidden in comparison to the gods of the people surrounding Israel. The pagan nations had visible idols that seemed to be everywhere, yet the God of Israel existed behind the scenes.

Throughout history, humankind has always struggled with an invisible God. Those of us who are sighted find it difficult to have a personal relationship with someone we can't see. As H. G. Wells illustrates in his classic science-fiction novel *The Invisible Man*, it's hard to trust someone you can't see. It's also more difficult to feel that you know someone you can't see, as anyone in a long-distance relationship can attest.

Moses had witnessed the powerful works of God, but as he led the Israelites out of Egypt, he wanted to see more. "Show me your glorious presence," he asked God (Exodus 33:18). And as for the Son of God, it was a privileged few who knew Jesus the man and lived around him. But as Jesus himself said, blessed are those who believe without seeing him (see John 20:29).

Peter instructed his audience to trust the very one they can't see, for in doing so, they will be filled with joy. Why? Because what they *will* see are the results. We may not see the one making those results happen, but our joy comes as we see our visible lives under the control of the invisible God.

One day you will see Jesus face to face (see 1 John 3:2; Revelation 22:4), and until then, your relationship of love can grow. Just as I learned while dating my wife long-distance, if we learn to love and trust God now, when we do see the Lord, our union will be all the sweeter.

God Loves . . . Crybabies?

Like newborn babies, you must crave pure spiritual milk so that you will grow into a full experience of salvation. Cry out for this nourishment.

1 PETER 2:2

We all—especially those of us who are parents—know how much babies love milk. They want it in the morning, in the evening, and in the middle of the night—and you bet they'll cry out for it. Every part of a baby's body will long for that milk. Peter is telling us that in that sense, we should be like a baby. Our longing for God should be like that of a newborn who craves nourishment.

One of the greatest things I love about the group of people I shepherd is their hunger for spiritual food. When we recently started a new journey through the Scriptures, the entire church facility was filled to overflowing. Even on a Wednesday evening, there were still 150 people listening outside because they couldn't fit inside the church. Our group of believers has repeatedly shown how they crave the Word of God.

Spiritual maturity and growth are always marked by a strong appetite for God's Word. It's one of my saddest moments when I see Christians begin to want something other than the solid food of the Word of God. The desires of such believers have changed so they want entertainment instead of enlightenment, spiritual fluff instead of spiritual food. They're like children who have no appetite for dinner because they've been snacking on junk food. Have you lost your hunger for pure spiritual truth? Do you find Bible study boring and prayer meetings dull?

Follow Peter's advice in today's key Bible verse. Before you open your Bible and before you enter your car to go to church, cry out to God for spiritual nourishment. The transformation may not be instant; you may have to wait for God to whet your spiritual appetite. But over time, you'll discover that God will meet you and grant what you ask.

December 4 READ 1 PETER 3:1-22

Explain Yourself!

You must worship Christ as Lord of your life. And if someone asks about your Christian hope, always be ready to explain it. 1 PETER 3:15

College can be quite a challenge. It certainly was for me. I was barraged with questions about my faith in Christ, and at first I didn't have any answers. Then I determined that good questions deserve good answers. I sought explanations to the issues being raised. I thought, *I have faith in Christ, and if my faith is worth anything at all, then it deserves to be carefully explained to those who don't believe.*

If you are a Christian, whatever your situation, you should be in contact with at least one person who doesn't share your faith. In this type of relationship, you cannot shirk your responsibility as perhaps the only representative of Christ in that person's life. And if you don't know how to explain your faith, keep in mind that for the Christian, ignorance is *not* bliss. Spiritual illiteracy hurts believers and unbelievers alike.

The English word *apologetics* comes from the Greek word that Peter used for "explain." Even though Peter meant it informally here, the ability to explain and defend the Christian position is needed more now than ever before. All Christians should know what they believe and why they made the choice to follow Christ. Then, they should learn to articulate their beliefs when someone asks about them. You should be able to talk about your beliefs in a reasonable and humble manner.

When someone says, "I think that the Bible was just written by men," what will you say? When someone comes knocking at your front door, denying the deity of Jesus Christ, how will you respond?

But don't confuse your duty to share with a duty to convince. Your answer may not convert anyone on the spot, but that's okay. A reasoned response could help the other person clear up honest doubts about a particular issue. And don't forget another benefit: your own additional clarity on what you believe.

Firestorms

Dear friends, don't be surprised at the fiery trials you are going through, as if something strange were happening to you.   1 PETER 4:12

When the firestorms of life come our way, the apostle Peter tells us, we shouldn't be surprised. It's hardly a strange occurrence for a Christian to have such experiences. Because there is so much at stake in the cosmic battle between good and evil, right and wrong, truth and deception, it's little wonder that believers get caught in the crossfire from time to time.

Because I'm a pastor, people in crisis often come to me. For one week, I decided to keep track of all the fiery trials I heard about or dealt with directly over a seven-day period. I had just started my log when the phone rang. The local hospital's chaplain informed me about a couple from our church in the emergency room. When I arrived, the mother was holding her dead three-day-old baby girl in her arms. Her husband dared to utter these words in faith: "I know God has a purpose."

That same week, I also received word of my wife's grandmother's death, two different situations involving child abuse, and a death threat on missionaries I know in the Philippines. I counseled an older couple who were divorcing after twenty years of marriage and a younger couple who were living together while she was married to another man. Finally, an acquaintance was in a serious automobile accident.

While these terrible life situations can happen to anyone, they can be especially disorienting to anyone with a warped expectation that God owes him or her some kind of immunity. We can expect God to be with us always. But we must realize that he sometimes allows fiery trials in order to strengthen us. During such times, your faith will be tested, but only a faith that is tested is a faith that can be trusted. Don't be surprised by trials—be assured that the one who sees all is with you, and he has a purpose for your trials.

December 6 READ 1 PETER 5:1-14

Watch Out for Lions

Stay alert! Watch out for your great enemy, the devil. He prowls around like a roaring lion, looking for someone to devour. 1 PETER 5:8

Once, in the Kenya bush, the tour group I was with spotted a lioness with her cubs. My window was down, and I hung out the side of the car with my camera. My guide quickly and firmly rebuked me, warning that an attack from the lioness could be imminent.

The Bible says that the devil is prowling around like a lion—an attack from him could be imminent. But our enemy knows human nature well, and his attacks come when we've been lured by our own temptations: places we wander, images we see, thoughts we dwell on. Are you careful to guard against spiritual attacks, or are you essentially hanging out the window?

Many people see Satan as a mythological figure concocted by guilty imaginations. A steady stream of pop songs involving a downplayed devil reveals that people are oblivious to his destructive power. But laughing off the devil is no joke. He is real, and the damage he can inflict is too—for Christians and non-Christians alike.

Believers are special targets of Satan and his minions because God loves us and is advancing his Kingdom through us. Our high value from God makes us targets; Satan wants to hurt God in any way he can. That's why he attacked Job, harassed Paul, and inspired the killing of millions of martyrs. The word *devil* literally means "slanderer," and one of his methods of attack is to accuse us before God, and even before ourselves, so we'll be discouraged (see Revelation 12:10). If we obey God—and repent, asking his forgiveness, when we fail to obey—we'll keep our consciences clean and clear of the accuser's reach.

Each of us needs to keep the windows of God's protection rolled up. Don't dangle yourself in front of Satan. Don't stroll into his territory, thinking he won't notice. When it comes to temptation, live with care and caution.

Failing Eyesight

Those who fail to develop in this way are shortsighted or blind, forgetting that they have been cleansed from their old sins.   2 PETER 1:9

Many of us experience failing eyesight, whether at an early age because of nearsightedness, or in older age as our eyes grow weaker. It's also possible to experience compromised spiritual eyesight. Spiritual shortsightedness produces selfishness, with our focus limited to our own interests. But it doesn't have to be this way. Though poor eyesight is almost a universal condition in the physical realm, it is a personal choice in the spiritual realm.

How do we prevent failing spiritual eyesight? First, we need to look backward. Peter tells us that we should never forget what God has done for us in the past. Through Jesus, he cleansed us of our sins. Many of us have heard these words so many times that they fail to make the impact that they should. Our sins had cut us off forever from God and from the privilege of living in heaven. We were lost! But our lives were transformed when we received Christ. Never forget the day you made that choice and how that choice affected your eternal standing.

Second, we need to look forward. Peter instructs us to keep adding to our faith. This doesn't mean that simple faith in Christ is lacking on its own, but that spiritual growth should never stop. We must be looking for ways to grow closer to Christ and to become stronger in our faith. When we stop moving forward with our spiritual lives, we stop developing, and that's when myopia can set in.

Make a decision to be proactive in your spiritual growth. For example, you could take a discipleship class or a course on how to share your faith or on another spiritual discipline. You could join a home Bible study or take a short-term mission trip. Don't be content with just "having faith." Make sure your faith is alive and growing so that your spiritual vision is clear.

Dogs and Hogs

They prove the truth of this proverb: "A dog returns to its vomit." And another says, "A washed pig returns to the mud." 2 PETER 2:22

To the Jewish Christians Peter is addressing in today's Scriptures, dogs and pigs were considered unclean animals—filthy and defiling. Peter is going for the gut with this unflattering metaphor, a visceral image of the sorry state some believers return to. He goes on to say that it is actually better to have never received the grace of God than to have received it and thrown it away by returning to the waste and filth of their former lives.

This message comes at the end of an entire chapter-long warning against false teachers, who earn their own unflattering, bestial description: They are "like unthinking animals," who have no true understanding—"and like animals, they will be destroyed" (verse 12). Why does Peter bring up these dogs and pigs at the end of the chapter? Because people who are ignorant of the truth aren't the only ones to fall prey to false teaching. Even those who already know Christ can be susceptible.

Peter warns that not only will false teachers themselves be punished but also those who leave the truth for a false way: "When people escape from the wickedness of the world by knowing our Lord and Savior Jesus Christ and then get tangled up and enslaved by sin again, they are worse off than before" (verse 20). They're like unclean animals, having tasted health and cleanliness but choosing to go back to their filth.

Take a moment and evaluate your own spiritual life. Is there an area where you have chosen a false way? A mud puddle you've let yourself go back to since encountering the cleansing power of Jesus Christ? Do not fall prey to false teaching, no matter what form it takes. And remember that the Lord is faithful to rescue his children, as he did with Lot, plucking him out of the disaster surrounding him (see verses 6-8). Ask him for his help.

Madame Tussaud's Nightmare

Since everything around us is going to be destroyed like this, what holy and godly lives you should live. 2 PETER 3:11

One of the most popular London tourist attractions is the world-famous, original Madame Tussaud's wax museum. My family and I have been there and seen the amazing likenesses of people such as John F. Kennedy, the Beatles, and Diana, Princess of Wales. I wonder what would happen to this array of famous men and women if someone turned up the heat. Before being modeled into the figures, wax is heated to about 165 degrees Fahrenheit, poured into a mold, and left to harden for about an hour. Obviously, wax can withstand fairly rigorous, extreme temperature changes without being essentially changed—though if it were heated again, the shapes it has taken at Tussaud's would literally have a meltdown.

But according to the Bible, one day the wax itself will disappear—along with everything else. The entire earth will face a meltdown in which the elements that make up the material universe will be dissolved. All atomic particles will deteriorate and burn up everything on the earth as God readies the universe for the new heavens and the new earth. The prophet Isaiah foretold this event: "The heavens above will melt away and disappear like a rolled-up scroll. The stars will fall from the sky like withered leaves from a grapevine, or shriveled figs from a fig tree" (Isaiah 34:4).

With this view of the future, what kinds of lives should we be living? Not materialistic ones! If we're living for this present world and its pleasures, the meltdown will be a nightmare.

Peter insists that we should live for something more enduring than the physical. Our lives should reflect eternal values because one day we will leave this world to live forever in the next. The transitory nature of our world and the ultimate reality of the world to come encourage us to pour the wax of our lives into an eternal mold.

Full Grown

You must grow in the grace and knowledge of our Lord and Savior Jesus Christ. All glory to him, both now and forever! Amen.   2 PETER 3:18

I'll never forget when I approached the great author and theologian J. I. Packer and asked him to sign my Bible. He graciously agreed and scribbled this reference next to his name: 2 Peter 3:18. I quickly looked up the verse, and after meditating on it for a while, I decided it should become a major theme of my own life. Pursuit of Christian maturity, through growth in God's grace and in the knowledge of Jesus Christ, should be a hallmark of every believer.

Peter's exhortation in this verse is twofold. First, we need to grow in grace, God's special favor. We were saved by God's grace, and it should mark our lives. As we grow in our faith, we should become more gracious toward others. And trials and hardships are a few of his tools to ensure that this process happens. But second, we must also grow in the knowledge of Jesus Christ: his person, his nature, his will, and his plans.

Sometimes we get out of balance. We want to be gracious and loving, yet because we aren't also growing in knowledge, we lean in the direction of doctrinal instability and are easily led astray. Or, we grow in knowledge but not in grace, and "while knowledge makes us feel important, it is love that strengthens the church" (1 Corinthians 8:1).

We need the combination of these two characteristics. Growth in either without the other produces a terribly shallow person. But when blended together, these two qualities produce a beautifully attractive life, attentive to right teaching and doctrine and yet filled with the grace to forgive those who falter around us. Let us all be able to say, "I've been studying the Bible and underlining it for years!"—and yet remember to emulate the Author of the Bible, who is himself full of grace and mercy.

Agreement with God

If we confess our sins to [God], he is faithful and just to forgive us our sins and to cleanse us from all wickedness.   1 JOHN 1:9

It's a great irony. We Christians have sin living in us, but we don't have to live in sin. As someone once said, it's not falling into the water but lying in it that drowns.

Take a moment and slowly read through today's key Bible verse. You're probably familiar with the words, but let's take a closer look. The word *confess* means more than "to admit." It means agreement with God that we have sinned, not just praying, "*If* I have sinned . . ." But it also means to name sin what God names it: such as envy, hatred, deceit, fornication, or adultery.

Long ago, there was a preacher who didn't mince words. He defined *sin* as "that abomination that God hates." When a leader in his congregation urged him not to speak so strongly about sin, to just call it a mistake or a twist in our nature, the preacher went to his desk and took out a bottle of strychnine. "Notice this label reads 'poison,'" he said. "Would you suggest that I change it to 'wintergreen mouthwash'?" The more harmless the name, the more dangerous the dose will be.

Confession comes from the repentant heart of someone who acknowledges sin and desires to turn from it. The Lord is faithful to cleanse such a heart. In King David's famous confession of his sin with Bathsheba, he finally cries out to God, "I recognize my rebellion; it haunts me day and night. . . . Purify me from my sins, and I will be clean; wash me, and I will be whiter than snow. . . . You will not reject a broken and repentant heart, O God" (Psalm 51:3, 7, 17).

As we confess our sins to God, we restore our relationship with our heavenly Father. Take some time to confess anything you need to. Then thank God for his faithfulness and forgiveness.

The Pantry Door

I have written to you who are God's children
because you know the Father.
I have written to you who are mature in the faith
because you know Christ, who existed from the beginning.
I have written to you who are young in the faith
because you are strong.
God's word lives in your hearts,
and you have won your battle with the evil one.

1 JOHN 2:14

In the house we lived in while our son, Nate, was growing up, we had a kitchen-pantry door marked with an array of pencil lines and dates—each one documenting Nate's height at different ages. He loved going to the pantry door and looking at that visual picture of his growth over a period of years. Today's Bible verse is like a spiritual pantry-door measure, dividing our development into three general groups.

Children are those who know that God is their Father. Though infants and toddlers may not know a lot about life, they can easily recognize their parents. But with young children around the house, life can be a combination of excitement and challenge. Spiritually, too, children need extra care, nourishment, and guidance.

Adolescents are those believers with a few more miles under their belts. While these Christians are stronger, they still have much growing to do. One of the marks of a young adult, both physically and spiritually, is muscle development, which produces a lot of energy. At this stage, feeding regularly on God's Word, the adolescent is well on the way to a stable spiritual life.

Elders are the mature believers who have become role models and are worthy examples. They have plumbed the depths of Christ and know him intimately. They don't just know the Word of God; they know the God of the Word.

Have you noticed that there is an expectation of growth? The difference between our physical and spiritual growth is that we must never stop growing in Christ. No matter what stage you are in this lifelong growth process, God is committed to your maturity. Are you?

When Christians Shouldn't *Love*

Do not love this world nor the things it offers you, for when you love the world, you do not have the love of the Father in you. 1 JOHN 2:15

Love is the hallmark of Christianity because it reflects the nature of God. We are commanded over and over to love God and others—our spouses, our neighbors, even our enemies. And we're told that the greatest of all the gifts is love. But even in love we need focus and discernment. If we love the evil in the world, which is hostile to God, we defile our love for God himself. So although we are to love the people of this world for Christ's sake, we are not to love the world's value system.

J. B. Phillips renders Romans 12:2 masterfully: "Don't let the world around you squeeze you into its own mould." While on earth, Jesus prayed to the Father, asking him to help his disciples stay holy as they lived in the unholy world (see John 17:15). He knew how easily distracted they were while he was physically with them—and how much we, in his physical absence, would need the steadying presence of his Spirit (see John 14:16-17). Glittering temptation in this world is ready and able to stamp us with its mold. But we were created to bear only one image—Christ's—and the best way to do that is by reflecting his love.

Take a moment and evaluate your affections. In your quiet moments, where does your mind wander? Like a compass, your mind can focus on a number of things in a given day. Yet at rest, a compass will always point back toward its magnetic pull. Be careful not to allow your affections to revert to pointing to false loves. Through regular study of God's Word and communion with him, you will keep the love of the Father as your true north.

Tiptoes

All who have this eager expectation will keep themselves pure, just as [Christ] is pure. 1 JOHN 3:3

In today's set of Scripture verses, John describes the future hope for every believer, who, upon seeing Jesus face-to-face, will be instantly and totally transformed. The earliest readers of this short epistle would have been greatly encouraged to see themselves as part of a process that has its goal in glory. We should too.

As Christians, we're not what we used to be—and thank God for that! But neither are we yet what we're going to be. Looking forward to that ultimate change should push us onto our tiptoes and fuel our desire for Christ's return.

Many people criticize Christians who hold to this doctrine about the imminent return of Jesus Christ. They say such a doctrine produces lazy believers. I beg to differ: I believe the opposite is true. According to the apostle John, one of the greatest and most purifying incentives is the hope that Jesus will return and change everything from the way we now know it. In fact, it could be argued that if you *don't* hold to the imminent return of Jesus, you could grow sluggish. After all, it was the wicked servant in Jesus' parable who thought, "My master won't be back for a while" (Luke 12:45).

A soldier far away from home avoided all sensual temptation. When his buddies asked him about it, he replied, "Back home there's a girl I love with all my heart. When the war is over, I'm going to be married to that girl, and I'm keeping myself just for her." It should be that way for believers in Jesus. Just around the corner of life is a Savior who loves us and is coming for us. Let's stay pure, and let's wait on our tiptoes in expectation of that day!

Jesus Christ or Antichrist?

If someone claims to be a prophet and does not acknowledge the truth about Jesus, that person is not from God. Such a person has the spirit of the Antichrist, which you heard is coming into the world and indeed is already here. 1 JOHN 4:3

The apostle John, author of today's reading, had a contemporary named Cerinthus, one of the teachers proclaiming the false "gospel" of Gnosticism. Gnostic teachings about Jesus made their way into many Christian assemblies in the second and third centuries. The Gnostics taught that Jesus was born a natural man who was especially obedient to God and that during Jesus' baptism the "Christ Spirit" came on him, enabling him to do and say many wonderful things. They believed that at the Crucifixion, this "Christ Spirit" then left Jesus and returned to heaven, leaving Jesus to suffer and die as a mere man, with the divine Christ remaining untouched and removed from suffering. This ancient form of philosophical dualism denied the Virgin Birth and the incarnation of God to become man.

While these concepts were more prevalent during John's day, they are still at large today. Many religious cults today deny the deity of Jesus Christ and his atonement, with various fantastic arguments about how he was conceived and how he lived his life. Deception about this central issue of Jesus Christ is one of the devil's specialties. Any teaching about Jesus Christ that is contrary to the teaching in the Bible should be rejected.

Jesus asked the Pharisees, "What do you think about the Messiah? Whose son is he?" (Matthew 22:42). The Pharisees' answer was essential—and so is ours—because it is through belief in Jesus that we are saved. It's vital that we believe in the right one. When you boil all religious beliefs down to their irreducible minimum, there are only two alternatives: They either exalt the biblical Jesus and his work or they deny it. It's either Christ or the Antichrist.

American Idols

Dear children, keep away from anything that might take God's place in your hearts. 1 JOHN 5:21

Today's Bible verse might seem like an abrupt way to end a letter. You might wonder if John was in a hurry. But this ending is a logical conclusion to a chapter that follows this line of encouragement: What you know is right, do.

Many scholars believe John is referring to idols that were a prominent part of life for these early believers. For example, the city of Ephesus held the massive Temple of Artemis (the goddess Diana), which was one of the seven wonders of the ancient world. People throughout the region traveled to the town and purchased idols of Diana, which they put on their chariots and in their homes.

But this last verse of 1 John is also a reminder that anything we set in higher esteem than the Lord our God is an idol. As John says in verse 20, "He is the only true God, and he is eternal life." Christians worship the original and authentic God, not some false image we create ourselves—whether out of stone or metal, or merely out of our own imaginations. When we choose not to believe what God says about himself, we are in danger of creating for ourselves an idol that suits our own image of God.

Maybe you've heard people say, "It doesn't matter what you believe as long as you're sincere." But it *does* matter. When Jesus Christ walked the earth, he referred to himself as "the true light," "the true bread which comes down from heaven," and "the true vine." These images might be difficult for us to grasp, but as we read about his life, his character, and his Kingdom purpose, an accurate picture will come together. God does not hide behind cryptic idol masks. The Holy Spirit will reveal himself to us if we seek him.

We know better than to worship anything that takes our focus away from God. So what we know—we need to do.

Learn to Discern

If anyone comes to your meeting and does not teach the truth about Christ, don't invite that person into your home or give any kind of encouragement. 2 JOHN 1:10

Nineteenth-century German philosopher Arthur Schopenhauer (1788–1860) said that a man who has the right ideas, but sits among those who are deluded, is like the only person in town with a watch: He knows what time it is, but what good is that when no one else is on time? Schopenhauer's conclusion is that the whole world is guided by clocks that show the wrong time.

It can be frustrating to have the gift of discernment, especially when everyone else thinks you're being harsh or judgmental. Theologians often face this problem. Within the body of Christ, these scholars quite often function as the liver, which filters out the toxins that would otherwise threaten to destroy the church. Paul referred to this gift as "the ability to discern whether a message is from the Spirit of God or from another spirit" (1 Corinthians 12:10). John writes today's verse to a church meeting in a home and warns them to be selective about whom they permit into their fellowship—even a little leaven will leaven the whole lump (see Galatians 5:9).

It is essential that every Christian exercise some spiritual discernment because Satan still sends his messengers and tricksters out among us. But using discernment also requires wisdom, or else we're at risk of deteriorating into critical, proud self-righteousness. This, too, is a trap. Oswald Chambers said, "When we discern that people are not going on spiritually and allow the discernment to turn to criticism, we block our way to God. God never gives us discernment in order that we may criticize, but that we may intercede."

Rightly used, the gift of discernment brings great benefit to God's people, sparing the body from embarrassment and error and guiding it toward obedience. But remember that even those who are not naturally gifted with this characteristic must follow God's Word to increase it.

December 18 READ 3 JOHN 1:1-14

How to Make Your Pastor Happy

I could have no greater joy than to hear that my children are following the truth. 3 JOHN 1:4

Throughout the week, pastors work hard to prepare their sermons. These servants of God teach God's truth in hopes their teachings will transform the lives of the congregation. And the fruit of their labors—seeing people change in their attitudes, behaviors, worship, or involvement—makes it all worthwhile. As the apostle John watched the believers he ministered to grow up in the faith and walk the path he cleared for them, he had the greatest payoff this side of heaven.

Some time ago, a letter appeared in a British newspaper that minimized the work of preachers. It read, "Dear Sir: I notice that ministers seem to set a great deal of importance on their sermons and spend a great deal of time in preparing them. I have been attending services quite regularly for the past 30 years and during that time, if I estimate correctly, I have listened to no less than 3,000 sermons. But, to my consternation, I discover I cannot remember a single one of them. I wonder if a minister's time might be more profitably spent on something else. Sincerely . . . etc." Angry responses flooded the editorial desk of that paper for weeks, until one letter ended the furor. It read, "My Dear Sir: I have been married for thirty years. During that time I have eaten 32,850 meals—mostly my wife's cooking. Suddenly I've discovered that I cannot remember the menu of a single meal, yet I received nourishment from every one of them. I have the distinct impression that without them I would have starved to death long ago. Sincerely, . . . etc."

Take a moment today to encourage your pastor. Whether you send a handwritten note, an e-mail, or a phone message, try to be specific in recalling past lessons and how God used them to nourish and shape you. Your encouragement will make your pastor's day, and it might come at just the right time.

Call to Arms

Dear friends, I had been eagerly planning to write to you about the salvation we all share. But now I find that I must write about something else, urging you to defend the faith that God has entrusted once for all time to his holy people. JUDE 1:3

Christians aren't supposed to get uptight and fight—are they? Or are some things worth fighting for? It's more dangerous to lie around and be passive than to take up arms and stand up for truth. Taking a closer look at today's Bible verse, we can see that the word Jude used for *defend* means to "contend, with determination and intensity." Hearing this verse, the apostle Paul would have nodded in wholehearted agreement. In the book of Galatians, Paul wrote a polemic against the false ideas people had about the gospel. We should consider the short book of Jude as a call to arms for believers.

Why was Jude so adamant about the unchanging gospel? Because he knew God's revelation was complete—and he also knew that people were prone to make things up to gain an audience. As Mark Twain would go on to say, a lie can travel halfway around the world while truth is still lacing up its boots.

"The Anvil of God's Word," by John Clifford (1836–1923), declares,

> Last eve I paused beside the blacksmith's door,
> And heard the anvil ring the vesper chime;
> Then looking in, I saw upon the floor,
> Old hammers worn with beating years of time. . . .
>
> And so, I thought, the Anvil of God's Word,
> For ages skeptics' blows have beat upon,
> Yet, though the noise of falling blows was heard,
> The Anvil is unharmed, the hammers gone.

God has given you everything you need to live a fulfilled life. His Word says it all. Don't fall for the line "God has revealed something new to me." Make sure that everything you believe lines up with what God has already revealed, and defend it!

Walking with God

Enoch, who lived in the seventh generation after Adam, prophesied about these people. He said, "Listen! The Lord is coming with countless thousands of his holy ones."   JUDE 1:14

Enoch was an ordinary man who had a relationship with an extraordinary God: "Enoch lived 365 years, walking in close fellowship with God" (Genesis 5:23-24). This "walking" doesn't mean merely walking in honesty, flowing with the universe, or walking by your own moral code. Walking with God means that you prefer God, pursue God, please God, and proclaim his Word when you have the opportunity. That is great spiritual exercise.

How many people do you know who have spent money on expensive exercise equipment in January only to take it to a resale shop in April? Statistics say that 87 percent of Americans who own running shoes don't run. Likewise, a large percentage of American Christians who own Bibles never walk spiritually. That reminds me of the story of the retired husband and wife who decided to get in shape by walking two miles every afternoon. They planned to walk a mile down a country road and then turn around and walk the second mile back. The first day, they walked out to the mile marker, and just before they were about to turn around, the husband asked his wife, "Honey, are you doing all right? Do you think you can make it back?"

"I feel great. No problem!" she replied.

"Good," said her husband. "I'll wait here while you get the car and come back for me."

It's important not only to *start* walking with God but also to *keep* walking with him and to finish well. We can pace ourselves in a spiritual exercise program by preferring to follow God and to pursue him with the aim of pleasing him.

God's Keeping Power

All glory to God, who is able to keep you from falling away and will bring you with great joy into his glorious presence without a single fault.

JUDE 1:24

December 21 is the date that most often marks the first official day of winter on our calendars. In most regions, trees and plants lose their leaves and slip into a state of dormancy. During these bleak winter months, they may seem dead or at least in the grip of a long, unproductive nap, but that's not the case. Many plants only stop growing above the ground where you can see them. Below the surface of the soil, there is still much activity as the roots continue their growth until the soil freezes solid. But even then, the plant will be kept safe in this state until it's time to blossom once again in the springtime.

Jude points out that in the midst of the harsh climate brought on by false teachers, God is able to keep the believers flourishing. The secret to surviving and even thriving is to remain rooted in the soil of God's love and truth. The Gardener (see John 15) is most interested in producing fruit in our lives.

God is able to keep you, but you must want to be kept. Solomon tells his son to cry out for wisdom and instruction and to walk with God, for "he guards the paths of the just and protects those who are faithful to him" (Proverbs 2:8).

Even Christians stumble, and when that happens, the devil wants you to believe that you're like a dead tree—that it's over and you'll never have the right kind of life. But trust the Master Gardener! Confess your sin to God, and entrust yourself to his cultivating hand. As the psalmist declares, "Though they stumble, they will never fall, for the LORD holds them by the hand" (Psalm 37:24). As with a child learning to walk, our loving Father holds us by the hand when we stumble, and he is able to keep us from falling.

A Fading Love

I have this complaint against you. You don't love me or each other as you did at first! REVELATION 2:4

Love can grow cold. Sadly, it happens all the time in marriages. Spouses who once swore their unending love scowl at each other across the bench of the divorce court. What happened? Though each story has different details, what they all have in common is that the couple allowed their love to fade. It can also happen to us in our relationship with Christ. The fervor we once had grows stale and commonplace. As time marches on, it fades. This was happening in Ephesus, where both Paul and John once ministered.

The first part of Revelation addresses seven churches in Asia Minor experiencing different spiritual conditions. But the addresses also have timeless application to all churches and believers whose love for Jesus Christ ebbs and flows. Just as with failed marriages, when commitments to Christ wane, it's not because of a blowout. Most often the change comes from a slow leak.

The early church experienced many physical attacks, and it has seen many other attacks since then, both physical and philosophical. Yet the real danger to the church isn't always the frontal assault. The key danger for the church is often rooted in self-destruction. It is possible to get so busy doing the King's business that the workers forget the King.

The church's activity must never eclipse our loving adoration. But it's not an either-or situation. The balance between presence with Jesus and service to him is illustrated in the Gospel story about Martha and Mary (see Luke 10:38-42). Martha is distracted with much serving and tells her sister to help. She allows her work to distract her from the presence of Jesus. If our service keeps us from spending time in his presence, or if it makes us difficult to live with, something is terribly wrong. As Jesus concludes, Mary, sitting at his feet, has chosen better. In our service to him, we must not allow our love to fade.

The Gate of Heaven

As I looked, I saw a door standing open in heaven, and the same voice
I had heard before spoke to me like a trumpet blast. The voice said,
"Come up here, and I will show you what must happen after this."

REVELATION 4:1

Everyone has heard those lame jokes about Saint Peter standing at the gates of heaven with his clipboard, determining who goes inside. Throw out that mental image, because in truth, Peter will have nothing to do with your entrance into heaven. Jesus is the only person to determine that. As he said, "I tell you the truth, I am the gate for the sheep. All who came before me were thieves and robbers" (John 10:7-8). Jesus promised his faithful followers that they would one day enter into the joyful celebration of their Lord (see Matthew 25:21).

In today's verse, we get a clue to the significance of the door in the trumpetlike tone of the voice heard through it. Earlier in the New Testament, Paul had said concerning Christ's return, "The Lord himself will come down from heaven with a commanding shout, with the voice of the archangel, and with the trumpet call of God. . . . Then we will be with the Lord forever" (1 Thessalonians 4:16-17).

Paul's description seems to match John's experience. After writing about matters concerning his present era, John is "caught up" into a vision of heaven after a mighty trumpet blast. From this point forward, John will record events from a heavenly perspective. In his vision, John hears from heaven the angels and saints praising God mightily, and he watches as judgment unfolds on the earth and Jesus eventually returns there.

The New Testament warns that these final events will happen suddenly and without warning: "It will happen in a moment, in the blink of an eye, when the last trumpet is blown" (1 Corinthians 15:52). Are you prepared? Are you living today in such a way that when the trumpet blares, you'll be ready to meet your Lord at the gate?

The Lion Who Looks like a Lamb

"Stop weeping! Look, the Lion of the tribe of Judah, the heir to David's throne, has won the victory. . . ." Then I saw a Lamb that looked as if it had been slaughtered, but it was now standing between the throne and the four living beings and among the twenty-four elders.

REVELATION 5:5-6

Often we depict Christmas as the baby Jesus lying in a manger with farm animals all around. And though this is an idealized scene, in John's vision of heaven, two animals are indeed mentioned: a lion and a lamb. Both creatures are symbols of the same Person born at Christmas, Jesus Christ.

John the Baptist called Jesus "the Lamb of God who takes away the sin of the world" (John 1:29), and the book of Revelation refers to Jesus in this way twenty-nine times. To any Jew, this imagery was clear, because in their religious practices a lamb was sacrificed for sin.

Yet in this passage, John the Beloved, the apostle who received the revelation, hadn't been looking for a lamb. John had been weeping for someone to redeem the earth, to take its title deed and rescue its inhabitants. That's when he heard of the "Lion of Judah," which is an early messianic title connoting Jesus' strength and power (see Genesis 49). Because of the announcement, John turned and expected to see this Lion—but instead he saw a Lamb.

To John, it was an unmistakable picture of Jesus' mission. When Jesus came to the earth the first time, he was a Lamb led to be slaughtered for mankind's sins (see Isaiah 53:7). Now in John's revelation, Jesus had risen from the dead and reigned in heaven. Because of his work on the earth, the Messiah could assume the role as King over all the earth—the Lion.

Jesus is both the Lion and the Lamb. He came humbly, he died a sacrificial death, and he will come again and rule over the earth. How wonderful is our great Lion who became a Lamb!

The Hope of the World

She gave birth to a son who was to rule all nations with an iron rod. And her child was snatched away from the dragon and was caught up to God and to his throne.   REVELATION 12:5

The hope of every ancient Jewish mother was to give birth to the Messiah. Since the Garden of Eden, God had warned Satan (the dragon) that this child would be his downfall: "I will cause hostility between you and the woman, and between your offspring and her offspring. He will strike your head, and you will strike his heel" (Genesis 3:15).

Throughout the Bible, Satan tried to strike the Messiah. He motivated Pharaoh to order the death of all Hebrew boys under two years of age. Saul tried to kill David, which would have put an end to the messianic line. During the time of Joash, the line of David was only one baby away from extinction. Haman tried to wipe out the Jews. But God preserved the line through which the Messiah would be born. When Herod told the wise men he wanted to worship the baby born in Bethlehem, what he really wanted was to exterminate the hope of the world. But Jesus and his family escaped to Egypt.

When it came to the Cross, Satan may have thought he had dealt the final blow. But on the third day, Jesus conquered death and rose from the grave. The prophecy of Genesis had been fulfilled! The baby born in Bethlehem conquered sin and death for all who trust in him. Today, he sits on the throne beside God the Father. And one day, he will return to do away with Satan and his armies once and for all.

The Ultimate Counterfeit

All the people who belong to this world worshiped the beast. They are the ones whose names were not written in the Book of Life before the world was made—the Book that belongs to the Lamb who was slaughtered.

REVELATION 13:8

Do you think you could walk into a store and buy something with a twenty-dollar bill that bears the face of Bill Clinton or Ronald Reagan? A counterfeiter wants the counterfeit to be as close to the real thing as possible so no one can tell the difference. Satan will have a counterfeit too—the Antichrist—and he will be remarkable, even pictured as a heroic rider on a white horse (see Revelation 6:2). According to Scripture, he'll initially come on the scene and do something no man has ever been able to do: bring peace to a war-torn earth for three and a half years.

During this time, this counterfeit will help Jews to rebuild the long-awaited Temple in Israel. This person will rule the confederation of ten world powers, which will provide him the necessary military muscle. And he will institute a new monetary system to bring economic solidarity. Revelation tells us this counterfeit will be socially attractive with an unusual appeal—the ultimate wolf in sheep's clothing.

What's the solution to the problem of a counterfeit? The real thing. The Antichrist will be false, a fake, an impostor. But Jesus Christ is called "Faithful and True" (Revelation 19:11). In his wake, the Antichrist will bring war; in the wake of Jesus Christ, there will be peace. The Antichrist's deception will result in famine and death, but Jesus Christ said, "I am the bread of life. Whoever comes to me will never be hungry again" (John 6:35).

The Antichrist will be everything the world says it wants, while Jesus is everything the world truly needs. We must be prepared to recognize and take a stand against this counterfeit. But don't let the prospect of doing so steal your joy; live in an authentic relationship with the one true Savior, and rejoice in his plan for the world.

The Return of Christ

I saw heaven opened, and a white horse was standing there. Its rider was named Faithful and True, for he judges fairly and wages a righteous war.

REVELATION 19:11

Newspapers have a type of lettering they reserve for astounding news events: It's called Second Coming type. This is the kind of lettering that features extralarge, heavy, black letters and is used in banner headlines. For example, Second Coming type was used to announce the surrender of Germany and Japan to end World War II, the assassination of John F. Kennedy, successful flights into space, and other dramatic events.

Today's key Bible verse celebrates a "headline event" of God, and it's not the only one to do so. There are eighteen hundred references to this same event in the Old Testament, made in seventeen of its books. Twenty-three out of the twenty-seven New Testament books refer to it in a total of three hundred references.

What is that headline event? It's the actual Second Coming—the return of Jesus Christ. His return will mark the climax of God's redemptive movement in history; it's the ultimate answer to the prayer *Thy Kingdom come*, the ultimate bruising of the head of the serpent, Satan (see Genesis 3:15). This day will see the culmination of all Christian hope. Throughout the centuries, all saints of every age have hoped and prayed for Jesus Christ's return and have predicted and anticipated it through the prophets and the apostles. This will be the event to fulfill all our longings, the victorious second coming of Christ.

Julia Ward Howe (1819–1910) had this event in mind when she wrote "The Battle Hymn of the Republic": "Mine eyes have seen the glory of the coming of the Lord." And Isaac Watts (1674–1748) wasn't thinking of Christ's first coming but his second when he wrote "Joy to the world, the Lord is come!"

We're told about John's revelation so that we're prepared for this headline event. Are you?

Heaven on Earth?

Blessed and holy are those who share in the first resurrection. For them the second death holds no power, but they will be priests of God and of Christ and will reign with him a thousand years. REVELATION 20:6

Not every Bible scholar agrees that there will be a real Millennium— a thousand-year period on the earth following the second coming of Christ. Some prefer to think of it in the terms most people think of Utopia, which derives from two Greek words meaning "no place": an idealistic fantasy of heaven on earth. Yet the specific words *a thousand years* appear six times in seven verses, as if demanding a literal interpretation. Why should there be a Millennium? To redeem creation from curse and from judgment, and to fulfill all of God's promises to Israel.

Since the fall of man in Genesis, a curse was put on creation; and during the Tribulation, judgments will trash the earth. During the Millennium, God will restore and beautify what he has judged. The Millennium is God's answer to the phrase from the Lord's Prayer, "Thy will be done in earth, as it is in heaven" (Matthew 6:10, KJV). Also, the Lord promised a literal kingdom to David (see 2 Samuel 7), confirming his promise with an oath (see Psalm 89). In the psalms and through every Old Testament prophet, an earthly kingdom was predicted in addition to a heavenly one.

The Millennium is the earthly portion of this promise, when Jesus Christ as Messiah will reign from Mount Zion on a restored earth for one thousand years. When the thousand years are completed, we will enter into eternity with the new heaven, new earth, and new Jerusalem.

According to Scripture, we will reign with Jesus during that time. We should want to be faithful now, so that Jesus will say of us, "Well done, my good and faithful servant. You have been faithful in handling this small amount, so now I will give you many more responsibilities. Let's celebrate together!" (Matthew 25:21).

The City of the Future

I saw the holy city, the new Jerusalem, coming down from God out of heaven like a bride beautifully dressed for her husband.

REVELATION 21:2

Do you remember the opening words for every episode of *Star Trek*? "Space: the final frontier. These are the voyages of the starship *Enterprise*. Its five-year mission: to explore strange new worlds, to seek out new life and new civilizations, to boldly go where no man has gone before." Guess what? Eternity is the real final frontier, and for every believer that means heaven.

Revelation contains fifty-five references to heaven. It uses different descriptions, such as "around the throne of God" (chapters 4–5), "the wedding feast of the Lamb" (chapter 19), and "a new heaven and a new earth" and "the holy city, the new Jerusalem" (chapter 21). This describes the capital city of heaven and the headquarters for the new heaven and earth. This city was the hope of Abraham, for he was "confidently looking forward to a city with eternal foundations, a city designed and built by God" (Hebrews 11:10).

During the eternal state, the city will descend into the midst of the new universe. The apostle John saw the city as a fourteen-hundred-mile cube (see Revelation 21:16-17), and it could comfortably accommodate one hundred thousand million people, which is room for more than all of the people who have ever lived on the face of the earth. The city is made of pure gold and is built on foundation stones inlaid with precious gems. And it has no need for a temple or for light, for "the Lord God Almighty and the Lamb" serve those purposes.

A child looking at a star-filled sky said, "Daddy, if the wrong side of heaven is so pretty, what will the right side be like?" Heaven will be beyond our wildest dreams. John described the city as "a bride beautifully dressed for her husband." Today are you, the bride of Christ, living in preparation for this wonderfully strange new world?

While We Wait

He who is the faithful witness to all these things says, "Yes, I am coming soon!"

Amen! Come, Lord Jesus! REVELATION 22:20

A church located on a frequently traveled stretch of road had the misfortune of picking up CB radio frequencies on its PA system, unbeknownst to the CB users. One Sunday as the pastor prayed, "Lord, meet us here," his prayer was interrupted with a radio squeal and the words "Ten-four, ten four, I'll be right down."

The church has been anticipating Jesus' "coming back down" for two thousand years, echoing John's prayer: "Come, Lord Jesus!" We intensely desire to see our King face-to-face. We know that when the Tribulation ends and the judgment is over and the Millennium gives way to the eternal state, there will be unending joy and complete peace. We know that at that time anyone who has walked with Jesus through faith will then walk with sight in our eternal home. Until the arrival of this glorious event, we wait. How?

First, we should have the right attitude about the future, living as if we believe heaven is real and the Second Coming is certain. As Charles Spurgeon said, "When you talk about heaven, let your face light up with a heavenly glory. When you speak about hell, your everyday face will do!" When we live without the acute awareness of heaven, we use our "everyday face." But our attitudes should reflect the reality that one day we'll see our Savior and be gathered again with all believers.

Second, we should have the right attentiveness about our enemy. Enemies of our Father will consider themselves enemies of us, and in this world we will have trouble (see John 15:18; 16:33).

Finally, we should have the right approach to the present situation. While we are ultimately citizens of heaven, we are also temporarily citizens of earth. Soon we won't be able to tell others about Christ, to encourage, or to disciple others. So while we wait, let's get busy.

Out with the Old, In with the New

The one sitting on the throne said, "Look, I am making everything new!" And then he said to me, "Write this down, for what I tell you is trustworthy and true."   REVELATION 21:5

Today's date tells us that as the clock strikes midnight, we'll be living out the good old expression "Out with the old, in with the new!" People the world over will celebrate the beginning of a new year. There will be gatherings, fireworks, and confetti.

Celebrating New Year's Day is all about hope. We all look forward to making a fresh start. Perhaps this year you'll resolve to eat healthier or start an exercise plan. Maybe you've decided that this is the year you'll get that promotion or go on that trip.

Of course, starting fresh has deep spiritual resonance, too. Jesus told Nicodemus that he could be "born again" (John 3:7) and start a new life even though he was an old man. Paul tells us, "Anyone who belongs to Christ has become a new person" (2 Corinthians 5:17), because God is able to renovate us so that we "become like his Son" (Romans 8:29). Let's look at some of the other wonderful changes the Bible promises will happen when we become children of God:

- "He has given me a new song to sing, a hymn of praise to our God" (Psalm 40:3).
- "I am about to do something new" (Isaiah 43:19).
- "I will give you a new heart, and I will put a new spirit in you" (Ezekiel 36:26).
- "I am giving you a new commandment: Love each other. Just as I have loved you, you should love each other" (John 13:34).
- "Put on your new nature, created to be like God—truly righteous and holy" (Ephesians 4:24).

Better than any diet or exercise plan, God's makeover will transform you into a completely new person. Are you ready for this radical change? The best New Year's resolution you can make is to turn your life completely over to Christ. Then you'll experience newness of life.

DAILY SCRIPTURE INDEX

1 Kings 12:16 *March 30*
1 Kings 17:1 *March 31*
1 Kings 18:17 *April 1*
1 Kings 19:2 *April 2*
2 Kings 1:3 *April 3*
2 Kings 1:8 *April 4*
2 Kings 4:27 *April 5*
2 Kings 5:12 *April 6*
2 Kings 11:1-2 *April 7*
2 Kings 12:1-2 *April 8*
2 Kings 14:25 *April 9*
2 Kings 15:1 *April 10*
2 Kings 18:4 *April 11*
2 Kings 25:1 *April 12*
1 Chronicles 1:29 *April 13*
1 Chronicles 3:1 *April 14*
1 Chronicles 11:3 *April 15*
1 Chronicles 11:9 *April 16*
1 Chronicles 14:10 *April 17*
1 Chronicles 17:1 *April 18*
1 Chronicles 17:14 *April 19*
1 Chronicles 29:28 *April 20*
2 Chronicles 1:1 *April 21*
2 Chronicles 3:1 *April 22*
2 Chronicles 12:7 *April 23*
2 Chronicles 14:2 *April 24*
2 Chronicles 17:4 *April 25*
2 Chronicles 20:22 *April 26*
2 Chronicles 32:7-8 *April 27*
2 Chronicles 36:23 *April 28*
Ezra 2:64-65 *April 29*
Ezra 3:12 *April 30*
Ezra 5:1 *May 1*
Ezra 7:6 *May 2*
Ezra 10:1 *May 3*
Nehemiah 1:2 *May 4*
Nehemiah 2:4-5 *May 5*
Nehemiah 3:1-2 *May 6*
Nehemiah 4:1 *May 7*
Nehemiah 8:8 *May 8*
Esther 4:14 *May 9*
Job 1:20 *May 10*
Job 2:3 *May 11*
Job 16:2 *May 12*
Job 38:3-4 *May 13*
Psalm 1:1 *May 14*
Psalm 2:4 *May 15*
Psalm 23:1 *May 16*
Psalm 51:4 *May 17*

Psalm 73:16-17 *May 18*
Psalm 90:12 *May 19*
Psalm 150:5-6 *May 20*
Proverbs 1:7 *May 21*
Proverbs 2:3-5 *May 22*
Proverbs 3:5 *May 23*
Proverbs 4:10 *May 24*
Proverbs 6:10-11 *May 25*
Proverbs 16:24 *May 26*
Proverbs 31:10 *May 27*
Ecclesiastes 1:2 *May 28*
Ecclesiastes 5:1, 7 *May 29*
Ecclesiastes 12:1 *May 30*
Song of Songs 2:4 *May 31*
Song of Songs 5:3 *June 1*
Song of Songs 7:6 *June 2*
Isaiah 1:18 *June 3*
Isaiah 6:1 *June 4*
Isaiah 11:1 *June 5*
Isaiah 37:36 *June 6*
Isaiah 53:5 *June 7*
Jeremiah 1:6 *June 8*
Jeremiah 9:1 *June 9*
Jeremiah 18:2 *June 10*
Jeremiah 29:11 *June 11*
Lamentations 1:12 *June 12*
Lamentations 3:22-23 *June 13*
Lamentations 3:40 *June 14*
Ezekiel 3:17 *June 15*
Ezekiel 11:5 *June 16*
Ezekiel 28:12-13 *June 17*
Ezekiel 37:4 *June 18*
Daniel 1:8 *June 19*
Daniel 2:45 *June 20*
Daniel 3:25 *June 21*
Daniel 9:25 *June 22*
Hosea 1:2 *June 23*
Hosea 3:5 *June 24*
Hosea 14:1-2 *June 25*
Joel 2:25 *June 26*
Amos 7:14 *June 27*
Obadiah 1:2-3 *June 28*
Jonah 1:3 *June 29*
Jonah 4:2 *June 30*
Micah 6:8 *July 1*
Nahum 1:2 *July 2*
Habakkuk 3:17-18 *July 3*
Zephaniah 1:2 *July 4*
Haggai 1:4 *July 5*

Zechariah 1:3 *July 6*

Malachi 2:13 *July 7*

Matthew 1:1 *July 8*

Matthew 3:3 *July 9*

Matthew 5:4 *July 10*

Matthew 7:24 *July 11*

Matthew 9:9 *July 12*

Matthew 13:8 *July 13*

Matthew 16:15 *July 14*

Matthew 19:25-26 *July 15*

Matthew 24:3 *July 16*

Matthew 28:19 *July 17*

Mark 1:12, 18 *July 18*

Mark 3:29 *July 19*

Mark 5:9 *July 20*

Mark 7:8 *July 21*

Mark 9:31 *July 22*

Mark 10:18 *July 23*

Mark 12:17 *July 24*

Mark 14:50 *July 25*

Mark 15:38 *July 26*

Luke 1:3 *July 27*

Luke 2:14 *July 28*

Luke 4:19 *July 29*

Luke 7:47 *July 30*

Luke 10:29 *July 31*

Luke 11:9 *August 1*

Luke 15:32 *August 2*

Luke 17:2 *August 3*

Luke 19:3-4 *August 4*

Luke 24:32 *August 5*

John 1:1 *August 6*

John 3:3 *August 7*

John 4:13 *August 8*

John 5:6-7 *August 9*

John 7:38 *August 10*

John 11:25-26 *August 11*

John 13:17 *August 12*

John 17:21 *August 13*

John 19:30 *August 14*

John 20:31 *August 15*

Acts 1:8 *August 16*

Acts 2:42 *August 17*

Acts 4:24 *August 18*

Acts 6:1 *August 19*

Acts 9:4 *August 20*

Acts 13:3-4 *August 21*

Acts 16:7 *August 22*

Acts 18:3-4 *August 23*

Acts 24:25 *August 24*

Acts 28:30-31 *August 25*

Romans 1:22 *August 26*

Romans 3:23 *August 27*

Romans 5:1 *August 28*

Romans 6:18 *August 29*

Romans 8:28 *August 30*

Romans 9:3 *August 31*

Romans 12:1 *September 1*

Romans 13:6 *September 2*

Romans 14:5 *September 3*

Romans 16:23 *September 4*

1 Corinthians 1:12 *September 5*

1 Corinthians 1:27 *September 6*

1 Corinthians 2:15 *September 7*

1 Corinthians 6:12 *September 8*

1 Corinthians 7:7 *September 9*

1 Corinthians 9:24 *September 10*

1 Corinthians 11:1 *September 11*

1 Corinthians 12:7 *September 12*

1 Corinthians 13:13 *September 13*

1 Corinthians 15:55 *September 14*

2 Corinthians 1:4 *September 15*

2 Corinthians 2:14 *September 16*

2 Corinthians 4:16 *September 17*

2 Corinthians 5:21 *September 18*

2 Corinthians 6:14 *September 19*

2 Corinthians 9:7 *September 20*

2 Corinthians 12:7 *September 21*

Galatians 1:8 *September 22*

Galatians 2:16 *September 23*

Galatians 3:3 *September 24*

Galatians 4:4 *September 25*

Galatians 5:1 *September 26*

Galatians 5:17 *September 27*

Galatians 6:1 *September 28*

Ephesians 1:4 *September 29*

Ephesians 1:18 *September 30*

Ephesians 2:4-5 *October 1*

Ephesians 3:6 *October 2*

Ephesians 4:1 *October 3*

Ephesians 5:21 *October 4*

Ephesians 6:11 *October 5*

Philippians 1:6 *October 6*

Philippians 1:12 *October 7*

Philippians 2:7-9 *October 8*

Philippians 2:15 *October 9*

Philippians 3:1 *October 10*

Philippians 3:14 *October 11*

Philippians 4:6 *October 12*
Colossians 1:17 *October 13*
Colossians 1:20-21 *October 14*
Colossians 2:8 *October 15*
Colossians 2:14 *October 16*
Colossians 3:2 *October 17*
Colossians 3:23 *October 18*
Colossians 4:6 *October 19*
1 Thessalonians 1:3 *October 20*
1 Thessalonians 2:7, 11 *October 21*
1 Thessalonians 2:13 *October 22*
1 Thessalonians 4:3-4 *October 23*
1 Thessalonians 4:17 *October 24*
1 Thessalonians 5:2-3 *October 25*
1 Thessalonians 5:18 *October 26*
2 Thessalonians 1:9 *October 27*
2 Thessalonians 1:11 *October 28*
2 Thessalonians 2:4 *October 29*
2 Thessalonians 2:15 *October 30*
2 Thessalonians 3:1 *October 31*
2 Thessalonians 3:6, 11 *November 1*
2 Thessalonians 3:16 *November 2*
1Timothy 1:2 *November 3*
1Timothy 1:15 *November 4*
1Timothy 2:5 *November 5*
1Timothy 3:1 *November 6*
1Timothy 4:12 *November 7*
1Timothy 5:17 *November 8*
1Timothy 6:7 *November 9*
2 Timothy 1:5 *November 10*
2 Timothy 1:16 *November 11*
2 Timothy 2:2 *November 12*
2 Timothy 3:16 *November 13*
2 Timothy 4:7 *November 14*
Titus 2:1 *November 15*
Titus 3:10 *November 16*
Philemon 1:18 *November 17*
Hebrews 1:1-2 *November 18*
Hebrews 2:1 *November 19*
Hebrews 4:16 *November 20*
Hebrews 5:12 *November 21*

Hebrews 9:12 *November 22*
Hebrews 11:1 *November 23*
Hebrews 12:1 *November 24*
James 1:14-15 *November 25*
James 1:22 *November 26*
James 2:20 *November 27*
James 3:5 *November 28*
James 4:1 *November 29*
James 4:13 *November 30*
James 5:16 *December 1*
1 Peter 1:8 *December 2*
1 Peter 2:2 *December 3*
1 Peter 3:15 *December 4*
1 Peter 4:12 *December 5*
1 Peter 5:8 *December 6*
2 Peter 1:9 *December 7*
2 Peter 2:22 *December 8*
2 Peter 3:11 *December 9*
2 Peter 3:18 *December 10*
1 John 1:9 *December 11*
1 John 2:14 *December 12*
1 John 2:15 *December 13*
1 John 3:3 *December 14*
1 John 4:3 *December 15*
1 John 5:21 *December 16*
2 John 1:10 *December 17*
3 John 1:4 *December 18*
Jude 1:3 *December 19*
Jude 1:14 *December 20*
Jude 1:24 *December 21*
Revelation 2:4 *December 22*
Revelation 4:1 *December 23*
Revelation 5:5-6 *December 24*
Revelation 12:5 *December 25*
Revelation 13:8 *December 26*
Revelation 19:11 *December 27*
Revelation 20:6 *December 28*
Revelation 21:2 *December 29*
Revelation 22:20 *December 30*
Revelation 21:5 *December 31*

ABOUT THE AUTHOR

 As a young man, **Skip Heitzig**, a native of Southern California, experienced the volatile days of the counterculture in the late sixties and early seventies and got caught up in the drug scene. One day, while Skip was alone in his brother's apartment, a televised message by Billy Graham captured his attention. The gospel message penetrated Skip's soul, and he knelt and prayed to receive Christ. After his conversion, Skip studied under Pastor Chuck Smith of Calvary Chapel of Costa Mesa. In 1982, Skip began a home Bible study in Albuquerque, New Mexico, which eventually grew into Calvary of Albuquerque. In 1988 and 1989, Calvary of Albuquerque was considered the fastest-growing church in America. Today, Calvary of Albuquerque ministers to more than fourteen thousand adults and children every weekend. Skip continues to reach out to many people across the nation and throughout the world through his multimedia ministry, which includes a nationwide half-hour radio program called *The Connection*. In addition to teaching God's Word, Skip helps equip others for living according to God's principles through his writings. Recent books include *Upon This Rock, When God Prays, How to Study the Bible and Enjoy It* (revised), and *Jesus Up Close*.

Seek God Daily

The Daily God Book
Through the Bible

The Daily God Book
A Year with Jesus

The Daily God Book
Words of Wisdom

The Daily God Book:
A Year of Listening for God